This author, who has written about Francis Thompson, grants his readers an imaginary summary of things as if penned by his suspect.

'Black it is to describe this species, thus I shall begin with light. My own perspective on life has caused me to accept certain principles. Some of them have found favour due to their assistance when trying to solve problems. One, which has proved useful, is the knowledge that we can only see by the eye what the mind can bear to feel. Unless there are beings, such as I, to witness light, as motes of dust do, suspended in the still air of a sanctuary, even the rays of the blessed sun are made black. So, too, may light be flashed back from a void. For the ability to perceive what is gross illuminates what is dark and through illumination makes what is small and dull into beings both monstrous and radiant.

'Yet I tell you, those that do read on, that whatever does follow, although based on myself, has been *ghost written* by a mediocre poet, who to me is not unlike a particle; isolated and alone in a distant place and far-off time. He is a man of little or no originality and of finite personality. He speaks of me only because fear has bent him to his knees; not all the perfumes of all the world can remove his stench of fear. Prick his words and they will lie bleeding. So what if there is a little blood?

'It has been many years now since this world has been born through me. My day has come and, pity for us all, I must die. Let my tears be his blackest ink and as I attempt to write in the blood of my five sisters, allow his fingers on the keys to impress upon you what I think. It is for this reason that I, Francis Thompson, have become breathless and to the author resign my breath. It is he who tries to grapple my crown of death though he knows that his success is all my power, but knowing this and despite knowing this, he shall speak for me and make his confession as he wears my life as one would a shroud of white.'

Dedication

Mary Ann Nichols, Annie Chapman, Elizabeth Stride,
Catherine Eddowes and Mary Kelly. Also the
Metropolitan Police, the City Police and Scotland Yard.

Richard Patterson

JACK THE RIPPER, THE WORKS OF FRANCIS THOMPSON

AUSTIN MACAULEY
PUBLISHERS LTD.

A CIP catalogue record for this title is available from the British Library.

ISBN 9781786934499 (Paperback)
ISBN 9781786934505 (eBook)
www.austinmacauley.com

First Published (2017)
Austin Macauley Publishers Ltd.
25 Canada Square
Canary Wharf
London
E14 5LQ

Acknowledgments

Joseph C. Rupp, M.D., Ph. D, for finding the dragon

Foreword

The original article proposing Francis Thompson as a Jack the Ripper suspect was published in 1988; the centennial year of the crimes. In the intervening years a number of books have been published, each naming a different Ripper suspect. Unfortunately, not many of the authors relate what circumstances, insights or facts led them to their proposed suspect. This is something that the more than casual reader would be interested to know.

In this case, Richard Patterson has given me the opportunity not only to publish the original article again but to allow me to explain what natural proclivities and training ted me to Francis Thompson as a Ripper suspect.

As a forensic pathologist for over fifty years I have personally with my own two hands performed approximately one autopsy a day, that is a total of about 9,000 autopsies performed during my working life. Performing an autopsy is a skilled task. If someone came to me and offered a king's ransom to perform a partial autopsy (evisceration) in the dark, on the ground, bare handed with only a surgical knife and no assistance plus a time constraint of a few minutes, my answer would be, "Certainly not, are you crazy?" And yet such a feat was accomplished not once but at least four times. It is almost impossible to even contemplate such a feat of daring and dexterity.

How could such a thing be possible in the near darkness with slippery blood all over the scene from the slashed aperies in the neck, the body fully clothed and all of the London police force out searching for you. Yet, Jack did It. Now take look at Francis Thompson, our suspect, with six years in medical school, three times through the medical curriculum which meant that he may have taken the anatomy course three times, a person severely addicted to laudanum, determined to gain the fame he knew his poetic genius deserved even if it meant a Faustian pact with the forces of evil. Yes, he was more than just familiar with the occult. Here in Thompson we have a man of unbalanced mind, with a chaotic sexuality, unable to support or care for himself who had a hatred of the women of the streets, but a poetic genius possessing all the elements fitting him for the role of a serial killer and driven by his drug addiction and the resulting delusions, to commit these crimes regardless of the risks and possible consequences.

As a medical examiner we learn from experience that there is virtually no crime that the drug addict may not be driven to commit, including parricide, the killing of one's mother and father, in order to support his addiction. Compared to killing a parent, the killing of a few downtrodden would be of no consequence, if his reward were to be recognition of his poetic genius, which he wanted above all else. His ultimate goal was to be ranked with the poets like Byron, Keats, Shelley and Coleridge.

When I entered college, my aptitude for mathematics led me to major in chemistry. The love of poetry, instilled in me by my mother, led me to minor in English Literature. This combination of science and poetry led me to understand who Francis Thompson really was. It was in a survey course of English Literature that I first became acquainted with Thompson's poetry. His most famous poem was 'The Hound of Heaven'. A poem which compared the all-forgiving love of God to the relentless pursuit of a criminal by a bloodhound. God's all forgiving love bent on saving a human soul from hell. Thompson was a poetic genius but a mad one and drug driven striving to obtain the fame and celebrity he desired beyond all else.

At about this same time I began to take a serious interest in criminology and to study the Ripper case. This interest was to the extent that in the company of a friend, we visited the University of Pennsylvania library several times and hand copied the articles about the Ripper murders that appeared in the issues of the Pall Mall Gazette in 1888.

Then in 1967, my relationship with the Ripper case was forever altered. In 1965, a book was published authored by Tom A. Cullen titled 'When London Walked In Terror', all about Jack the Ripper. This was followed in 1967 by a biography of Francis Thompson, by John Walsh titled 'Strange Harp, Strange Symphony'. These books were read at approximately the same time and I was amazed at the similarities between many of the elements in the two books. The more I learned about the Ripper murders and the life of Francis Thompson the more certain I became that Thompson was in fact Jack the Ripper.

The centennial of the Whitechapel murders was approaching and it was time to further muddy the waters with the name of yet another suspect. By this time, I was a busy medical examiner with a growing family to provide for and no spare time to write a book. With these things in mind, I opted to write an article for a publication devoted to criminology.

The story does not quite end there. The article was written and published in the winter 1988 issue of The Criminologist. As the result of my article, there was not one single letter of praise or criticism. I did get paid for the article but was so disappointed I never even cashed the check, it still resides in my filing cabinet. There the matter rested for twenty-eight years. Then in 2016 I received a call from Richard Patterson in Australia who had come to the same conclusion about Francis Thompson independently only to find that my article had secured for me bragging rights and I was still alive and kicking.

All the information presented here will be found by the critics hard to refute because it is in the suspect's own words, in his own handwriting. He left manuscripts, notebooks and letters behind and nothing has appeared or come to light that does not support the premise that Francis Thompson was indeed Jack the Ripper.

I was never happy about my discovery for as I got to know Thompson, his life, his works, his genius, and his terrible suffering, I felt sorry for him. If we are correct in our suspicions he will receive the fame he so sought but not for his poetic genius as he had hoped. I can only think of a quotation from a poem by John Dryden that can bring a fitting end to my little story, "Genius is near to madness oft allied and thin partitions do their bounds divide." God bless you Francis Thompson and forgive you if I am right and God forgive me if I am wrong.

Joseph C. Rupp, M.D., Ph.D
October 5, 2016

Introduction

In London, the largest and most powerful city in the world, on a very dark night, well over a century ago, the body of a woman was found. Although there were murders before, and after – what became known as the canonical five – this one was the first. She lay on a footpath. Her throat had been cut and although they could not find the knife, the police first thought that it was simply a case of suicide. The woman was obviously very poor and there was no reason to rob and kill her. Back then, in 1888, there were hardly such things as serial killers. Today, there are thousands all over the world. They kill between three and hundreds of people, and they seemingly kill for almost any reason: because they do not like blonde-haired people, or tall women, nurses, people called Ann or Margaret, anyone who resembles their mother, or women with bows or ribbons. It is felt that they kill for the sake of killing. They find it fun to watch the blood spurt. It thrills them to hear their victims beg for their lives. Such evil is hard to comprehend now, when this woman was found dead on the pavement, it was inconceivable. People back then killed for known reasons. They did it for money, for revenge, when they were fighting in a war, or if they had gone mad with a brain disease or unfettered power. Either way, the crimes of the murderer could, even if not forgiven, be understood. Violence was no stranger to the Victorians and the area where the woman was found was feared as a hotbed of crime. The earth's fractured history had brought forth genocides geared by a legion of murderers and cutthroats, and all similar evils – society was already soaked in it. Suicides were often found on the streets of London and it was common for drunken violence to lead to a stabbing. Scant attention was at first shown to this one dead woman. Little did they know that upon her death there began the actions of a new breed of criminal. One who seemed to want to settle an old score.

It was not until the police had taken the body to the morgue, and attendants undressed her, that they found her stomach had been cut open and her intestines protruded from it. Then the police realised that the woman had been murdered. It was possible that she had cut her own throat, but it was highly unlikely to accept that she had also cut her own stomach and pulled out part of her intestine. The police guessed that the murder was the random act of someone who had gone insane and it was a freak event, but then, about a week later, the killer struck again.

The area that these murders were taking place was rather small, less than a square kilometre. This second woman was found in the backyard of some flats and, like the first, her throat had been cut and her intestines dragged out. It was then that the police understood that there was a killer on the streets. The slayer was someone who was willing to kill repeatedly with no known motive. The police stepped up their patrols and paid particular attention to anyone acting suspiciously or appearing unusual, but they could not find the murderer.

How the Ripper murders stand, in relationship to what is now called the Victorian era, is well expressed by the British writer Sir Francis Osbert Sitwell in his 1929 book *The Sober Truth*. In the preface to his book about 19th-century enigmas, Sitwell concentrated on the Ripper crimes, explaining how, by the third murder, a consistent pattern emerged.

'By now, all three murders were recognised as the work of one man – a criminal of a very different stamp from the ordinary Whitechapel rough. During that year there happened to be an extraordinary outbreak of crime and the first two murders passed almost unnoticed among the many that were daily reported in the press. But the uniformity in the details of these tragedies could not fail to attract attention. One account would do for them all. The victim was a middle-aged woman, widowed or separated from her husband, barely subsisting on her earning as a prostitute. On the night of the crime she was drunk and penniless. The murderer was a stranger to her until a few minutes before he seized and killed her noiselessly, within earshot of at least half a dozen people. Then, careless of detection, he proceeded to mutilate her body.'

The American actor, director, and presenter Leonard Nimoy introduced these crimes in the 1978 television episode *In Search of Jack the Ripper*, with these words, 'London. The centre of the Victorian empire on whose colonies the sun never sets. The home of kings and queens, of magnificent monuments that only a thousand years of royalty could build, but it was also a city of cruel paradoxes.' These hard contrasts were shown by London's ability to display great wealth and poverty. The English writer Sir Sitwell elaborated on the differences within its empire in his treatise to one of the history's most perplexing mysteries.

'What a romantic epoch that is that unfolds itself? The world could not be changed, as each generation trusted it would be, by a few years of gaslight and steam-engines or telegraph and electric light. A thousand false messiahs born into this arid, sure and religious century. The same period which was the first, perhaps, to organise an efficient police… watched the noiseless and remorseless operations of Jack the Ripper... That series of anonymous and sequent murders that is the most frightening in the annals of English crime. Indeed as this dim, jaunty figure of vengeance slinks down the crooked, rat-ridden alleys, through the beautiful courts of older London, his murders seem to transcend crime and to attend by some of the monstrous and diabolic. Jack the Ripper displayed an anatomical knowledge that could not have gained in any other epoch. This fact, indeed, while it narrows down the field for inquiry only makes the figure of the murderer more mysterious. Did he belong to the professional classes, this terrible, quiet monster? Was he a doctor, a medical student, or a student of a veterinary college and, if so, for what purpose did he write the horrifying letters?'

The police who investigated what was formally named the Whitechapel Murders were at a loss as to what to do when they had what was thought to be a stroke of luck. The killer wrote a letter for the police to read. He called himself Jack the Ripper and he told them that he loved his work and his knife was nice and sharp. In another letter, the Ripper also let the authorities know what night he was going to kill again. He promised that he would slaughter two women this time, writing, 'Just for jolly wouldn't you.' The police were shocked at such jests, but also relieved that they could be ready to catch him. They sent out even more constables, with each officer having a lantern and a whistle. They made sure that they patrolled every street and that they would be in hearing distance or in sight of each other. If the murderer attempted to fulfil his promise of a double killing, then he was sure to be caught. Then, one night, the police found the body of a woman with her throat cut and another body a seven-minute walk away. The second woman had been cut up so badly that, as well removing parts of body and taking them away, he had cut small shapes under her eyelids. Beneath all this slaughter, it was discovered that the killer had such knowledge of anatomy to have caused in her instant death with little more than a nick in her neck. The surgeons, who had years of experience, said they could only have made the same injuries in just under half an hour in a brightly lit operating theatre. The killer had done this in less than fifteen minutes, in almost total darkness. It was then that people began to panic.

The newspapers told of rumours that the killer was possibly not human. How could anyone slip past so many police, kill these women and simply disappear? People began to act in odd ways. One woman, unrelated to the crimes, died of shock, simply from a newspaper account of them. Some of the most destitute and depressed prostitutes were overheard begging and praying that the murderer would take them next and end their horrible existences. Some men secretly dressed as women, pretending to be prostitutes, in the hope that they could lure and capture the killer.

All through London people grew fearful. Citizens banded together in mobs and searched the streets at night. In a city of five million people, almost every woman felt unsafe to be alone outside. Even if she were to live across the road, many asked to be escorted when walking home at night. Families fled the city. The Queen grew concerned and urged that the killer be stopped. Radicals and extremists used the murders to justify the failure of authorities to protect the people and they called for revolution. The highest officials in the land warned that these murders might topple the government. During all this commotion, people at least felt safe in their homes. The killer had struck on the streets – in alleyways, backyards and courtyards – but it was thought that as long as you stayed indoors, you were going to be all right.

The last, and the most horrible murder, happened in a bedroom. The woman had been cut up so badly that some of the people who saw her remains later killed themselves. It has been reported that bits of her flesh were found hanging from nails on the walls. Her breasts had been cut off and her arm pushed into her stomach. Her heart had been removed and her womb had been taken. Her face had been so badly cut that her partner could only identify her ears and eyeballs. The Queen called the head of the police, only to be told that he had quit. In a time of worldwide military and political conflict, Britain fought to control its dominion against a legion of warring armies and armed anti-colonial radicals. However, India and Africa were very far away. People were used to feeling safe at home in England; now it seemed as if the murderer besieged the entire city and everything had fallen apart. Then, when all hope was lost, the killings stopped. Things came back together and the wanted man simply vanished. But his legacy lingers.

Today, many serial killers all over the world worship and envy Jack the Ripper. That he successfully eluded so many gives them hope and spurs them on. Many of their killings are copycat murders of his. Numerous serial killers, when they are finally caught, admit their admiration of his deeds. For a hundred years, the best and brightest scholars and researchers have sought to find out who he was. It is reasoned that if we could only know his name then we could gain an insight, not only of him but also into the mind of all serial killers. We could find out what drives them and what makes them tick, and maybe stop them, even before they begin, and save possibly many thousands of lives. Some believe such monsters have no souls, that they are possessed or out of their minds. Humans are not perfect. We all have or are missing something. Our mistakes make us human, but what if serial killers are simply not endowed with what makes us human? They are the modern horror. They are feared and reviled universally. They gain no sympathy and nothing they say could redeem them.

In our civilisation, worse than terrorists, traffic accidents and cancers, must be the idea that the stranger you pass is a serial killer. Our society, with all its elegance and subtlety, has in its own centre such fears. Humanity revolves thus about inhumanity like lights about a black hole in the sky. Uncovering the invisible mask with which the serial killer hides would mean all this would be undone and a new star would dawn; if one could only find the key and wind the instrument right.

Those who already know something about the Ripper case will tell that pointing to a suspect is pointless. They say it has been too long after the event. In the absence of forensics, anyone who hated prostitutes could have been the murderer. All they would need was to have a knife, some skill and a good excuse for being in the area. They needed to be like Francis Thompson. When the murders happened, Thompson, then an ex-medical student, lived just a 15-minute walk to where all five women were knifed. The bed of this man, whose writing shows a hatred of prostitutes, was only 100 meters up the street from the last victim. At this time Thompson was carrying, under a long coat, a knife, which he kept razor sharp. All while he was hunting for a prostitute after their failed relationship.

After the press-frenzy generated by the Ripper murders, the papers soon turned their attention to other news items and scandals; the ghastly events surrounding these five victims were soon forgotten. Other distractions ensued, including the recently published works of a young Lancashire man.

Since coming onto the writing scene, Francis Joseph Thompson had made a name for himself with his passionate religious verses. There is confusion about the exact date that he was born in Preston, Lancashire. Most probably, it was on the 18th December 1859. He was the son of Charles Thompson, a medical doctor, and Mary Morton, a governess. Their first son, Charles Jnr, had died after his birth and Francis was their second and, subsequently, only son. Francis Thompson's parents were both converts to Roman Catholicism. His father considered that it was only natural that he would become a Catholic priest, but after several years of study it was deemed that it was not the will of God that he take on holy orders. So Thompson, at his mother's insistence, instead went on to study medicine in Manchester. Problems at home and distractions caused him to eventually give up medicine and, in 1885, he drifted to London where one calamity after another brought his downfall. Thompson soon became a vagrant living in destitution on the streets. A change of fortune in 1888 came to Thompson, with some of his first poems being published. The charitable editor rescued him from homelessness. Thompson recovered in body and mind and went on to produce many more pieces of verse – which later gained him a reputation as one of the great modern poets –before his early death in London of tuberculosis and complications from long-term opium abuse.

Out of all the people suspected of the Whitechapel crimes, it would be hard to imagine anyone less likely to fit the image of a rough and strong armed assassin – like the papers described – than this mild-mannered poet. The prime concern when describing Thompson in terms of guilt for the murders is that, as a poet, he is already famous. It is reasonable to assume that successful people have satisfied their desire for dominance and are therefore less likely to want to be any sort of murderer. This might be why it is statistically less likely that famous or successful people turn out to also be killers. Understandably, people would think it is unfair to choose a random, now long-dead, popular person, like this poet and journalist, and pin the crimes on him.

It is hard to believe that someone who had gained the public's trust and admiration could secretly kill five women without anyone noticing. Thompson was different because, even at his peak of fame, hardly anybody knew him. His fame was largely posthumous. After his rescue, he produced and published many poems and essays but it was not until the 1940s, many years after his death in 1907, that he became well known. In 1888, when he was a London vagrant, only a handful of people knew he was even alive. Having lost all ties with his former life and trying to live on the streets, most people had either forgotten him or thought he had died of exposure or starvation. All his life Thompson was a solitary, private person. He largely kept out of the limelight and refused all requests by the press to interview him. After 1888, there are no group photos of Thompson. He did not let any artists take his portrait. He let his memoirs be burnt and did not consent to biographies on himself. All his fan mail could have fitted in a single envelope; all his life's work did fit in a tin box. When he died in 1907, he had a small, private burial with only a handful of mourners.

Presently, hardly any credible experts on the murders, whom the writer Collin Wilson dubbed 'Ripperologists', give Thompson a brief glance. When they discuss strong suspects, Thompson is overlooked because of his celebrity. His poetry is his life's facade. It is what he is known for. As an example, when he died in 1907, the *London Times* wrote of him, 'entirely free from timidity in matters of poetic form… the poetry was at once great and sincere.'

What most people do not know about Mr Thompson, of course, was that up to the weeks preceding the murders he was a homeless bum. It was not until the eve of the Ripper murders that he could throw away the worn rags he had been wearing and buy himself a new suit. However, because he went on to be famous, he is largely ignored. The public has already seen the US crime writer Patricia Cornwell blame the well-known painter Walter Sickert for the murders. They have heard before the speculations that the murders were by a member of royalty like a prince, or that a high-ranking physician or powerful Freemason did it. Over the years, amateur sleuths and seasoned professionals alike have put forward names as a possible solution to who the Ripper was. Those suspected have ranged from illiterate seamen to high-standing doctors, police officials and academics. Almost no one has been spared accusation: poets, priests, politicians, petty thugs, prince and pauper have all been the subject of articles, books, plays and films asserting various people's guilt.

When someone reads that Thompson might have ripped five women apart, they rightfully hesitate. This dismissal is accentuated by our thinking that writers and especially poets are largely effeminate and they avoid life's harsher realities. Until Thompson's candidacy hit the news, most web searches on this book's suspect were in accord with the newspaper *Speaker'* that wrote of this man, 'Mr Thompson's poetry, at its very highest, attains a sublimity unsurpassed by any Victorian poet.' Most researchers think that the suggestion that Thompson also got around to killing and cutting-up five prostitutes is absurd or incredibly naive.

Researchers find it difficult to see Thompson as more than a man of letters and certainly not as the infamous letter writer Jack the Ripper. To make matters worse, soon after Thompson died, his life was re-written and sanitised for easier public consumption by his editor. Those few people he knew said he avoided his medical studies and hated the sight of blood, that he was a weak, aimless, innocent man. His editor, who happened to be a keen follower of the Victorian sensation that was the Ripper murders, managed Thompson's affairs. He took part in burning most of the damning of Thompson's written works, including many letters – those pieces in his writings that talked about strangling women or living in Crispin Street in the centre of Spitalfields where the murders happened were carefully edited and cleanly removed. His editor, who became his literary heir and made a fortune decades after Thompson's death, insisted that his gentle poet could not harm a fly.

Thompson is famous, and so is untouchable by mere mortals. It almost does not matter that he has a childhood of starting fires and performing acts of mutilation on dolls. Forgiven is his history of drug abuse, or that he consorted with prostitutes and had prior run-ins with the police, whom he has said were 'against him'. It seems to be not worth noticing that he borrowed more than four times the amount of money needed during his six years at medical school to purchase extra cadavers. This gave him more than one hundred bodies to cut up for hour after hour, while all alone in the basement mortuary of the Manchester Medical College.

After Thompson's death in 1907, the 1913 three volume *The Works of Francis Thompson* released by his editor who hoped to show Thompson as an intellectual who was mostly concerned with poetry about flowers and sunshine and literary criticism. By 1938 the reinvention of Thompson from the wayward, troublesome drug-addicted doctor's son into a pious, religious poet was complete. It would not be until after the 1950s that proper research would uncover that his editor and others made changes to Thompson's words after his death.

Nobody wanted to know how a poet who appears the most in anthologies might have been a serial killer. It shouldn't be true that a man who has gotten away with murder can be the same man that popular magazines like the *New Chronicle* and *Bookman*' praise with words such as,

'In all sobriety, do we believe him of all poets to be the most celestial in vision, the most august in faculty ... In a word, a new planet has swung into the ken of the watchers of the poetic skies ... It is patent on the first page that there is genius of rare inspiration ... page after page reveals the rich and strange, and the richer and stranger ... the reviewer feels the necessity of caution ... He is an argonaut of literature.'

Most people like to think the murderer was just another nobody, that he was an otherwise nondescript figure – one who faded away amongst the crowds. It takes a close look at Thompson's timeline to see that, when the murders happened, he was nobody and unknown to anyone where he lived. His past life as a vagrant for three years and its sordid details faded from the crowds as he became reborn as a poet. Universally, Thompson's innocence was praised. His goodness became saint-like and the image of a man steeped in biblical history whose only wants were spiritual became the standard view. Now there is this book. It aims to give a true account of who was probably Jack the Ripper.

Chapter 1

A Murderous Impulse

'I have never killed anything in my life.'

Francis Thompson, quoted from Wilfrid Blunt, "My Diaries: being a Personal Narrative of Events 1888 – 1914" (1908)

'He was one of the most innocent of men.'

Alice Meynell. "Some memories of Francis Thompson", Dublin Review (Jan. 1908)

Francis Joseph Thompson was born in Preston, Lancashire. His birth certificate is missing and different biographies and plaques give incorrect dates for his birth. The son of Thompson's publisher, Everard Meynell, in his 1913 biography of Thompson, has recorded him as saying,

'I was born in 1858 or 1859 (I never could remember and don't care which) … the house wherein I was born; and it seemed to me disappointingly like any other house.'

It was probably on Sunday 18 December, 1859, on an exceedingly cold and frosty day, that Thompson came into the world, in the family home at Number 7 Winckley Street, Preston. Thompson was born into banality. His birth was a quiet and private affair, with his father acting as the midwife. His baptism was performed at Preston's St Ignatius Church, though even this is in doubt. His record of baptism misspells his name as *Thomson*. His mother's maiden name is wrongly spelled too, as *Moreton* when it was actually *Morton*. This book follows the tradition of calling Thompson a Catholic, though the errors in his baptismal record challenge that he was even of the faith. The Catholic Church, for the most part, has had a glorious history, and if this book promotes Thompson as a suspect, it does not condemn Catholicism. It is this writer's opinion that Thompson's unique brand of religion did not represent Catholics. Rather, it was an aberration of this religion.

Thompson's parents were recent Catholic converts and for their part, true believers. Their home was a gathering place for the local clergy. Preston has been long held as a very Catholic city, and is in fact believed to be the most Catholic city in England; its Catholics had formed a close-knit community. Since the Reformation, Catholics had been barred from many professions. These included that of doctors. Though recent laws introduced only a few years before Thompson's birth had repealed these restrictions, Catholics still bore the stigma of persecution.

Francis's father, Dr Charles Thompson, (1823-96), at the age of 36, was a homeopathic doctor. Dr Thompson was also a lay healer, taking on religious responsibilities such as baptising dying infants. Before setting up practice with a dispensary and surgery at the rear of his house, the doctor began his career in Bristol. His brethren saw Dr Thompson as affordable and hardworking. Poetry and literature held little interest for him, unlike three of his five brothers. The surgeon John Costall Thompson esteemed him for his 1848 poem *A Vision of Liberty*. Reverend Henry Thompson published his sermon *The New Birth by Water and Spirit* in 1850. Edward Healy Thompson, once an Anglican curate, was a professor of English Literature at the University of Dublin. He was also a sonnet writer whose verse was upon religious topics. Edward Healy was co-editor of a series of pamphlets known as the *Clifton Tracts*. These publications were controversial due to the radical Catholic views they expressed. Finally, James Thompson began a biography on his nephew Francis but died serving as a police officer in the Boer war before his work could be published.

The poet's mother, Mary Morton Thompson (1822-80), converted to the Roman Catholic faith when she was 32. After failing in her attempt to become a nun, Mary became engaged to a fellow Catholic. In response, Mary's Protestant family disowned her. Soon after, her fiancé died. Mary spent time as a governess before marrying Dr Thompson. After her first son lived for just one day, at the age of 37, Mary gave birth to a second and thereafter only son, Francis.

Francis is a very popular name for Catholics. The most well-known Francis, apart from the current Pope Francis, was Saint Francis of Assisi. Francis Thompson was largely interested in this saint and would one day write an essay on him. This Italian saint was the first person to manifest the wounds known as stigmata. This was spontaneous bleeding from locations corresponding with the five wounds of the crucified Christ. The constant pain took two years to kill him. One day Thompson would grow up to write an essay on Saint Francis. Considering that this book chooses to see that Thompson was Jack the Ripper, a maniac who killed at least five women, we should ponder why, in his essay, Francis happily praised this saint's suffering. He wrote that, 'the pain of his stigmata was agonising, but was accompanied by a sweetness so intense as made it ecstatic to him ... Pain may be made the instrument of joy.' Everard Meynell, in his biography on Thompson, tried to understand this poet's disturbing world-view, 'The something awry, the disordering of sympathy, the distorting perspective, is hard to name. Perhaps loneliness, perhaps disease, perhaps his poetry, perhaps the devil.' {LIFE}

Despite the death of an elder brother he never knew, Francis Thompson would not be an only child. Three sisters would follow – Mary, Helen and Margaret. In 1864, when Thompson was five years old, Helen, aged 15 months, caught tuberculosis, then known as consumption, and died. Tuberculosis was a prevalent lung disease, typified by the wasting away of the body. Dr Thompson, despite all his homeopathic remedies, was unable to save her. With a vaccine for tuberculosis not available until 1944, sufferers faced a grim outcome. Some 42 years later, this disease would be blamed for taking the life of her brother, Francis, in 1907.

The first of many strange coincidences involving Francis Thompson is probably that one of his playmates would himself become a Ripper suspect. James Kelly was a fellow Preston Catholic – born four months after Thompson – and lived only a few blocks away. Undoubtedly, both the Kelly and Thompson family attended the same church. Kelly grew up to become a hardened criminal and was discussed as a suspect in James Tully's *The Secret of Prisoner 1167 - Was This Man Jack The Ripper*.

In 1864 the Thompson family moved to Ashton-under-Lyne, near Manchester. As he had done in Preston, Dr Charles Thompson opened his homeopathic surgery from their new residence in Stamford Street. Unlike Preston, in which Catholics felt a sense of security, if not acceptance, Manchester was considered a Protestant stronghold. Catholics were viewed with distrust. The family was shunned and so their social life was restricted to clergy. Thompson's sister Mary said, 'We did not have any friends apart from the priests of four or five who would gather to dine and pass the evening' This restricted existence was remembered by Francis' sister Margaret who said of it was 'a horrid little place'. John Carroll was one priest who made friends with the family. One day he would prove instrumental in helping Thompson's rescue from London's streets in 1888.

Francis Thompson's development was different to others' early on. He was quickly seen as an awkward and secretive child, and the move to Ashton only increased his reserve. As he matured, Thompson continued to become increasingly strange, with habits such as smiling and talking to himself. In 1867, he was again marked by death when his maternal grandfather, Joseph Morton, a bank clerk, died in the Thompson's Ashton home. There is little to indicate that Joseph Morton and his daughter, Thompson's mother Mary, had previously reconciled their religious differences. Thompson dealt with his passing by becoming more withdrawn and controlling. His sister Mary wrote of how an agitated Thompson would take charge over her and her sister Margaret, compelling them to play games that centred on military conflicts, 'In our playroom he used to get Maggie and me to join him in mimic sieges,' she said. His two younger sisters learned not to say no to him, with Mary recalling, 'He could get into a temper when roused.' His outbursts of anger often turned to resentment, and in competitions he proved to be a sore loser.

Once the children's governess offered a prize for the best pupil and despite Francis excelling his sisters in class, the prize, a clockwork mouse, went to Mary for her good walking pace during outings. Even though many years later Mary could not remember why she had won it, she was not surprised that her brother still did. In a letter she wrote she said, 'But Francis never forgot it;

he could never see the justice of it, he said.' When his mood changed and he became withdrawn and uncommunicative, the phrase for this was that Thompson was 'up in the moon again'.

Francis Thompson's moodiness, need to control, secrecy and withdrawal might have been a phase he was going through. It might have all gone away, allowing him to become a well-adjusted individual. He might have been the product of a sad but otherwise peaceful childhood, but destiny had other plans. Ever since Jack the Ripper, arguably the first modern serial killer, people have tried to fathom what sort of mind would be compelled to commit crimes of this nature. With around 2,000 people killed by these folk annually in the United States alone, this wish to understand these murderers is not simply an academic one. Through countless interviews with convicted killers, forensic psychologists have concluded that the formative years are considered important to the making of an adult of sound mind. When criminal psychologists ascertain the mental state of a suspect, they often look to the client's childhood. They look for mutilation themes in their play. As an example, there is the United States serial killer Edmund Kemper III. The theme of childhood acts of mutilation is echoed in Kemper. During one Christmas, when Kemper III was a child, his grandparents gave his sister a doll. Kemper desired and stole it and it was only to be found by the sister decapitated and handless. A few years later Kemper would move from removing the heads off dolls to humans.

This destructive sign in Kemper's childhood is very similar to Francis Thompson's. He once complained to his doting mother about why only his sisters were allowed dolls. Finally his mother relented and he was given a series of dolls. None of them lasted very long, after being subject to his particular method of play. A method that would be of particular interest to child psychologists today. Of one doll in particular, which he had become overtly fond of, Thompson would write many years later,

'With another doll of much personal attraction, I was on the terms of intimate affection, till a murderous impulse of scientific curiosity incited me to open her head, that I might investigate what her brains were like. The shock which I then sustained has been a fruitful warning to me, I have never since looked for a beautiful girl's brains.'

Psychologists, when studying subjects with passion for violence, will look at their childhood and signs of some trauma. Although some serial killers can have a perfectly uneventful upbringing, most have suffered or witnessed overt violence, causing deep-seated fear and aggression. In the case of Francis Thompson, such violence is not hard to find. It was not in the form of a sadistic father, drunken mother or beating. It revolved about an episode for which Francis Thompson could find no comparison apart from an apocalypse.

In May 1868, when Francis was almost nine years of age, he became part of a full-scale and bloody riot. In that year, an anti-Catholic agitator, named William

Murphy, brought his propaganda to Ashton-under-Lyne. His rabble-rousing heralded a chain of events that would lead to violent ends. Murphy made a series of fiery speeches, expounding his hatred for Catholicism. The Catholic religion to Protestants was then shrouded in mystery and secrecy. Fear of the unknown had caused wild rumours to spread. There were claims of a conspiracy headed by the Pope in Rome against the people of England; even worse, some said that the rites and rituals practiced by Catholics involved horrible acts including infanticide.

Murphy appealed to the largely Protestant crowd to riot against the Catholics. On 10th May, a mass of people rushed through streets attacking almost every Catholic house. Wielding hammers, hatchets and knives, the rioters wreaked havoc; furniture was overturned and household items and bedding were strewn onto the roads and gutters. Scores of people were shot and stabbed. They included Thomas Summer, a clothier who suffered scalp wounds from a bullet while walking in Stamford Street, the street that Thompson lived. Dr Thompson would have been quickly summoned to treat the wounded in his back-room dispensary. It would have been impossible to shield his son from the carnage. A large mob descended upon the two small Catholic churches of St Mary and St Anne. The interior of St Anne, in nearby Cavendish Street, was destroyed. The *Manchester Guardian* newspaper gave a detailed account of the damage,

'The appearance of the chapel could not easily be forgotten by anyone who had the opportunity of seeing it shortly after the event. The floors in every part were strewn with broken glass, stones and brick-bats; benches were broken, pictures torn down and destroyed; a brass bell used in divine service had been taken from the alter steps and broken into fragments; an oil painting of the Sacred Heart was cut through and torn; a holy water font broken; the alter in the chapel dedicated to St Joseph destroyed and a figure of the saint removed and broken to pieces; and the whole of the canvas matting in the aisles had been taken up. The figure was seen to be carried off by one of the rioters and dashed to fragments against the street pavement.'

As houses continued to be broken into and people attacked, the Thompson family, with Francis in tow, ran with other parishioners to the comparative safety of the surviving church of St Mary. The enraged mob, who numbered almost 3,000, then attempted to storm the little church, while families, including the Thompsons, sealed the doors and mounted a guard inside. The rioters attacked with bottles, stones, burning timber and gunshot. The constabulary could not control the crowds and the Riot Act was read. The siege continued and military personnel had to be called in. It took trained militia three days to quell the bloodshed. By the end of the chaos, 111 houses of the Catholic congregation had been broken into and gutted.

Such events might have sent any normal boy mad. There were no counsellors to comfort Francis. Neither were there the familiar faces of priests; for months the entire clergy, fearing for their lives, were obliged to leave town. Francis's only relief was to turn to the pages of the bible for comfort, but the section, which he could not help returning to repeatedly, was the Apocalypse. This details the reign of the antichrist and the end of the world. Francis Thompson had already concluded by the age of 10 that, 'The world – the universe – is a fallen world.' When he would grow up to write about these passages, it is little wonder that Thompson seems to recall the Ashton riot,

'An appalling dream; insurgent darkness with wild lights flashing through it ... on the earth hurryings to-and-fro, like insects at a sudden candle; unknown voices uttering out of darkness darkened and disastrous speech; and all this in motion and turmoil ... Such is the "Apocalypse" as it inscribes itself on the verges of my childhood memories.'

In the summer of June 1870, Francis, upon meeting her, became entranced with a girl named Lucy Keogh. He had met and was instantly smitten with this friend of his sister, Mary, at an outing. He did not inform Lucy of his feelings and a second meeting was interrupted when he was sent away to college. The memory of that single meeting would become forever fixed in his consciousness, he recording the briefest glance she threw to him in his poem *Dream Tryst* of a fantasy in which he encountered Lucy once again:

'There was no change in her sweet eyes

Since last I saw those sweet eyes shine;

There was no change in her deep heart

Since last that deep heart knocked at mine.

Her eyes were clear, her eyes were Hope's,

Wherein did ever come and go

The sparkle of the fountain-drops

From her sweet soul below.'

Before the end of the summer of 1870, Thompson took the long train journey to the northern county of Durham. The institution, which was chosen by his father who had dreams of his son becoming a priest, was St Cuthbert's in Ushaw. This was a Seminary College and boarding school, which prepared novice priests to take Holy Orders. Thompson's general hatred for his classmates, who described him as 'abnormal' was an indicator of one he held for most other people later in life.

'...a veritable demoniac revelation. Fresh from my tender home, and my circle of just-judging friends, these malignant school-mates who danced around me with mocking evil distortion of laughter ... devilish apparitions of a hate now first known; hate for hate's sake, cruelty for cruelty's sake. And so such they live in my memory, testimonies to the murky aboriginal demon in man.'

Although Thompson was sometimes seen at the courts and showed proficiency in sports like racquet or handball, he spent most his time in the school library. It held 45,000 volumes. This was a huge selection of books, for a school back then. The library boasted a good range on ecclesiastical and general history. Even in the library Thompson felt that his classmates were out to get him. He was often found at a desk with spare books set up as a barrier to shield him from possible paper bullets, catapulted from other pupils.

Despite Thompson's difficulty in socialising at St Cuthbert's, his rate of learning was remarkable. By the age of 14, he knew how to speak, read and write in Sanskrit and French, and he excelled in Latin, English and Greek. In a school that had about 1,000 students, Thompson won 16 of the school's 21 competitive exams in essay writing. The school's English master said, in 1872, that Thompson's essays were, 'the best production from a lad his age I have ever seen in this seminary. Thompson's writing all showed a fascination for war and the more bloody battles of history. His essays, with titles such as *The Storming of the Bridge of Lodi*, based upon a Napoleonic battle, earned him the nickname of *L'homme militaire*, which meant *Our Soldier*.'

Chapter 2
Twisted Fire Starter

'Mystic images, inhuman, cold. That flameless torches
hold. But who can wind that horn of might. Open for
him shall roll the conscious gate; and light leap up from
all the torches there, and life leap up in every
torchbearer.'

Francis Thompson.

During the Christmas break of 1872, Francis Thompson
returned home and presented to the world another well-
known trait of serial killers – arson. The start, of what is
now known as the canonical-five Ripper murders, was
announced by a red glow in the night sky. This was from
not one but two warehouse fires in the nearby docklands.
It all started a few hours before the 31st August murder
of Mary Ann Nichols. The fires happened in the West
India docks, a huge and sprawling Thameside complex.
When the warehouses were first built in 1802, they were
the largest brick buildings in the world. The first fire was
in the dry docks of Shadwell. The second fire was in the
Spirit Quay, in which a three-storied warehouse had

caught fire. The West India London Docks were about a 30-minute walk from the murder.

There was the real danger of an explosion. Beneath the quay's warehouse were vaults containing brandy, a drink made from 40% flammable alcohol. The vaults held around 200 kegs that housed 27,000 litres of liquor. Beneath this warehouse was kept enough explosive bottled alcohol to tear down buildings. The blaze could be seen for kilometres and by 10 o'clock thousands of curious onlookers were at the scene. These fires, which erupted on a gloomy night, drew thousands of people in, all in search of free entertainment. Police from nearby Whitechapel's H Division were called in to assist in the emergency. Further police, from other divisions, were also enlisted to control crowds and clear streets for rescue vehicles. This left mainly inexperienced recruits or replacement police from other districts to patrol Whitechapel. J Division police, of the adjacent Bethnal Green, where the first victim was found. They also had to hastily reorganise their nightly patrols. Being new, many of these police could not have known the difference between a local or a stranger. Anything unusual would have been unnoticed. The fire was fierce and was not brought under control until well after midnight. So much mayhem from one little matchstick would have provided a wary killer with the perfect diversion. The fire too had brought in people from other parts of London, who wanted a better view. Despite the power and the danger of the blaze, the fiery colours and smoke mingling in the sky gave a vaguely festive air to the East End. The flames were described as 'gigantic and fantastic' by a reporter standing on London Bridge. Whitechapel's prostitutes must have welcomed having more customers to earn enough for a night's lodgings and a little more money besides.

By most accounts, when the fires were raging, Thompson was then living at 21 West India Docks Road. It was here, in the district of Limehouse, that he was staying at the newly opened Salvation Army Homeless Shelter. This refuge was around four kilometres southeast from the murder site and Limehouse was the district adjacent to the fires.

Thompson was born into an ultra-conservative Catholic family, and it was they who sent him to study as a Catholic seminary student for the priesthood. It would seem natural that he would stay away from the Salvation Army, a protestant religious organisation, but it was this organisation's military air that attracted him. We know this from his 1891 essay, 'Catholics in Darkest England'. In the essay, Thompson applauded the military persona of this charity. He signed his essay 'Francis Tancred'. He got that name from the crusading knight who lived from 1076 to AD 1112. This knight helped capture Jerusalem from the Muslims and was, for a short time, Prince of Galilee. His essay championed the word 'army' in Salvation Army. He described the condition of poverty in occult terms. He suggested that the work of the Salvation Army be converted into a weapon and that the poor, particularly prostitutes and their issue, should be thrown into the Thames.

Thompson's, who lived so close to the dock fires, was a serial fire-starter from a young age. He began two separate blazes, before the age of fourteen. Here is an account by Mr. E. Byrne, a childhood playmate that describes Thompson's tendency to start fires, in 1869, when Thompson was 10,

'He asked if he could not have a red cassock. He was told he could not, he was too tall and the candle bearers were the only ones in red. He admired James Clayton's cassock (a pretty purple one) but Clayton was the boat bearer (the smallest boy) and walked with the thurifer [a container on a chain used to hold burning incense]. With bad grace Thompson donned a black cassock and surplice. The Host day [the Sunday] passed over very well, but the following Sunday, quite unexpectedly, he seized a long metal taper holder, went on the side altar and began to light up the big candles. Frank MacFarlane, head clerk, rushed on and took the taper from him, before the whole of the candles and sticks might have been spread about the altar.'

Mr Byrne was also present and witnessed the second fire, begun by Thompson, upon his return home in July 1872 for the summer break. What is interesting is how, in this second incident, Thompson afterwards returns to his seat as if nothing had happened, appearing completely innocent.

'Later on, I was promoted to be thurifer, with Clayton still as boat boy. But Thompson used to tell us at low mass that he was a nobody and had nothing to do. The thurifer spent much time in the vestry keeping his charcoal in good condition, sometimes dropping the lid of the thurible to swing up the light.

'Thompson quite unexpectedly came to the side of the altar and saw me revolving the thurible. In a minute he had hold of it, opened the thurible, and ere I could protest he was whizzing it round. He caught the floor and all the charcoal was scattered over the vestry floor. I ran to the housekeeper's room and she came with a shovel, stamped out what she could and carried away the rest, while I was heating more charcoal. When I returned Thompson had gone back to his seat on the altar.'

The second attempt got him into the local paper, the *Ashton Reporter*, in December 1930, with E. Byrne's article, *Boyhood Days in Ashton: Francis Thompson*, which detailed Thompson's charcoal burner fireball and the general panic it caused. This incident may be played down as a minor childhood prank by some, but Thompson cherished it, remembering to imbed the incident in his most well-known poem, *The Hound of Heaven*, with these lines,

'In the rash lustihead of my young powers,

I shook the pillaring hours

My days have crackled and gone up in smoke,

Even the linked fantasies, in whose blossomy twist

I swung the earth a trinket at my wrist.'

The writer, GK Chesterton, when writing about this poem, saw the significance Thompson accorded it. To Chesterton, this spiteful rebellion was not just against a small church on the outskirts of town. He saw it as a potent symbol of Thompson's greater defiance to the wider world. Chesterton said of the *Hound of Heaven*,

'He was describing the evening earth with its mist and fume and fragrance, and represented the whole as rolling upwards like a smoke; then suddenly he called the whole ball of the earth a thurible'

Some years after the murders and warehouse fires, Thompson held a double event on one night when he used a match to set fire to some curtains in his lodging house. He then kicked over a lamp, setting fire to his lodging room. He left his landlady to die in that fire and later jested about it. Of the fire, a business associate, Lewis Hind, asked Thompson, 'But Francis, did you not rouse your landlady?' Thompson's reply was typical of his callous view on outsiders. 'My dear Hind, a house on fire is no place for tarrying.'

Thompson's history of such fire-starting is restricted to what was made public and seems minor in comparison to the great conflagrations of the West India Docks. Fires such as these though, with their destructive beauty, held a special appeal to Thompson. Our suspect for the Ripper murders, because he had intimate knowledge of London's streetscape due to his three years of destitution on them, was once asked to write upon his experiences. It was to be for an illustrated book called *London at Night*. Thompson's letter to William Hyde, the illustrator, spoke of his fascination of such fires. He told which illustrations took his interest. 'I plan to write on, *Houseless wanderer sleeping in the streets* and *Factory at Night*, since I have in mind such a factory across Westminster. And I intend to describe a night fire. It is effect I wish to dwell on; the character of horror, sombreness and suggestiveness of London, because I have seen it most peculiarly under those aspects.'

Nobody has so far seen anything but a coincidence in there being two dramatic incidents that night – the first murder and these dock fires.

That the serial killer, Jack the Ripper, may have also been the fire starter is not ever considered by most Ripperologists. Even though most serial killers are also fire starters. One of the most common warning signs that potential serial killers show is a passion for setting fires. We can see this in many serial killers including New York's David Berkowitz, the 'Son of Sam' killer, and San Francisco's David Carpenter, the 'Trailside Killer'

Thompson's childhood history, that included fire-starting, mutilation of dolls and refusal to communicate, showed an unsound mind, but is it fair to paint him as a possible psychopath? Paul Van K, in his 1973 *Francis Thompson a Critical Biography*, wrote that while Francis Thompson studied at Ushaw College as a priest his strange, secretive, behaviour 'gives evidence of a schizophrenic tendency in him.' {Paul Van K p28}. This opinion was backed up by respected psychiatrists Thomas Verner Moore. He wrote of Francis Thompson's personality in the fifth volume of the 1918 *Psychoanalytic Review*. In his article, *The Hound of Heaven*, Moor wrote of Thompson that, 'At Ushaw he manifested that shut-in reaction type which might readily have developed into a full-grown dementia praecox.' [childhood psychosis]. Moore explained in his article that the 'shut-in' personality 'tends to become psychopathic.'

Doctor William B. Ober, followed suit. Dr Ober was an internationally recognized Director of Pathology in New York. In 1968, in the *New York Academy of Medicine* journal, his article *Drowsed With The Fume Of Poppies*, appeared. It was on opium-addicted poets. His summary of Thompson was damming. Dr Ober wrote, of the poet's life.

'Francis Thompson (1859-1907) was that of an overt psychopath and known addict'

Of Thompson's poetry, such as his *Hound of Heaven*, which has the words, "Naked I wait Thy love's uplifted stroke!" the good doctor continued,

'An expression of the most masochistic attitude ever adopted by any poet who has written in English, even beyond the customary limits of self-flagellation or martyrdom.'

In July 1877, as Thompson entered his adult years and his fellow scholars took their Holy Orders for a life in the priesthood, his parents received a report from the school. The letter was from the president of the college, who wrote to Dr Charles Thompson telling him, as kindly as possible, that Thompson was not suited to become a priest.

The reason for this was put down to 'idleness' though this description hardly suits a high achiever whose previous reports home said, 'Frank gives the greatest satisfaction in every way.' The confidentiality of his schoolmasters forbid us knowing the exact truth, though later John McMaster, the shoemaker who hired Thompson in 1886, remarked of him, 'There was something wrong between him and the priests.' Perhaps they sensed or saw that there was something not quite right about him. Regardless, the head of the school wrote to his father, Dr Thompson,

'With regard to Frank ... I have been most reluctantly compelled to concur in the opinion of his director and others that it is not the holy will of God that he should go on for the priesthood ... he has the ability to succeed in any career.' {LIFE p32}

Chapter 3
Apt Pupil

'How praise the colour of her eyes, uncaught
while they were coloured with her varying thought.'

Francis Thompson.

In September of 1878 Thompson returned to his Stamford Street home, and his mother, forever forgiving of her son's faults, desired that he become a surgeon. In the same month as his return, Thompson passed the entrance examination to Manchester's Owens Medical College, with honours.

Catholic priests are forbidden to marry, and this would have been the case for Thompson if he had been accepted to the priesthood. All through his teenage years, Thompson would have been led to believe that he would never engage in sex with a woman, let alone marry one. Now suddenly, with his rejection from a life in the church, came the prospect that he would be expected to one day wed and settle down. While other men, at the age of 19, were either married or courting, Thompson chose to find the perfect match by asking God for help. As Thompson would later relate, 'It was my practice from the time I left college to pray for the lady whom I was destined to love – the unknown She.'

While he prayed nightly for a suitable woman and waited for college to begin, Thompson launched into his favourite pursuit of immersing himself in great battles. In 1878, the year of his return home, Russia and Turkey were at war. The conflict culminated in a drawn-out siege lasting from July till December. When the Russians attacked Plevna, a fortified Turkish town, with 35,000 men and 170 heavy guns, the Turks fought back with lesser force of 22,000 men and only 58 heavy guns. The toll against the Russian army was great, with 7,300 men dying daily. After three weeks of fighting, in which the Russians lost 27,500 men, they were forced into retreat. It took almost half a year until the Russians captured the town. While most Englanders with an interest in the battle simply read about it in the daily papers, Francis Thompson displayed his typical initiative. He was then aged 19, when he commandeered the ground floor of his family's home and requisitioned all the furniture available to build a replica of the beleaguered city. Using planks of wood and chairs made into walls and towers he recreated and fought the battles, taking turns of the Russian and Turkish sides. As his family and servants continued with the running of the household, navigating his 'city' Thompson again lived up to the words of Canon Henry Gillow. He was school prefect when Thompson was at the seminary. Gillow told of Thompson's obsession for war, 'His tastes were not as ours. Of history he was very fond, and particularly of wars and battles …to put some of their episodes into the concrete.' This is a telling description of young Francis Thompson, who would one day walk the streets of Spitalfields, where terrified citizens would feel as if they were under siege by the Ripper.

Thompson's homemade battlements could not protect him from responsibilities. Owens college, was one of the most modern and progressive. It was here, for the next six years, that Thompson was instructed and practised the latest surgical techniques. To become a student doctor at the college it was mandatory that applicants possessed a high physical strength. This was so they could handle the physical workload and struggling patients. The arduous years spent there were one steeped in the growing sciences of dissection and anatomy. His college stressed practical learning over bookwork and the college register for attendance shows Thompson was as committed to his studies as any student could be and spent six years here training to be a surgeon. Here is a description of life at college for Thompson from 1878 onwards. It is from the writer Bridget Boardman's 1988 biography on Thompson, called 'Between Heaven & Charing Cross', she described the curriculum and working conditions of the lecture theatre, autopsy rooms and the busy Manchester Royal Infirmary where he worked as a student surgeon.

'Anatomy had always occupied a central place in training and the dissecting of cadavers was accompanied by far more practical experience in assisting at operations ... his time was almost equally divided between the college and the hospital.'

Boardman explained in her biography that anatomy was central to his studies, 'Before the discovery of x-rays, it was the only adequate means for students to gain the knowledge they needed.' There rose the belief that Thompson, because he became a celebrated writer, spent his years reading in the college library. This image of the book loving class dodger is very unlikely. Boardman wrote that, since the college stressed practical anatomy and work on cadavers, students 'were deliberately discouraged from using the library in preference to the dissecting room.' {Charing p41}. From 1878 to 1883, Francis Thompson studied to be a surgeon. Any idea that Thompson's love of books meant he slinked off to the library during those six years at medical school is unfounded. College attendance rules were so strict that if Thompson had skipped a day of school, his father would have been informed. The regulations at Owens Medical College, at Thompson's time as a student, state, 'A daily record is kept of the attendance in the lecture room. Absences will be reported to the principal, who will, at his discretion, cause the same to be notified to the parent or guardian of the defaulting student.' Thompson is listed as a student in all the university calendars of those years, with attendance for most terms credited to him. This attendance requirement was strengthened by a peculiarity of his instructor, Dr Julius Dreschfeld. He was so vehement that students attend his rounds and lectures that he was known to refuse giving instruction if a single student was absent.

Dr Dreschfeld, a professor of pathology, was Thompson's lecturer of pathology and his infirmary director. A brand new method taught at Thompson's medical school when he attended was the Virchow technique. It was taught in England, exclusively in Thompson's student college. Dr Julius Dreschfeld had instigated this technique into the college. The professor had just returned from Germany when Thompson began his studies. Dreschfeld had studied in Germany as a pupil of the esteemed pathologist Rudolf Virchow. Having learned the Virchow method, Dreschfeld taught it in Thompson's classes and in the infirmary's surgery. He was said to be a brilliant and popular instructor who was followed by a trail of students. They took notes from his demonstrations on patients and cadavers, and were in awe of his photographic memory for the science and practice of pathology. Dreschfeld was seen as the authority on the Virchow method and was instrumental in introducing it into England.

At college Francis Thompson focused on the craft of a doctor, and presented himself as the typical student. At home, though, Thompson swapped his medical text for romance novels and Elizabethan novels and plays. Now a young man, Thompson, who had never had a girlfriend, lost himself between the covers of the three volumes of *Cassell's Illustrated Shakespeare*. Printed in 1875, it held black and white drawings from the plays by the English painter Henry Courtney Selous. Thompson, who had never been with a woman, was limited by this book. His view of them was formed from this book's representations. Its depictions of women, from two centuries earlier, only caused his understanding of them to become increasingly separate from reality. The divide between the images conjured up by seventeenth-century Shakespearean books and women in the latter half of the nineteenth century vexed Thompson. That these women he would meet in his daily transactions did not meet up to his idealised expectation was blamed by him on one event which had meant a disaster to all Catholics in England. The sixteenth-century English Reformation was when the Church of England broke away from the authority of the Pope and the Roman Catholic Church. It was a time of violence and brought about the English Civil Wars, which ended when the last Roman Catholic monarch, James II, was beheaded. To Thompson the reformation, as well as crushing his beloved religion, forever changed the character of women. His nostalgia for these pictures from Cassell's book was kept close to his heart and increased his bitterness toward the modern Anglican England in which he, a born Catholic, had to live. Here Thompson records the lasting effects of those three volumes,

'I understood love in Shakespeare ... Those girls of floating hair I loved; and admired the long-haired, beautiful youths whom I met in these pictures which I connected with the lovely, long-tressed woman of FC Selous' illustrations to Cassell's Shakespeare, my childish introduction to the supreme poet ... Comparing the pictures of medieval women with the crinolined and chignoned girls of my own day, I embraced the fatal but undoubting conviction that beauty expired somewhere about the time of Henry VIII. I believe I connected that awful catastrophe with the Reformation.' {LIFE}

Francis Thompson's brooding over these women that he could never have took up most of his time. He did nothing to participate in the running of the household or in helping his father in his backroom surgery. Thompson's loathing of participating frustrated his family. His sister, Mary, who saw he did little to commend himself for family responsibility said, 'He required looking after, almost like a child, though he was the eldest in the family.' Even if his own family tried to deny it, Thompson's peculiar behaviour could not be long hidden. Neighbours would remember that Thompson would leave his house on weekends with untied laces and make his way up Stalybridge Road, muttering to himself, in his quick odd step, to wander Manchester's public art gallery.

Everard Meynell remarked on Thompson's strange love obsessions in his 1913 biography on this book's suspect.

'The actor in unreal realities. Already he had been thrice in love with the heroine of Selous' Shakespeare, with a doll, with a statue.'

Modern psychologists would now see something pathological in someone fetishizing over inanimate objects. Thompson's attraction to dolls had culminated in him opening up their heads. His love for a book's Shakespearean illustrations had convinced him that modern women were dammed to hell. His third and final love, apart from with his prostitute in the years of the Ripper murders, was the bust of a woman. He found it in the plaster section of the Manchester art gallery. This long room with high ceilings held copies of great sculptures for art students to study and draw. Francis believed that no living woman could equal the plaster bust, 'for she was a goddess.' The statue was called the *Vatican Melpomene*. *Melpomene* was one of nine muses of Greek mythology. *Melpomene* was a mystical being and she bestowed artistic creativity. This entity, whose name means 'to sing', was the muse of tragedy, song and harmony. Known as the saddest muse, Thompson's attraction to it was from what he felt was a mistake in the casting procedure causing damage to the mouth. It meant that one corner showed the hint of dreamy happiness, while the other drooped as if from some suggested sadness. By viewing the statue from either a left or right, two different expressions could be seen, but when it was viewed straight on the two corners of the mouth combined to produce an emotion in him 'which was inexpressible'. Was this fleeting and tantalising feeling the balance of mind of a normality that eluded him? On weekends and throughout the evenings of weekdays, Thompson would go to the gallery to stare transfixed at the statue. He would remain standing until evening, though he would tell his parents he was studying for his exams. He would wait in anticipation for the sun to set while he stared into the plaster eyes, as they seemed to come to life. This is how he described it,

'Thither each evening, as twilight fell, I stole to meditate and worship the baffling mysteries of her meaning: as twilight fell ... the eyes broke out from their day-long ambuscade [ambush]. Eyes of violet blue, drowsed-amorous, which surveyed me not, but looked

62

ever beyond, where a spell enfixed them. Waiting for something, not for me … Between us, now, are years and tears; but the years waste her not, and the tears wet her not; neither misses she me or any man. There, I think, she is standing yet; there, I think, she will stand for ever: the divinity of an accident, awaiting a divine thing impossible, which can never come to her, and she knows this not.'

This statue, and how in the gloom of twilight it seemed alive to Thompson, shows us not only his fascination of lasting inanimate lifeless females, but also his growing dissatisfaction with changing living women. We see him return to this theme constantly in his writing. We see it in his only murder story. As the following passage from it shows. After his story's 'hero' kills his love, he cannot stop seeing her eyes in the gloom of night, even as her dying makes her immortal to him.

'Whereat she cried; and I, frenzied, dreading detection, dreading, above all, her wakening, struck again, and again she cried; and yet again, and yet again she cried. Then—her eyes opened. I saw them open, through the gloom I saw them; through the gloom they were revealed to me, that I might see them to my hour of death. An awful recognition, an unspeakable consciousness grew slowly into them. Motionless with horror they were fixed on mine, motionless with horror mine were fixed on them, as she wakened into death.'

In June of 1879, Thompson went to London for his medical exams, but while other students tried their best to pass, Thompson instead skipped them and went to look at the exhibits of the South Kensington Museum. Passing would have meant him leaving the cadavers he worked on, and his refuge of home and the mother that doted on him.

The name Jack the Ripper, so clearly designed to install fear in the listener, would seem a piece of melodrama if it were not associated with very real murders. It was created through a series of horrible, joking letters sent to individuals and authorities. Although its origins have never been adequately explained before, it seems to ideally suit these atrocious and bloody knife murders. That the name itself may have been lifted from some horror-crime novel, might be where, strangely, answers are to be found.

A horror novel is exactly what the public, at the time of the murders, first thought of when their consciousness tried to grapple the criminal's wanting brutality. The nature of these murders could find no comparison in real crimes. This led to newspapers like *The Star* being forced to turn to the pages of fiction to find any likeness. The paper conjured up the American author of the macabre, Edgar Allen Poe, to comprehend what was happening on the London streets. It also gave mention to the English author of the weird and morbid *Thomas De Quincey*,

'Have we a murderous maniac loose in East London? It looks as if we have. Nothing so appalling, so devilish, so inhuman – or, rather non-human – as the three

Whitechapel crimes has ever happened outside the pages of Poe or De Quincey.'

De Quincey is known for his dark and fantastical *Confessions of an Opium Eater* and his sardonic work *Murder Considered as one of the Fine Arts*. To the press it seemed that the entity Jack the Ripper was the physical embodiment of horror fiction. Could it be that the Ripper murders were the work of same deranged fan of De Quincey? It appears laughable that someone like this might exist, let alone possess the capability to trap and kill women, as if they were simply some physical extension of the horror genre. As it happens, Francis Thompson was one of De Quincey's biggest fans.

Nine years before the murders, Thompson came to know about De Quincey and his works. It was in 1879 that Francis fell ill with a long bout of fever. To aid his cure, laudanum was first administered to him. Thus began his lifetime habit of addiction. Now considered a harmful drug, when Thompson consumed his first doses, it was widely accepted and thought to be beneficial. Laudanum was sold at pharmacies for pain relief, to aid in sleeping and relieve menstrual cramps. It was spoon-fed to babies, by nurses, to ensure a deep sleep. It was sold in bottles made from a mixture of nine parts wine and one part opium powder, the chief component of modern heroine.

It was as Thompson took his first droughts of opium-laced wine that his mother, Mary Thompson, gave him her last gift before her death the following year. It was De Quincey's book, *The Confessions of an English*

Opium Eater. Thompson immediately became obsessed with De Quincey's narrative. Even though De Quincey's narrative was written 50 years before Thompson's time, much of it matched his own circumstances. Particularly of how De Quincey also lived rough in London as he tried to become a successful writer. Thompson, from the outset, endeavoured to emulate De Quincey's life. Thompson's uncle, Edward Healy Thompson, afterwards remembered that, *Opium Eater* was his favourite book, and said of his nephew, 'We had often said his experiences would surpass those of De Quincey.' Thompson so often quoted the works of Thomas De Quincey, that Everard Meynell was brought to remark upon the relationship as being like that of an elder and younger brother, and that, 'De Quincey's words become his own by right of succession.' The connections between Thompson, who first discovered De Quincey as he began his medical studies in Manchester, and the gothic writer who died in Manchester the year that Thompson was born are almost too many. Both, for example, fled to London where they became vagrants. Both fell for a prostitute and each relationship ended badly. Both were addicted to forms of opium. Both wrote murder stories. However, this book asks if Thompson took this a step further with committing murder beyond the printed page. Another connection between both is that Thompson lived in Whitechapel, in the parish of Spitalfields, where the Ripper struck. Thompson, of course, would, a year after this, write his own murder story, *The Final Crowning Work*. De Quincey too is known for his writing on a murderer whose crimes were also in Whitechapel. The murders that De Quincey wrote about happened in 1811, yet they were so horrible that the *Star* newspaper, in 1888, could not avoid referencing John Williams who, until the Ripper, was the East End's most well-known killer, when talking of the current slayings,

'There is another Williams in our midst. Hideous malice, deadly cunning, insatiable thirst for blood.'

De Quincey's murder essay was upon Williams, and was called. Within *Murder Considered as One of the Fine Arts* De Quincey employed his macabre wit to suggest that murder should be ranked with the fine arts such as painting, music and theatre. As an example for his premise, De Quincey looked at what are called the Ratcliffe Highway murders. This was when a draper, his wife, their baby and an apprentice were killed by an unknown intruder. The murders were blamed on Williams, who committed suicide before his trial. De Quincey, in dark tongue-in-cheek, wrote about these awful events, and how the design of proper planning made a world of difference.

'People begin to see that something more goes to the composition of a fine murder than two blockheads to kill and be killed, a knife, a purse and a dark lane. Design gentleman, grouping, light and shade, poetry and sentiment, are now deemed indispensable to attempts of this nature.'

Like De Quincey's opium confessions, Thompson greatly enjoyed this murder essay. When it came to

Thompson writing on his beloved literary 'brother' he dwelled on this work on these earlier East End murders.

'The famous *Murder as One of the Fine Arts* is the only specimen which we need pause upon ... The passage which describes how murder leads at last to procrastination and incivility – "Many a man has dated his ruin from some murder which he thought little of at the time".'

Thompson's essay on De Quincey was written after 1888 and the Ripper terror. In it Thompson hinted that recent events had made De Quincey somewhat redundant,

'In this, as in other things, De Quincey was an innovator and, like other innovators, has been eclipsed by his successors.'

Did Thompson mean that one of these 'successors' was he, carrying out the 'art' of murder in real life? Today, it is common to think that serial killers always come with a nickname. We see this time and time again, with killers like Son of Sam, The Zodiac Killer and the Yorkshire Ripper, but before the 1888 crimes, killers were not in the habit of writing letters advertising their deeds. In fact, using non-de-plumes was unheard of, apart from in the writing of Thompson's much-admired De Quincey. It so happens that we see this naming trait first appear in De Quincey's short story *The Avenger*. It was about a serial murderer who, like the way people thought the Ripper was on a deluded moral crusade, believed his crimes were for the greater good. The opening lines of *The Avenger* are,

'Why callest thou me murderer and not rather the wrath of God burning after the steps of the oppressor and cleansing the earth when it is wet with blood.'

The killer takes on the name Avenger to inspire fear in the city's populace. This, if we believe the words within the infamous *Dear Boss* letter, seems to be the case with the Ripper. It is almost as if the Ripper, if he were a fan of De Quincey, were taking De Quincey's murderers' aims to heart.

This all may be true but why use Ripper as a name? One needs only to return to De Quincey and his fine art murder essay – the one Thompson so much admired – to know. The Ratcliffe Highway murders, the essay's focus, involved a murder weapon that was a tool of 51 centimetres in length. It was found lying next to the wife's body, and had been taken from a chest of tools owned by her draper husband. Guess what the name of this tool was? A ripping hook. It is easy to think that the writer of the *Dear Boss* letter chose the name Ripper as a Jack-the-Knife homage to these earlier crimes. All in hope that the good citizens of London would cower in fear.

On 19th December, 1880, after suffering a complaint of the liver, Mary Morton Thompson, Francis' mother died in the family home at Ashton, Mary was aged 58. It was the day before Francis Thompson turned 21; he had effectively come of age, but in many ways he was still a child, having never known a woman, a day's work or the independence of fending for himself. The day after though, his fantasy world began to fall apart. To Thompson, his mother's death was a nightmare become real. Mortality through liver failure is not a pretty sight. What Thompson would have witnessed of his mother's final hours would have included the jaundiced yellowing of the skin, bleeding, vomiting, swelling and reduced brain function. Thompson would have been familiar with death in the sterile conditions of the hospital, but like it had with his baby sister and his grandfather, death had again visited his home.

Outwardly, Thompson seemed to be little affected. He had already learned how to bury his feelings. As he once wrote he was, 'expert in concealment, not expression, of myself. Expression I reserved for my pen. My tongue was tenaciously disciplined in silence.' Publicly, Thompson never brought up the subject of his mother's death. The nearest thing he shared was when, at the age of five, he lost her while shopping. It happened at the town of Ashton's marketplace. This short time of separation was devastating and the memory haunted him. He told of its lasting impact, 'world-wide desolation and terror of, for the first time, realising that the mother can lose you, or you her, and your own abysmal loneliness and helplessness without her.'

To turn 21 in 1879-England granted adult status. A person of lesser faith may have doubted why a just God would kill their mother the day after this most important of birthdays. Thompson never lost faith, though a fragment of verse on her passing, found in his papers after his death, explained in visceral terms how his mother's awful suffering and the disintegration of her flesh only served to please a jealous God who took her life.

Thompson's un-published *This is my Beloved*,

'Died; and horribly

Saw the mystery

Saw the grime of it- ...

Saw the sear of it,

Saw the fear of it,

Saw the slime of it,

Saw it whole!

Son of the womb of her,

Loved till the doom of her

Thought of the brain of her.

Heart of her side,

Joyed in him, grieved in him-

God grew fain [pleased] of her,

And she died.'

It must have been difficult for Thompson to reconcile his image of the unchanging ideal women from his dolls, books and gallery statues, with the sordid destruction done to his mother. It was his mother, Mary's wish, of course, that her son become a doctor, and so at the end of the Christmas break Thompson returned to the infirmary of Manchester's hospital and lecture theatres of Owens. The conditions of the hospital, with its endless traffic of sick and dying, must have afforded little respite.

Finally, the years of hospital work and his lasting grief proved too much for the medical student. It was early in 1882 that James Thompson, uncle to Francis, told that his nephew 'had been afflicted with a nervous breakdown before leaving Manchester, from the effects of which he never fully recovered' {Charing p50-1)

The Owens' college attendance register records his absence from the summer session. Little time was given for his recovery, for he was back in the surgery for the autumn session, and by near the year's end Thompson was sent to Glasgow for his second attempt at the medical finals. When Thompson had failed his first London exams he had not told his father, he had simply missed them. His only words upon returning home were, 'I have not passed.' Dr Thompson organised for his son to make his second attempt in Glasgow because it was considered that the exam was easier. 'I have failed,' was Thompson's repeated answer when he returned to Ashton once more. It is more likely he never actually sat the exam. As 1883 began, and with his father growing more perturbed by his son's failure to pass, Thompson buried himself in his hospital studies. It was easier to face the sawdust floors of the surgery and distressed patients coming in on wagons than his father's disappointment. Thompson compensated with longer and longer hours in the hospital's mortuary, cutting into hundreds of corpses with his dissecting scalpel. So many did he dissect that his sister Mary could not help but complain,

'Many a time he asked my father for £3 or £4 for dissecting fees; so often that my father remarked what a number of corpses he was cutting up.' {Harp.p.35}

A fellow student remembered Thompson at this time, 'a vacant stare, weak lips, and a usually half-open mouth, the saliva trickling over his chin.' {Charing p.52)

In 1883 Thompson welcomed a novel distraction from life's grim realities. It was when he first read a magazine called *Merry England*. This monthly periodical was the second and more successful publishing venture of husband-and-wife writers who had converted to Catholicism. After Wilfrid and Alice Meynell had wrapped up their first short-lived *The Pen* their next venture was the *Merry England*. *This new* magazine aimed to re-introduce the innocent and virtuous days of Catholic-dominated medieval England with modern social reform to protect the poor from exploitation by the new middle class. The first edition stated the magazine's aims,

'We shall try to revive in our hearts and in the hearts of theirs, the enthusiasm of the Christian Faith ... to recover the humour and good humour of the Saints and Fathers.'

This magazine, with its nostalgia for pre-reformation England, suited Thompson. He became an avid reader of the essays and poetry that the Meynells included. He also began to read the contributions of other Catholics. A host of well and lesser-known writers included such names as Coventry Patmore, Katherine Tynan, Wilfrid Blunt, Hilaire Belloc, Lionel Johnson and Cardinal Manning. Even Francis Thompson's uncle, Edward Healy Thompson, was able to see one of his poems printed. Thompson was a loyal reader and admired Wilfrid Meynell's articles. Thompson wrote, 'I was, myself, virtually his pupil, and his wife's long before I knew him.'. Four years later and a few days after the murder of Mary Kelly, Wilfrid, Thompson's 'teacher', would be called to drag his exhausted 'pupil' off the Spitalfields streets.

Wilfrid Meynell, born William Francis Butler, was of Protestant-Quaker origins. His mother was one of the Tuke's of York. This was a family of prosperous coffee merchants. They had made a good name through the founding of England's first humane lunatic asylum in 1792. He was born in Newcastle-on-Tyne in 1852, the seventh child of a colliery owner. Although Wilfrid had become a journalist and editor, he too was once destined to be a doctor. At the age of 15 he met Sir James Simpson, the inventor of chloroform. Its use to anaesthetise patients undergoing operations revolutionised surgery. Simpson asked Wilfrid to kneel down with him and offer prayers that he might also be a healer. When Simpson rose he said to Wilfrid, 'Pain, my boy, I have made it an oblivion; it is for you to make it an ecstasy.' After moving to London Wilfrid converted to Catholicism. Wilfrid was known for his controlling nature and his work in aiding 'lost causes, lame dogs and forlorn friends.' In his first years in London Wilfrid worked in aiding the poor. By 1888 Meynell knew half of the most powerful people in London. He was a friend of William Gladstone, the then liberal opposition leader and future prime minister. Other friends included Irish nationalist leader Charles Stewart Parnell and British Statesman Lord Randolph Churchill.

In 1877 Wilfrid married Alice Gertrude Christiana Thompson (no relation to this book's suspect). Alice was a poet and essayist, born in 1847 at Barnes near London. Alice's family knew many of England's best writers. Charles Dickens was a close family friend and confessed his love for her mother. Alice Thompson settled in London in 1864 and converted to the Catholic faith in 1872.

At the end of 1883 Thompson again failed to attend his medical examinations. His father gave up on his son ever passing to become a doctor. He insisted that Francis Thompson find any job. To satisfy his father's demands Francis applied for the position of an encyclopaedia salesperson. His income would have come from a commission on the books sold. Francis was given a two-month deadline to sell the encyclopaedias. The excessively shy and withdrawn Thompson instead locked himself in his room. Eight weeks later Francis emerged having sold none of the books, having instead read every word and volume. It is unknown which encyclopaedia Thompson had read, but the most popular was the *Encyclopaedia Britannica*. The latest complete edition then available was the eighth, which consisted of 24 volumes containing roughly 33 million words. If Thompson were to have spent eight hours a day, without stopping, over the eight weeks and finished reading the complete set, his reading speed would have been at least 20 words a second.

Dr Thompson, dismayed at his son's performance, used his contacts to find another job for his son in the same year of 1883. This time it was at a local factory that made medical instruments. Some may say that this was where he sourced the dissecting scalpel he carried with him when he would become homeless in London. It would have been relatively easy to fish one he liked from the factory's assembly line. It is more likely though that the one he carried 'to shave with' was kept as a memento from his medical student days. Thompson managed a fortnight's work before being dismissed.

Thompson had already begun writing poetry when at the seminary. These poems were mainly about his schoolmasters or on wars and historic generals. After returning to Manchester, Thompson tried his hand again at poetry and sent off several submissions to various publishers and editors in the hope that he would be 'discovered', but nothing came of it. Francis sent his submissions without his father's knowledge. 'If the lad had but told me!' Dr Charles Thompson would one day implore when asked of his efforts to assist with his son's aspirations of becoming a poet. It was one of these comparatively early poems that saved Thompson's first successful submission from the flames, and Thompson from death on the streets, or worse. On Sunday 19th September, 1885, one of the Ashton's priests and consequently a friend of Dr Charles Thompson, Fr Richardson, gave a sermon. It inspired Thompson to take some notes on it, which, two years later, would be used for his poem *The Passion of Mary*. At the time of writing Thompson did not know that this priest's sister would one day become his stepmother. In the poem Thompson describes a dying mother of Christ as she is bleeding to death. It would not be until three years later in June 1888. Two months before the Ripper claimed his first of five female victims, the world would read how he has a female suffer the five wounds of Christ's crucifixion. Part of the poem tells,

'Thou hung'st in loving agony …

'The red rose of this Passion-tide

Doth take a deeper hue from thee,

In the five wounds of Jesus dyed,

And in thy bleeding thoughts, Mary.'

Another year would drag by, with relations between father and son soured even further. Home life was changing. Devoid of a mother, his sister Mary was planning to leave to become a nun, and his other sister Margaret had married Canon Richardson's brother and moved to Canada. Worst of all for Thompson, he was informed that his widowed father had become engaged to Ann Richardson, the sister of Cannon Richardson. Now there was no one to care for him. His security at home was coming to an end and he was let known that his father's new fiancé wanted Francis out of the house before she moved in. Richardson felt that Francis Thompson had no future and was a failure in all things. She suspected he was hooked on opium and believed him to be a drain on the finances of her future husband.

On 8th November, 1885, things came to a head. Dr Thompson confronted his son. He accused Francis of being drunk, Francis, knowing that the cause of his flushed appearance was opium, at first denied the accusation. When he admitted to taking laudanum, his father then accused him of stealing laudanum from his own supply of medicine. Francis was also expressed as bitter over his father's plans to remarry. His sister Mary wrote about the argument, telling that this second marriage was the cause of it. 'My father may have given Frank some reason for thinking that he may have been in the way.'

The animosity between Francis Thompson and his stepmother only increased. In 1891 Richardson convinced her new husband to cut Thompson out of the

78

family will. In 1896, when Thompson's father died and he returned to Manchester for his funeral, she would not allow him into the home. Ann Richardson's loathing of Thompson meant that he was forced to find paid lodgings. It is probably pertinent to remember that 'Mrs A Richardson' was written on the front of the Hanbury Street building where the second Jack-the-Ripper victim, Ann Chapman, was cut open. It seems more than odd that the name of the victim, Ann, and the name of the place of execution, Richardson, both make up the full name of Thompson's stepmother. Of the 16 residents at this address were a Francis and a Thompson. Another correlation is that the night Thompson ran away from home, 9th November, was the same date that, three years later, the Ripper embarked on his most bloody murder of his fifth victim, Mary Kelly, less than 100 yards from where he was staying at the Providence Row refuge.

Chapter 4
Dirty Old Town

'The boy shall traverse with his bloody feet. The mired and hungered ways, three sullen years, of the fell city: and those feet shall ooze crueller blood through ruinous avenues.'

Francis Thompson.

Thompson stayed a further week in Manchester before heading to London and attempting to settle in the district of Soho. This was because a superstitious Thompson had the idea that, if he followed in De Quincey's footsteps, he would likewise achieve fame or be charmed by the ghost of his admired dead writer. Here Thompson cared for hansom cabs, which graced the Drury Lane or Haymarket theatres, earning a sixpence per week to hold a horse's head. Eventually, even these efforts proved hopeless and his failure to gain a publisher or find a career was not helped by his increased reliance on opium.

From November 1885 Francis Thompson stayed at a number of cheap lodgings, paid for by his father. Thompson gained no steady employment and his income was minimal. Thompson tried his hand at shining shoes as a bootblack. His efforts resulted in his first run-in with the police. A nearby shopkeeper reported Thompson to the police. Most likely, he did so because Thompson was pestering the shopkeeper's customers and blocking access to his shop. A constable arrived and forced Thompson to close his makeshift shoeshine stand and move from the corner where he had started his business. Thompson next tried to make money from tips for carrying people's luggage, but the coins that were thrown to him were too few.

In April 1886 Dr Charles Thompson travelled to London. He met with his son and informed him that a date for his wedding with Ann Richardson had been set for the April of the following year. His father may have also visited two other relatives who also lived in London. These relatives could have helped Thompson as he drifted further into destitution but not once did Thompson contact or visit them. For a time his father provided Francis with a small allowance to claim from the desk of the Reading Room of the Clarendon library. By July 1886 Francis, his clothes unkempt at the best of times but now reduced to rags, grew fearful that he might be dragged out of the Reading Room, so he ceased calling to claim the money.

Months later, Thompson was still homeless. At this time even the despised workhouses were full. The master of Paddington Workhouse, for example, let the papers know that he had been forced to turn many vagrants away. The nights of Thompson's torment in hunger and addiction appeared endless and then a minor miracle occurred. He was walking, more to keep warm than in any particular direction, along a crowded street when he heard a clinking sound and saw a coin rolling in the gutter. He watched as it weaved itself about the feet of the passing pedestrians and revolved to a stop. Thompson picked it up and because no one approached him to claim it, he kept it. Believing that the coin was a newly minted halfpenny, Thompson put it in his waistcoat pocket and walked on. Then he decided to turn back the way that he had come. When Thompson reached the same spot where he had found the first coin, he saw another coin glittering on the road. Thompson, thinking that it was another halfpenny, picked it up as well. He looked at the coin in his hand and saw a golden sovereign. Francis took the first coin from his pocket and when he held both coins together, he saw that they were both gold. Everard Meynell recorded, in his biography on Thompson, of the homeless poet's reaction to the finding of the equivalent of two pounds, which was equal to a fortnight's working wage,

'"That was a sovereign too, Evi; I looked and saw that it was a sovereign too!" he ended with a rising voice and tremulous laughter.'

It only took a few weeks before the windfall of the 'miracle' coins ran dry. As a homeless man in a last attempt to maintain some respectability he tried newspaper selling. He must have presented a pitiful sight, this once aspiring doctor and priest now reduced to crying out the latest headlines of a broadsheet, his calls from a street corner all but lost in the bustling din of the great city. His hope that he would not become yet another street beggar was taken from him inadvertently by a small act of kindness from a prominent financier. A passing banker, who was a member of the Rothschild, that Thompson recognised, grabbed a paper from a stack beside Thompson and gave a coin, before walking on. It took Thompson a moment to see that even though the paper only cost a penny, the banker had thrown him a florin that was worth 20 papers. In 1888 the Rothschild had become the world's most powerful bank. In Thompson's case this rich tipper may have been Ferdinand Rothschild (1839-1898). Thompson was well aware of the part that this banking family had played in history; he had read Lord Byron who said of the Rothschilds.

'every loan

Is not merely a speculative hint,

But seats a nation or upsets a throne.'

To Thompson the pity of this piece of silver highlighted how the world saw him as nothing but a ragged panhandler. It was a stark reminder of his plight. Such an act of charity was, as he said, 'a little sweetness making grief complete.' Years later, when Thompson learnt of the death of the banker who had tipped him, he expressed anguish that he could never repay him. This florin must have only served as a sharp reminder of his plight. Even as he struggled to prise himself away from the crowds of the destitute with his newspaper selling, a shining, unwanted charity let him know that others saw him as simply a beggar. Such an act of charity was a 'little sweetness making grief complete.'

Everard Meynell recorded that it was soon after the episode with the florin that Francis became delirious. A bizarre metamorphism occurred in him where the hunger of food, addiction and the accompanied anxiousness crumbled as his mind gave way. His biographer and colleague Everard described this as follows, 'His weakness has passed and he is drifting along the streets, not wearily but with dreadful ease, with no hope of having resolution to halt.' For perhaps minutes, days or weeks, Thompson literally became lost, not knowing where he was or where his feet took him. Common things like his sense of time, place and even those people about him merged into an incomprehensible and jumbled blur. Within him the last vestiges of his sanity slowly ebbed away. This could have lasted forever if it wasn't for the intervention of a good-hearted but naive man of charity.

In early August 1886 the shoemaker John McMaster hired Thompson to work at his Panton Street shoe shop. At the back of McMaster's shop was a workroom. McMaster was also the Protestant churchwarden for Haymarket's St Martins of the Fields. McMaster was a charitable man and as well as running his shop he spent his spare time seeking out young men who needed help. When McMaster first found Thompson, the Manchester runaway had been homeless for a fortnight. When Thompson first arrived in London he had brought with him well over 100 books. Just some of the authors that graced the spines included Blake, Aeschylus, Edmund Spenser, Zola, Goblet D' Alvella, Keats, Byron, Crashaw, Coleridge, Shelley, Thomas Babington, Thomas Brown, Walter Scott and Wordsworth. The days in which he could find odd jobs grew further apart. His dependence on laudanum, the necessity of buying food and paying rent was met by Thompson selling 95 of his books. His well-stocked personal library had dwindled down to less than a handful.

McMaster first sighted Thompson wandering the Strand, attempting to sell matches to people passing. Apart from his few books Thompson had sold all his other goods and this single matchbox was his only possession. It was then, through the crowded street's noise, that McMaster, bursting with Protestant faith and goodwill, called out to him, 'Is your soul saved?'

The Roman-Catholic born, seminary-trained Thompson gave a curt reply, 'What right have you to ask me that question?'

McMaster must have sensed immediately that arguing theology with this particular homeless man was useless, so instead he made this offer, 'If you won't let me save your soul, let me save your body.' Thompson relented and he was hired by McMaster to work at his shoemaker's shop.

This shoemaker's first impressions of Thompson were grim. McMaster said that he was, 'a damp rag of humanity ... He was the very personification of ruin, a tumbledown, dilapidated opium-haunted wreck.' McMaster thought Thompson resembled more of an escaped convict than the son of a respected doctor. He had the police check that he wasn't, and wrote to Thompson's father to confirm Francis' story. Satisfied that Thompson was who he said was, McMaster hired Thompson to work in the back room and run errands. Thompson soon found that the shoemaker's back workroom held other young men that McMaster had rescued from the streets. For extra pay these men were given extra duties.

Thompson's response to receiving a small but regular income was to rely even more heavily on laudanum, much to the dismay of his employer. It was during his time at the shoe shop that Thompson first became interested in the occult. Most probably, its promise of gaining special powers seemed to answer his need to escape the mental misery he felt. His gateway into the supernatural and magic was by reading the works of Edward Bulwer-Lytton. This British author, who had died in 1873, was notable for his diverse range of fantasy and horror stories. Lytton is famed for penning the famous first line, 'It was a dark and stormy night.' Lytton was an avid occultist with a fascination in psychic phenomena and magic. Everard Meynell noted of Thompson, and how his passion for gothic writer became lifelong 'Bulwer Lytton was devoured, then as in later years.' Thompson also learnt how Lytton's and his other occultist friends practised secret magical ceremonies. Most of these rituals involved necromancy in which they claimed to raise and control the spirits of the dead.

Thompson had already formed the conviction that the cause of England's social woes and spiritual decline could be blamed on the Protestant Reformation and England's rejection of the once all-powerful Catholic Church. Now the hardship of living off the streets had forced him to seek shelter under the roof of a devout Protestant. It is even conceivable that Thompson, himself, accepted the added pay that McMaster offered his employees for extra duties. These included singing with St Martins choir, ringing the church bells or tending the St Martins graveyard. The shoe shop, as well as offering its workers church-related tasks, was unusual in its clientele. It turned out that the shop specialised in making and repairing the shoes of well-known writers and publishers. This must have appealed to Thompson, but now that he harboured hopes to one day become a poet, it must have been irksome knowing that the front room of the shop served the famous writer of the day. Thompson, who once aspired to be a priest or surgeon, was left in the back room. He found himself to now be so close to fame, but separated by a tremendous gulf of misfortune. Instead of cutting into patients with his dissecting knife, Thompson was left cutting into leather with a shoemaker's knife. He had dreamt of becoming a doctor or the next De Quincey, a literary superstar. Now it seemed he was destined to be forever the shoeshine and the errand boy.

Up till now, Thompson's fantasies had been relegated to queer romantic notions of women and a belief that hidden in the old plays he read, the military histories he learnt was the secret to realise his heroic destiny. He had struck out on his own, waiting for fortune to stoop down and lift him up from mediocrity and the common man. Instead, the tide of bad circumstance and poor judgment had brought him, a man steeped in Catholic rite and ritual, to becoming a mere servant boy to a Protestant master, whose very name McMaster was but a bitter added irony.

Any other man might have accepted his fate, but Thompson, in a last determined effort, took the most famous words of Bulwer Lytton to heart, 'The pen is mightier than the sword.' Overcome with an undying desire to achieve something in his life, Thompson grabbed one of the shop's old account books. Having already disposed of almost all his treasured books, he relied entirely on memory and the jottings from a few tiny notebooks which fit in the palm of his hand to begin writing. He began to piece together the poem *The Passion of Mary* out of the notes he had made in 1885 from the church sermon of the priest back in Ashton. He again wrote out his sad poem on Lucy, the girl he had once encountered at the age of 10. He relied on his adept skill at essay writing, mastered when he was a seminary student. His essay was an argument against bringing back Pagan eroticism, which he saw exhibited in French licentiousness. It argued that Pagan ideals needed to be infused with Christian beliefs if they were to be of any worth.

Thompson also tried his hand at a new poem. It was intended to include a modern styled twist that paid homage to the days of knights and chivalry. In Chapter 3, *The Gutters of Humanity*, of his 1988 book *Francis Thompson, Strange Harp Strange Symphony*, John Walsh wrote,

'The most painful of these poems was *The Nightmare of the Witch Babies*, never revived in a fair copy. But in the last of the notebook drafts, he added a reminder, rare for him, of the date of its completion: "Finished before October 1886" – that is within a year of his departure from home.'

It was probably while still apprenticed at McMaster's, that Francis Thompson penned it; while almost certainly written unhinged by the influence of drugs. There is probably no poem that came out of the nineteenth century to contend with its unbound revelry for carnage and bloodshed. It provides an awful glimpse into Thompson's mind and shows that finally the years of solitude, the riot faced by his family, the seeming wickedness of his stepmother, the cruel loss of his mother, had all unhinged him. With the *Witch Babies* his full depravity and abandonment of morality is revealed. It shows his rage against women who abandon and betray him. The poem begins with the protagonist, a 'lusty knight' on a hunt, but he hunts in London, after dark, and his game is women.

'A lusty knight,

Ha! Ha!

On a swart [black] steed,

Ho! Ho!

Rode upon the land

Where the silence feels alone,

Rode upon the Land

Rode upon the Strand

Of the Dead Men's Groan,

Where the Evil goes to and fro

Two witch babies, Ho! Ho! Ho!

A rotten mist,

Ha! Ha!

Like a dead man's flesh,

Ho! Ho!

Was abhorrent in the air,'

As he rides through a desolate landscape of the metropolis, the knight catches sight of a suitable prey.

'What is it sees he?

Ha! Ha!

There in the frightfulness?

Ho! Ho!

There he saw a maiden

Fairest fair:

Sad were her dusk eyes,

Long was her hair;

Sad were her dreaming eyes,

Misty her hair,

And strange was her garments'

Soon he begins to stalk her.

'Swiftly he followed her.

Ha! Ha!

Eagerly he followed her.

Ho! Ho!'

Then she disappoints him. He discovers she is unclean.

'Lo, she corrupted!

Ho! Ho!'

The knight captures her and decides to kill her. He slices her open and drags out the contents of her stomach. He guts her like an animal in order to find and kill any unborn offspring she may have. The poem ends with a macabre twist and his rapture at finding, not just a single foetus, but two.

'And its paunch was rent

Like a brasten [bursting] drum;

And the blubbered fat

From its belly doth come

It was a stream ran bloodily under the wall.

O Stream, you cannot run too red!

Under the wall.

With a sickening ooze –

Hell made it so!

Two witch-babies,

ho! ho! ho!'

The entire poem contains phrases like 'the bloody-rusted stone', 'blood, blood, blood', 'No one life there, Ha! Ha!' and 'Red bubbles oozed and stood, wet like blood'. It has a plot which reads like the description of a slaughterhouse. Those people who think poets always rely solely on imagination are not thinking of Thompson. To him, his poems were records of real events in his life, clothed in rhyme and symbolism. In a letter written years later to his editor, this is how Thompson explained that his poetry was always more fact than fiction, 'The poems were, in fact, a kind of poetic diary; or rather a poetic substitute for letters.' {Poems p436]

McMaster, who was probably oblivious to the contents of the scrawlings, had come to the realisation that Thompson was unfit in shoemaking too. He was tardy in running errands and never applied himself to the trades of mending and making shoes. 'My only failure,' was how McMaster would remember him. He would also recall how Thompson distracted the other shoemakers with conversation and shout in medical and other arguments. In the Christmas of 1886 McMaster arranged for Thompson to travel back to Ashton to celebrate with his family. He hoped that some family time would enliven Thompson's spirits. Thompson returned more despondent and reticent than ever. Evidently, the disappointment of Thompson's failure to make something of himself in London had only served to increase his alienation. McMaster grew more than he was usually concerned about Thompson's mental state and found his other behaviour strange, such as the audible prayers he would hold nightly, for 'She', the woman of his dreams. Finally, when, in mid-January 1887, Thompson injured a customer who had come to buy footwear by slamming a window shutter on his foot, McMaster dismissed him.

On 23rd February, 1887, five weeks after becoming unemployed by McMaster, Thompson bundled some of his work into a parcel for a submission to the editor of his favourite magazine. The editor's son verified that

Thompson was shrewd when it came to knowing who to write to, 'He knew the target at which he aimed.' {LIFE p86}. Thompson let fall the crumpled envelope into the *Merry England* Kensington letterbox at 44 Essex Street. He had once again spent almost all the money earned from working at the shoe shop and had just one halfpenny. As he said, 'Next day I spent the halfpenny on two boxes of matches, and began the struggle for life.' The parcel held the torn pages from McMaster's ledger books. Written on these pages was a letter of introduction and his essay, titled *Paganism Old and New*. In the same package he also included three poems – *The Passion of Mary* about Mary dying on the cross, *Dream Tryst* on unrequited love, and his poem on slaughtering corrupt woman. *Nightmare of the Witch Babies*. The Meynell's home-office was frankly a mess. Family and friends remember that tables and desks of the household were strewn with unopened letters, bound manuscripts and preview editions. Wilfrid, never the most efficient office keeper, often resorted to bonfires to clear all the clutter. Such a busy man, planning to open the package later, placed it in a pigeonhole – and there it would sit for many months.

In April of 1887 Dr Charles Thompson married his second wife, Anne Richardson. His son did not attend the wedding. Thompson's anger at his father's seeming ease of shedding his devotion to the departed wife and mother, Mary, gnawed at him. Whatever the truth of his father's intent or extent of grief for his first wife, Thompson's deranged outlook cast both his father and stepmother as villainous monsters. This is seen in another poem that never saw publication. *The Ballad of Fair Weather* typically presents those women whom Thompson has perceived have wronged him as evil witches. His father is described as a lackey to her sadistic and foul torture and killing of him.

'My father, too cruel,

Would scorn me and beat me;

My wicked stepmother

Would take me and eat me,

They looked in the deep grass

Where it was deepest;

They looked down the steep bank

Where it was steepest;

But under the bruised fern

Crushed in its feather

The head and the body

Were lying together, –

Ah, death of fair weather!

Tell me, thou perished head,

What hand could sever thee? ...

My evil stepmother,

So witch-like in wish,

She caught all my pretty blood

Up in a dish,

She took out my heart

For a ghoul-meal together,

But peaceful my body lies

In the fern-feather,

For now is fair weather.'

By the spring of 1887, Thompson, now aged 27, had become completely destitute. His pride did not allow him to beg and it was only on the rare occasion that he could scramble together the few pennies for the most basic foods to stave off nearing starvation. As for work, he was lucky if he could work holding the leads of horses as they waited fixed carriages while the owners enjoyed the latest West End plays. Thompson, in a city of five million was utterly alone. He was now completely set apart from ordinary men. He felt no kinship to those who shared his underclass status. While they, in his mind, through immorality, stupidity or laziness chose to live in the gutter, Thompson saw himself as an entirely innocent victim.

The hazardous 'pea souper' of Victorian London is well known to historians. This was the lasting smog, made from a mixture of chimney smoke and other pollutants of the industrial revolution. It hung thick in the air and settled on everything, coating roads, buildings and people in black, oily flakes of dust. When Thompson cast his mind back to the multitudes of poverty-stricken masses he struggled alongside to survive with, he saw them as the real toxicants. His disgust of his fellow tramps was offered years later in a private letter written to his editor,

'We lament the smoke of London – it were nothing without the fumes of congregated evil, the herded effluence from millions of festering souls. At times I am merely sick of it.'

To him, those he was forced to share the doss houses, kerbsides and doorways with, on nights of bitter cold, merged with the worst of his hospital experience. Their conversations were designed purely to cause sickness and disease. These people – the street beggar, chimney man, fruit seller, window cleaner, dustman – were not people. They were dumb beasts; insects that lived off rotten flesh. Their talk was, 'nothing but the vocabulary of the hospital, images of corruption and fleshly ruin. The very streets weigh upon me. These horrible streets with their gangrenous multitudes, blackening ever into lower mortifications of humanity! The brute men; these lads who have almost lost the faculty of human speech, who howl & growl like animals, or use a tongue which in itself is a cancerous disintegration of speech ... Seamed & fissured with scarred streets under the heat of the vaporous London sun, the whole blackened organism corrupts into foul humanity, seething & rustling through its tissues.'

Vagrants, even in modern society, are largely looked down upon. In 1888, in England, simply being a vagrant was a criminal act and would remain so until 1935. There was little now to prevent Thompson sliding into a bottomless pit of despair. His future lay in being put in a workhouse to die a pauper. Now his very existence was a crime, it seemed that at any time he would face arrest or some other disastrous outcome.

Then, in June of 1887, against all odds, a woman entered his life. Most unusually, the woman who reached out her hand and briefly cared for him was the very type that Thompson would have despised. The woman was a prostitute. The politer term for women such as her back then was 'an unfortunate', or 'a fallen' woman. Less impolite was 'whore'. Her lifestyle meant that she was one of the corrupt, the very creature that Thompson's 'lusty knight' had joyfully killed in his poem sent to the Meynells.

Nobody has ever found out what her name was. His hero, De Quincey, met and had an ill-fated relationship with a prostitute named Ann, so this is what biographers of Thompson have christened his friend. It is unlikely. Considering Thompson's evident dislike for his stepmother Ann, he would probably have avoided entering into a relationship with someone of that name. Almost nothing is known of her. Thompson always remained tight-lipped about her, but we do know she had lodgings in Chelsea and that she arranged to meet him regularly at an appointed place and hour. There she would take him home and was passionate in supplying him with affections that were 'both maidenly and motherly'. {LIFE p81}.

That from out of nowhere a girl would become Thompson's lover seems hard to believe. Some writers have even suggested that Thompson, for whatever reason, made her up and that she never existed. A close analysis of Thompson's writings and testaments of those who knew him, however, leave little room for doubt that in June began his yearlong romance with this woman. That a prostitute cared for this derelict, providing intimacy, company, food and her bed, has brought others to compare her as a saint. Everard Meynell, in his *Life of Francis Thompson* dubbed her 'a Sister of Charity' after the Catholic religious order of nuns that ran Providence Row night-refuge in Spitalfields. Thompson, on his part, never admitted that this woman was the unknown 'She' he prayed for, but when she left him, it proved no less terrible for him. That Thompson found relief in the very underclass he loathed must have mystified him and run against all his sensibilities. It seems, though, that when desperation was all his being, like how he, the Catholic, secured Protestant help, he was not against accepting aid from a sinner. The months that once consisted of fearful hunger and want, for a short time passed in relative comfort in his friend's lodging rooms in Chelsea.

Another occurrence in June of 1887, which happened without him then knowing, changed the roadmap of his life yet again. Back at the *Merry England* offices in Kensington, Wilfrid Meynell must have been having a slow day. He decided to have one of his regular burnings in which he offloaded piles of manuscripts and correspondence into the fireplace. With his paper bonfire in full swing, Meynell retrieved Thompson's now dusty parcel, which had lain forgotten for five months. Meynell skimmed through Thompson's query letter. There was little in it to give him hope that a writer of talent was behind it. The only literary reference within it was to the Shakespearean character Parolles. He was from Shakespeare's *All's Well That Ends Well*. He was a coward, a liar and a braggart. He is exposed and shamed as someone who pretends to be a great soldier. Meynell might not have seen this as an encouraging sign. Thompson's letter said,

'Feb 23rd, 1887—Dear Sir,—In enclosing the accompanying article for your inspection I must ask pardon for the soiled state of the manuscript. It is due, not to slovenliness, but to the strange places and circumstances under which it has been written. For me, no less than Parolles, the dirty nurse experience has something fouled. I enclose a stamped envelope for a reply, since I do not desire the return of the manuscript, regarding your judgement of its worthlessness as quite final. I can hardly expect that where my prose fails my verse will succeed. Nevertheless, on the principle of "Yet will I try the last," I have added a few specimens of it, with the off chance that one may be less poor than the rest. Apologising very sincerely for any intrusion on your valuable time, I remain yours with little hope, FRANCIS THOMPSON. Kindly address your rejection to the Charing Cross Post Office.'

Upon reading that Thompson himself did not expect his work to be accepted, Meynell prepared to consign the package and all its contents into the flames, when he spied on one of the soiled torn ledger sheets the title *The Passion of Mary*. As a Catholic convert, Meynell's heart was filled with the fiery enthusiasm of someone who believed they had found their true faith. The title – referring to the Mother of Christ and the Passion, the days leading up to and right after Christ's crucifixion – caught his eye. He proceeded to read the poem out loud, more as a joke than anything. Meynell did not expect a poem written with a scrawled, wavering hand on paper stained with laudanum splotches to be worth anything. As he read on, however, his curiosity increased. The poem seemed reminiscent of the great Latin hymns of the church and indicated that Thompson was a fellow believer of poetic skill, who had fallen on hard times. Of course, not all of the package's contents proved to have equal merit.

Later that night Wilfrid shared his discovery with his wife, Alice, who was already an esteemed poetess in her own right. There was already talk that she might become the next poet Laureate. She also saw that Thompson was worth publishing. Her reaction to the *Nightmare of the Witch Babies* poem, however, was what might have been expected. She too put the perverse verse down to the effects of laudanum. Their son, Everard Meynell, who was then only eight years old, had begun writing a diary. Here is his entry for the following day, 'Told by AM at 21 Philimore Place, Mother read in bed the dirty ms of Paganism and along with it some witch-opium poems which she detested.' Everard Meynell wrote a letter inviting Thompson to come and see him. Meynell had immediately concluded that Thompson's *Passion of Mary* poem and his *Paganism* essay would be suitable for publication in his *Merry England* magazine. He had begun proofreading them and his letter asked that Thompson come to check the proofs before they went to the printers.

By now Thompson, not receiving a reply, believed that his package had been simply tossed aside. Thompson had decided that, not only had Meynell rejected his submission, he had not even bothered writing to tell him this.

In October 1887 Meynell's letter of response was returned back to him as unclaimed. Meynell suspected that Thompson, who already seemed on the precipice, had succumbed to the elements. He thought Thompson had either ended his life through exposure, drugs or suicide, or otherwise become hopelessly lost amongst the numberless outcasts of London. The truth was not far from wrong.

By April of 1888 Thompson had reached the point where he had given up all hope. His submission to *Merry England* was not the only one sent; from her Chelsea room his prostitute lover had encouraged him to continue sending off various samples of his work. Month after month passed without any positive response. Thompson must have felt that he was a disappointment to her, his only source of affection. He no longer had the will to live. It was in the vegetable rubbish dumps of

Covent Garden Market, where Thompson had been used to sleeping, that he decided to end his life. In nineteenth-century Britain this was illegal and the maximum punishment was paradoxically the death penalty. For Thompson, such an action was worse than illegal. Suicide is considered a mortal sin and forbidden by the Catholic Church. At this point, for this failed priest, even the teachings of the Catholic Church and the commandments themselves had become meaningless. That Thompson, by now, had refuted even the teachings of the church and the morality it preached, was kindly alluded to by his future editor many years later,

'Of course as a carefully practising Catholic he knew suicide to be wrong, but there may have been occasions in his life in the streets when he lost his Catholic consciousness.'

Thompson's planned suicide was to be through an overdose, after dark, with enough laudanum to kill two men. Francis took the first half, which should have killed him when, as Thompson claims, he was saved by a phantom. It was the ghost of the writer Thomas Chatterton. He too was penniless in London. In 1770, at the age of 18, Chatterton, feeling that he would nevermore have his work published, killed himself by arsenic poisoning. As the full effects of the drug took hold he felt a hand upon his shoulder. Thompson turned and saw a boy standing before him in eighteenth-century dress. Thompson recognised him from his paintings. The boy reached out and took his hand. The image soon disappeared, but not before Thompson understood the full meaning of this apparition. The tale goes that it was the day after Chatterton's suicide that news arrived, to the loft in which he took his life, to tell him his poems had been published. Thompson saw that the message to him, of this silent ghost's visitation, was that if Thompson held off his self-execution, he too would be published. How different may have been this book, if Thompson had taken the second dose?

As it happened it was the next day Thompson got word he had been published. This occurred six months after opening the package, in April 1888, and more than a year after Thompson had first delivered it. Meynell published Thompson's poem *The Passion of Mary* in his monthly magazine. Meynell, who had not found the aspiring homeless poet, believed that by publishing the poem, one of his readers might be able to do what he could not. That is exactly what happened. One of the magazine's subscribers, Father John Carroll, was a friend of Thompson's father. Carroll had known Thompson in his youth. Carroll wrote to Meynell giving him details on Thompson's background and circumstances. Carroll somehow got a message to Thompson, telling him that one of his poems had made it into print. On 14th April another letter arrived at Meynell's office, in which Thompson wrote,

'Dear Sir ... I forwarded to you for your magazine a prose article ... and accompanied it by some of the verse ... To be brief, from that day to this, no answer has ever come into my hands ... I am now informed that one of the copies of verse ... is appearing in this month's issue.'

Thompson probably wrote this letter from the Chelsea rooms of the prostitute he was then seeing. He gave his postal address as a chemist in Drury Lane. Meynell approached the chemist and he was told that the poet still owed money for his previous purchases of opium. Wilfrid paid Thompson's debts and asked the chemist to direct Thompson to contact him at his *Merry England* office. When, a month later, Thompson failed to respond, Wilfrid Meynell published *Dream Tryst* in May.

In that same month a threadbare, shirtless Thompson first met Wilfrid Meynell at his office. Meynell offered to pay him a weekly sum of money, but Thompson refused and once more went back to the streets. Meynell's son, in his book on Thompson, wrote of the initial meeting between the vagrant and his father,

'There was little to be done for him at that interview, save the extraction of a promise to call again. He made none of the confidences characteristic of a man seeking sympathy and alms. He was secretive and with no eagerness for plans for his benefit, and refused the offer of a small weekly sum that would enable him to sleep in a bed and sit at a table … But the impression of the visit on my father was of a meeting that did not end in great usefulness, so much was indicated by a manner schooled in concealments.'

Thompson kept Wilfrid Meynell in the dark about his past. After the editor paid him for his two poems *The Passion of Mary* and *Dream Tryst,* Thompson quickly left. The editor essentially only knew a few bits and pieces about Thompson. Then, on 25th May Thompson's uncle, Edward Healy, who had also read Thompson's work in *Merry England*, wrote to Meynell, giving him a full history on his nephew. The poet and editor met again. Meynell paid him for his *Paganism* essay and, in June, Meynell published it in *Merry England*.

Chapter 5
Trail of the Murderer

'Yet none could have regretted their strange barter.'

Francis Thompson.

What happened next is as strange as the prostitute striking up a relationship with the homeless Thompson. Now that he had gained a foothold as a writer, he returned to the prostitute's lodgings in Chelsea to tell her the good news. Her response proved shocking. Everard Meynell was painstaking in his writing of the biography *The Life of Francis Thompson*. As had already been established, both Wilfrid Meynell and the Father Terrance Connolly of Boston College are guilty of making unauthorised alterations and deletions of Thompson's work. These changes were deliberately made to eliminate anything Thompson wrote that would reflect badly on Thompson or the Meynells. Whatever suggested that Thompson was not 'the most innocent of men', as Alice Meynell said of him, was removed from new editions of Thompson's works or works about Thompson. What is intriguing is that when the essay *Catholics in Darkest England*, written by Thompson for the January 1891 *Merry England* first appeared, Thompson described staying at Providence Row, the Spitalfields night refugee in the heartland of the Ripper murder territory. Theoretically, on the night that Mary Kelly was murdered, Thompson could look from the building where he slept, to the passageway that led to the room in which Mary Kelly slept. Later, though, in successive printings of this essay, after Thompson's death in 1907, the passages that spoke of this were entirely removed.

A comparison of Everard Meynell's first edition of his *Life of Thompson* – which his father oversaw – and later editions show this same removal of details, as well as particular terms that a suspicious or suspecting reader may interpret as hinting that Thompson was not as innocent as he seemed. Everard's biography went through five editions. Each was subject to minute editing with exactness one might expect exhibited in a Swiss watch or displayed in an intricate Chinese puzzle box. This care for detail by Everard on the contents of Thompson's biography filled most of his time in the last year before his death in 1926. The following is an example of the changes made to the original text. The 1913 edition gave the following description of Thompson's final meeting with his prostitute friend in June. The original version compares her leaving with the deaths of Thompson's mother, Mary, and his younger sister, Helen, who died in infancy.

'After his first interview with my father he had taken her his news. "They will not understand our friendship."

She said and then, "I always knew you were a genius." And so she strangled the opportunity; she killed again the child, the sister; the mother had come to life within her. She went away. Without warning she went to unknown lodgings and was lost to him.' {LIFE p83}

The words 'killed' and 'strangled,' by the fifth edition released in 1926, had disappeared entirely. These words one might think more apt when describing the Ripper murders, two months after his final meeting with his prostitute, were deftly removed. The revised passage now read.

'After his first interview with my father he had taken her his news. "They will not understand our friendship," she said, and without warning went to unknown lodgings and was lost to him.' {LIFE 5th Edition. p65-5}

Of course, we might expect that there are bound to be slipups when only a few people try to keep such a big secret, and at least one remark survived the white wash. For instance, here is Thompson describing in a letter how overthinking almost killed one of his planned poems, 'My fear is that thought in it has strangled poetic impulse.' {Letters p117}

This revisionism of Thompson's writing has concerned successive biographers and researchers. Biographer Bridget M Boardman, in her 2001 book *Poems of Francis Thompson* related how the 3 volume *Works of Francis Thompson* and other texts of Thompson's were tampered with, '... among those that were published by Meynell in Works or elsewhere, he made alteration to and deletion from the original texts that have so far gone unnoticed.' {Boardman xxii}. In his introduction to the 1913 *Works of Francis Thompson*, Meynell was careful to explain that the then deceased Thompson would have approved of all the changes. He wrote,

'In making this collection I have been governed by Francis Thompson's express instructions, or guided by a knowledge of his feelings and preferences acquired during an unbroken intimacy of 19 years. His own list of new inclusions and his own suggested reconsiderations of his formerly published text have been followed in this definitive edition of his Poetical Work.'

However, Boardman and others have declared that there is no reference in any of Thompson's papers or many letters to the Meynells. Also, that there was never instructions or suggested reconsiderations by Thompson to Meynell. Why the deletions and changes to Thompson's work were performed by the Meynells is explained by the husband and wife Wilfrid and Alice Meynell; they wished to preserve Thompson's reputation as 'the poet of Catholic orthodoxy.' {Boardman xxxi}.

Therefore, when in the summer of 1938 an American Jesuit priest went on a pilgrimage, from Massachusetts' Boston College to England, to retrace the poet's life there seemed to be no indication that there was little amiss about Thompson. Father Terrance Connolly worked for the college's English department. His travels stemmed from his frustration as a teacher in not finding enough material on Catholic poets. He also had the dim hope of acquiring enough of Thompson's paraphernalia for a planned display room. Connolly's previous experience in literature and as teacher of poets made him well suited to the task, but Connolly held an additional prerequisite. He had also worked for a time as a prison chaplain, counselling murderers and hearing their confessions on death row. He also advised the relatives of condemned men who confided their suspicions to him. The priest must have felt a strange sense of *déjà vu* when he came to meet an old classmate of Thompson's. The bizarre introduction between Father Adam Wilkinson and himself was recorded in his 1945 book *In His Paths. A Visit to Persons and Places Associated with the Poet,*

'We found the aged priest, sitting before a blazing hearth fire, reading a detective story in Braille. He was then eighty years old ... "Just a minute, Fathers, please. I must not lose my place. Oh, my! They're hot on the trail of the murderer." As he spoke, he marked the place in some mysterious way, placed the book on the mantel over the fire and then extended his hand in welcome.'

These cryptic remarks did little more than cause a raised eyebrow. Connolly later told how, when he gathered material from Meynell to bring back to Boston College, he could only accept Meynell's donation with a certain condition, 'I was admonished that if I discovered anything unpleasant in the notebooks it should be burned.' Boardman described Connolly's readiness to continue gutting Thompson's works and the removal from history of anything 'unpleasant' that might cause concern.

'By "unpleasant", Meynell appears to have meant anything that could detract from the image of orthodox piety which was endorsed by Connolly. Due to the number of mutilated notebooks and other manuscripts, it is impossible now to assess how much may have been destroyed ... Like Meynell, Connolly had little or no hesitation in adapting and making changes in the texts. ... there is no indication of the extent of the editing process.' {Boardman xxii}

In Bridget M Boardman's *Between Heaven and Charring Cross*, her 1988 biography on Francis Thompson starts with strong rebuke of the way his editor and the Boston academic priest handled Thompson's papers. Boardman wrote, '...the editing by Meynell and Connolly is indefensible. They felt free to make omissions, deletions and alterations ... there is no explanation given for omissions and deletions.'

Wilfrid Meynell, who was happy to do as he pleased with Thompson's literary bequest, was not averse to forging Thompson's signature. Connolly wrote of the editor's reaction to Connolly's discovery of this, in the introduction to his book *In His Paths. The Life of Francis Thompson.*

'When I had finished reading the last line of the manuscript, I glanced at the signature beneath it and then looked up at Mr Meynell. I am sure that my eyes expressed my thoughts before I said: "Why! This is the strangest Thompson signature that I have ever seen!" Mr Meynell's eyes danced with delight as he chuckled and said: "The poet gave me the copy unsigned, my dear Father, and I put his signature onto it before sending it to *Merry England* for publication".'

The years rolled by after Thompson's death in 1907 and the East End of London, which bore the myth of these murders, underwent great change. By the Second World War, social reforms, and new infrastructure in Whitechapel to improve conditions, rendered it hardly recognisable from the age of the Ripper. All that remained to be seen of the Ripper's defenceless victims were some simple cemetery plaques. By the end of the war the assault of Hitler's bombings, concentrating on the East End, changed Whitechapel irrevocably. Standing there today it seems as if the Ripper's gaslight realm is a world away. The squalid streetscapes where the Ripper plied his ghastly trade was on the other side of the world from Boston College in the New England state of Massachusetts. It was here, in 1959, that a group of Thompsonians celebrated the coming into existence of the Francis Thompson Room. His admirers opened it on the centenary of Thompson's birth. Here, in a building that looks more like a medieval keep than a library, books by Thompson and of Thompson lie in solid wooden bookcases. They represent the largest collection of the poet. Carefully maintained, these shelved books are locked behind secure metal screens. Above them hang large portraits of him on the thick sandstone walls. The imposing appearance is made more so by a lofty ceiling room. Several tall stained-glass windows, portraying literary epics, illuminate everything here. The whole effect is as if one has entered a sanctuary for some heavenly creature and/or pious martyr to literature. Thompson is protected and bolstered by fame so he remains impervious to any attempt to say he may have done wrong. Others have tried and failed.

In 1965 the eminent American historian John Evangelist Walsh was researching the life of Francis Thompson for a planned biography. He found in a bookshop a recently released work by the English author Tom Cullen. Walsh's research on Thompson is considered definitive and his conclusions on the facts of Thompson's life are accepted in places of learning like Boston College. The staff, who oversee the magnificent Francis Thompson Room and his special collection at the Burns Library, consider Walsh's biography to be the best book on him. This prestigious academic, Walsh, when writing Thompson's biography, had permission of the director of libraries of Boston College to examine the Francis Thompson collection held there. Walsh was given access to his papers and he had the trust of Thompson's most heartfelt supporters. In preparing his book, Walsh visited places and people associated with Thompson. He was allowed to handle Thompson's papers at Greatham. This country cottage and large estate was purchased by his editor with the proceeds of sales of Thompson's written works. Wilfrid Meynell had already died so the editor's daughter granted him permission. Here Walsh took notes of Thompson's time on the streets around the years of the Ripper murders. Walsh examined Thompson's papers at Chichester, kept by a granddaughter of the publisher. In London Walsh went through the papers on Thompson, which were held by another granddaughter. While in the city Walsh also visited places associated with Thompson including the Guildhall Library and the British Reading Room. Walsh travelled throughout England, researching Thompson. This included visiting St Mary's Priory in Storrington, where Thompson was sent at the start of 1889. He made an extensive search of their archives. Walsh interviewed Norbert Thompson, the half-brother of Francis Thompson, who supplied him with further information. Walsh also examined written material kept on the estate of New Buildings in Sussex, the city of Manchester, and in the adjacent town of Ashton-upon-Lyne. Walsh visited the monasteries at the townships of Pantasaph and Crawley. He looked at the records and papers on Thompson held at Ushaw College, where Thompson unsuccessfully studied to become a priest.

The true-crime non-fiction that Walsh plucked off the store bookshelf in 1965 was called *Autumn of Terror: Jack the Ripper, His Crimes and Times*, written by Tom Cullen. Inside it Walsh read an account of a suspect that eerily matched that of Francis Thompson. Cullen wrote that the man gave an alibi when he was interviewed by two city police officers. They had been tipped off that their suspect would try to trick prostitutes to go along with him by offering highly polished farthings, made to look like sovereigns. A London newspaper reported that with Chapman's body, two bright pennies were found. Upon questioning the man was discovered to be an ex-medical student. He had been in a lunatic asylum and had spent all his time with prostitutes. Despite this history, the man explained how he could never have done the crimes and the police accepted his alibi.

Walsh had only recently learned, in researching his own book, that Thompson had been living in Panton Street, Haymarket, in 1886; and in 1888 he gave his address as Charing Cross, as he collected his mail from the Charing Cross Post Office. This office was about 150 meters from Haymarket's Rupert Street. The street the police's suspect was found in. Panton Street, where Thompson once resided, was less than a two-minute walk from Rupert Street. What was even more odd was that the description of the man and that of Thompson closely matched. Thompson was an ex-medical student; he had taken the summer of 1882 off from medical school due to having a mental breakdown. Thompson's only relationship had been with a prostitute while she resided in West End Chelsea, before she fled and hid from him, most probably in East End Whitechapel. To add another bizarre similarity, Walsh already knew the tale of Thompson and the 'miracle of the halfpennies'. In an earlier 1913 biography on Thompson, written several years after his death, his editor's son told of a windfall of money that Thompson came to. It was while he was living as a vagrant in London,

'They came to him on a day when he had not even the penny to invest in matches that might bring him interest on his money. He was, he told me, walking, vacant with desperation, along a crowded pavement, when he heard the clink of a coin and saw something bright rolling towards the gutter … As he neared the place where he had found the first coin, he saw another glittering in the road. This, too, he picked up, and again thought he held a halfpenny. But looking closer he discovered it to be golden and a sovereign, and only after much persuasion of his senses would he believe the first-found one to be likewise gold.'

Walsh saw that both the police's murder suspect and Thompson, one of the most widely known modern Catholic poets, told stories about switching coins. The suspect with his quarter-penny farthings, that were highly polished and made to appear to be sovereigns, and Thompson with his half-pennies that were miraculously made into sovereigns. It was all very interesting, but could Walsh have abandoned his work on his academic biography on this poet? Could he, instead, launch into an *exposé* on a brand new Ripper suspect? Let us pause to consider what it would have done to tell people this in 1967. When Walsh read Cullen's book, with contents that might have linked this esteemed Catholic poet with multiple murders, the political landscape was very different. In Northern Ireland, in the 1960's, tensions between Catholics and Protestants were at an all-time high. By the end of the decade, in August of 1969, rioting during civil rights marches rocked Northern Ireland. Protestors demanded an end to discrimination against Irish Catholics. Several people were killed and hundreds wounded. Antagonism against Catholics had a long history. In 1868, when he was a boy in his hometown, Francis Thompson himself was caught up in a three-day anti-Catholic riot. In addition, in 1967, Thompson's poetry was part of compulsory learning topics in Catholic colleges all over the world, and loved by millions of the Catholic faith. Was telling all this worth it, after all? What Walsh did, instead, about his little discovery was regulate it to a footnote in the appendix of his biography *Strange Harp Strange Symphony. The Life of Francis Thompson*. The footnote on this 'most bizarre coincidence in Thompson's life' told of Thompson and the Ripper. It spoke of a suspect who was found to be close to John McMaster. This was the Panton Street bootmaker who Thompson had worked for, before being fired when he had injured a customer. Walsh's footnote said,

'During the very weeks he was searching for his prostitute friend, London was in an uproar over the ghastly deaths of five such women at the hands of Jack the Ripper ... The police threw a wide net over the city, investigating thousands of drifters, and known consorts with the city's lower elements, and it is not beyond possibility that Thompson himself may have been questioned. He was, after all, a drug addict, acquainted with prostitutes and, most alarming, a former medical student! A young man with a similar background and living only a block away from McMaster's shop was one who early came under suspicion. {Walsh.p256}

Funnily enough, nobody seemed to take much store in this little footnote by Walsh. This selective comprehension, about Thompson, was not helped by twists and turns in cartography. Walsh, in his reading on

Thompson, had come to find out he stayed, in the Providence Row night refuge. When it was first opened in 1860 this homeless shelter, run by the Catholic order the Sisters of Mercy, was situated in London's West End, in the small lane that it was named after. When it moved to Number 50 Crispin Street, Spitalfields, in 1868, it retained its old name. Walsh, probably, like any good researcher, would have consulted a map of London. This would have led him to mistakenly think the shelter was still in the West End and so not connected with Jack the Ripper. Sadly, Walsh died in March of 2015. The man, who first saw the significance in the proximity to Thompson in Panton Street and the Metropolitan Police's Rupert Street Ripper suspect, failed to see the even more profound significance of Thompson's Providence Row address – how it was not miles away from the murder in the West End, but instead situated right in Whitechapel during the time of the murders.

Such wrong conclusions contributed to the wall of silence regarding Thompson as a contender for the Ripper. There may have been other reasons why, when Thompson could have been exposed as the nefarious Jack the Ripper, some might have thought it better to let sleeping dogs lie. To have said, in the 1960s, when Walsh's biography came out, that Thompson was the wanted man would have led many others to have a closer look at this poet and question, not just his links to the crimes, but possibly other aspects of his life.

In 1967, when John Walsh released his book on Thompson, it was a time of fearful religious violence against Catholics, and when paedophiles under cassocks were the Catholic Church's open secret. Highlighting a praised Catholic poet as a murderer could invite all sorts of prying eyes to examine all aspects of Thompson's life. At risk were, not only Thompson's legacy, but also the reputations of a great many important and powerful people. This man's poetry was loved and followed by millions. His verse is even today in the mandatory curriculum of renowned universities. If he is indeed an infamous serial killer, when will his books of poems be moved to the other section of libraries? Alongside with his prodigy. Those multiple murderers who also wrote poetry. Killers such as Israel Keyes, Dennis Nilsen, Joel Rifkin, Ted Bundy, Jack Unterweger, Dennis Rader, and the Zodiac Killer.

Many more years were destined to pass until a milestone was reached when 1988 came around. It was the centenary of the Ripper murders. This was commemorated by a new series of books on the crimes and documentaries with experts re-examining the evidence. This international interest in the unsolved murders caught the attention of Doctor Joseph Rupp, an American forensic pathologist. His many years of experience told him that skill was more important than strength when it came to the use of a dissecting knife. He was reading a book on Thompson. It acknowledged he carried a knife but the verdict was that after three years living on the streets he was too exhausted to do anything. The doctor did some more research on Thompson. His article *Was Francis Thompson Jack the Ripper?* was published in the UK journal *The Criminologist,* in 1988. Dr Rupp gave an accurate surmise of why people should stop pretending about this famous poet,

'Francis Thompson spent six years in medical school, in effect, he went through medical school three times. It is unlikely, no matter how disinterested he was or how few lectures he attended, that he did not absorb a significant amount of medical knowledge. Indeed, we know that he learned enough medicine to deceive his father, a practicing physician, for a matter of six years … The Ripper was able to elude the police so many times in spite of the complete mobilisation of many volunteer groups and the law enforcement agencies in London. If we look at Thompson's background, having lived on the streets for three years prior to this series of crimes, there is no doubt that he knew the back streets of London intimately and that his attire and condition as a derelict and drug addict would not arouse suspicion as he moved by day and night through the East End of London ... Francis Thompson was at least as good and perhaps a far better candidate for the role of Jack the Ripper than was the Duke of Clarence or any number of suspects that have been put forward over the past one hundred years.'

Dr Rupp's excursion into crime solving was met by the same wall of silence. When this author first spoke with him on the phone, early in 2015, Rupp, now a very old man, was surprised to hear from anyone and told that, after 27 years, this author had been the first person to respond to his article.

In 1997, not knowing about the research done by John Walsh and Dr Joseph Rupp, when Mr Richard Patterson (the writer of this book) concluded that Francis Thompson could be a Ripper suspect, he thought he too was alone in doing so. Patterson was then a 27-year-old student of philosophy at Melbourne's La Trobe University and he was just completing his second year of a three-year Bachelor of Arts Diploma. Patterson had also just finished a minor in English literature, which focused on early twentieth-century British poets. A tutor of his, who had taught his class in aesthetics, had approached him, asking if he would like to help him complete a book he had been writing on murderers. His tutor had been interested because of a statement that Patterson had made: that the reason certain criminals got away with their crimes was not because they were 'evil geniuses' but because their motives were so alien and horrible that those investigating their crimes, subconsciously, did not wish to understand the criminal. It is as if those investigating some crimes bring with them a psychological blind spot where the killer seeks refuge. Patterson decided to test his belief on the Jack the Ripper murders. With this in mind, at this time, he also happened to have bought a slim volume of poems by Francis Thompson. Although an English literature student, Thompson was a poet he was unfamiliar with. Patterson thought him to be nothing more than simply another forgotten Victorian poet. Then he read, in the little book, what seemed to be a harmless romantic poem of his. It is called *An Arab Love Song*. It is set in the Arabian desert and has the narrator try to persuade the object of his affection to return his desires. Part of it reads,

'Now while the dark about our loves is strewn,

Light of my dark, blood of my heart, O come!

And night will catch her breath up, and be dumb.

Leave thy father, leave thy mother

And thy brother;

Leave the black tents of thy tribe apart!

Am I not thy father and thy brother,

And thy mother?

And thou what needest with thy tribe's black tents

Who hast the red pavilion of my heart?'

A beautiful poem, surely, but also one filled with subterfuge and sacrifice. In it, the writer asks the listener to sacrifice and risk everything – family, friends and more – while the seemingly gently imploring and adoring poet risks nothing. The logic and premise of this poem is 'love nobody but me!' Patterson asked himself, who would fall for this poem? Surely most people would see through the poem's elaborate language to its selfish core, but what if the listener was a near-homeless prostitute? Patterson wondered, what if the audience was a fearful Whitechapel woman, one who had been taught to fear a brutish butcher or strong tattooed foreign sailor for the murders in the East End? Patterson imagined that such a desperate soul, who walked the streets at night, is tapped on the shoulder. She fears the worst before turning, only to see a well-dressed Englishman. The stranger asks her in a gentle voice if she would like to hear a poem. Is this what happened? Was Thompson able to use words to trick these unfortunate women to their doom?

The small book Patterson had read had a short biography in point form. It told that Thompson had been living homeless in London and that he had trained as a surgeon. Patterson decided to research this poet himself and write down why he might be the Ripper. Patterson promised himself he would stop when he encountered a fact that showed Thompson to be innocent. That was almost 20 years ago and he has kept his promise.

Chapter 6
With Dreadful Ease

'But here the gates we burst, and to the temple go.'

Francis Thompson.

When Francis Thompson's prostitute lover told him, in the first week of June 1888, that she would leave him, he was devastated. Evidently, this woman, who had encouraged him to send submissions to publishers, did so knowing from the very start that their acceptance would bring him fame. The shock of Thompson's life, and he had already been subjected to many, was all this time she planned to leave him. Her inadvertent admission, that she knew him always as a genius, was that while he believed their love could be everlasting, from the very beginning she foresaw that she would desert him. This occasion is subject to varying versions and a veil of secrecy so there is no way to tell if Thompson saw this as yet another betrayal from a woman. We do not know his reaction when this prostitute, who made him betray his own vows of chastity, threatened to leave him. We also know after that fateful meeting, she vanished and was never recorded to be seen alive again.

The Meynell's like to suggest, her leaving was because she was worried, that their relationship would give him a bad name. It might have been the other way around. Although Thompson's *Nightmare of the Witch Babies* had been sent to the Meynells before she had met him, she may have learned of it from his small notebooks or conversations with him. If so, then she would have known that her prostitution, in his religious doctrines, would be viewed by him as corrupt, and also that he had written about killing and disembowelling corrupt women. If his poem had gone nowhere then she could have ignored it and played down any anxiety felt. Now that it seemed his fame was near, such a poem's prominence, as well as Thompson gaining leverage in their relationship, may have been something to fear, and with good reason.

Because her fate is unknown and all we are told about comes from Thompson, everything ever said about her is speculation. Here is some more. Did Thompson react with anger and strike out at this woman who threatened to desert him? Did he snap and kill her? Or did she indeed flee from him without his knowledge? If the truth was the former, then in a murderous rage he may well have sought out women who represented her, to kill again and again, until his guilt had been overrun and his anger at her and at himself had been satiated. Both scenarios would have brought him to where she would most likely have gone – Spitalfields, where there were women of her type the greatest chance of finding similar prey. It was where he did in fact go. If a West End prostitute wanted to disappear, yet continue in her trade, there was no better place than the East End's Whitechapel, a place known as the centre of London's vice and prostitution. The parish of Spitalfields, in particular, held thousands of women like his friend. Here was a greater concentration of prostitutes than in any other part of London. If she was still alive, then Spitalfields was the perfect place for her to – as he said, 'fled, a swift and trackless fugitive,' – disappear in the crowd. Thompson shifted his home ground from west to east. By the first Ripper murder in August, he was sleeping in the Limehouse Salvation Army refuge that had opened their first homeless shelter earlier that year. Then, by the last Ripper murder in November he had moved into the heart of Spitalfields.

During June and July Thompson continued to visit Meynell at his office and then his home. There was only Wilfrid and Alice in the house at the time, because his children had been sent with their nurses to holiday on the Isle of White for the summer. In their home Thompson bathed, was fed meals and was made presentable. Meynell was already, courtesy of Francis's uncle, aware of Thompson's background, but he did not know why Thompson refused his offer to provide him with accommodation. Thompson wished to stay on the streets. Everard Meynell told of how the poet, from very early on, showed the habit of leaving their house when the hour grew late. His excuse was not so he could hunt down his lost prostitute, but to earn money, which he had refused from Meynell, by minding carriage horses. In his biography on Thompson, Everard said,

'... of his history he said nothing ... reluctant to admit that he might become a worker and quit the streets, so fixedly reluctant that some strong reason was conjectured. He would visit my father, then living in Kensington, but it was long before he would accept substantial hospitalities; coming in the evening or afternoon, he would leave to return to his calling, literally a calling of cabs. That he was also, during this time, either parting with or searching for his Ann is not unlikely... he went frightened and brave at once, at war with peace, at peace with war.'

Although Meynell did not know about Thompson's failed relationship, he did rightly suspect that Thompson was an opium user. He insisted that Thompson stop using; Thompson, for the time being, complied. That he had become published gave him renewed hope that he could escape the streets and make himself respectable. This and Meynell's urgings was the impetus to no longer take laudanum. From July 1888 until 1890 Thompson was essentially drug free. While laudanum puts the user in a sleepy, dreamlike state, its stopping use also holds side effects. Abrupt withdrawal, after long-term usage, causes hyperaesthesia. This is when the former addict's senses become highly receptive; noises become intensified and even the skin becomes highly sensitive to touch. Other symptoms are an increased sex drive, nightmares and hallucinations of smell and disturbances of vision. The physical symptoms can last for weeks, with mental symptoms lasting indefinitely.

Arguably, the British surgeon Dr Thomas Bond made the first ever criminal profile when he outlined whom the police should be seeking for the Ripper murders. He was the registered police surgeon for A Division, Westminster. Some say he was the closest real thing to the fictional Sherlock Holmes. By the culmination of the murders, Bond was called in to examine the medical reports of all the slayings. He performed the autopsy on Mary Kelly. Dr Bond wrote in his report to the police,

'I think he must be in the habit of wearing a cloak or overcoat or he could hardly have escaped notice in the streets if the blood on his hands or clothes were visible.'

Thompson was known for his insistence on wearing a long, dark brown inverness-style coat in all weather. Thompson, in 1888, was without regular employment and living homeless on the streets of London. His only small income was cash given to him for the first publication of two poems and essays in a magazine; this was used to buy new clothes. Thompson had very few friends and lived virtually as a hermit. Of the Ripper, Bond wrote,

'… he would probably be solitary and eccentric in his habits … also he is most likely to be a man without regular occupation, but with some small income or pension.'

In the days following the final murder, most likely Sunday 11th November, Wilfrid Meynell, who was concerned about Thompson's physical and mental condition, had him hospitalised for six weeks in a private sanatorium. Four days after his release he relapsed into life back on the streets, so by the year's end the Meynell's had him sent to a country monastery. When his editor had published Thompson's first poem in April 1888, he knew precious little about Thompson, even though he had seen that one of his poems, *Nightmare of the Witch Babies,* was about killing women with a knife and disembowelling them. Despite this, the editor, out of goodwill, paid off Thompson's debts accrued through his laudanum habit, and made him look respectable. It was his editor's good name, vouching for Thompson, that enabled him to gain entry to the night refuge on Crispin Street, situated not more than a 15-minute walk to all the Ripper murder sites. It is possible that this editor, who followed the Ripper murders in the press and spoke about it, at some point, may have suspected that he had inadvertently published the Ripper's poetry, and effectively helped to make him appear respectable so that he could lure his victims. Revealing this would have ended the career of both him and his wife. Given the furore that these murders had generated, it could even have meant a jail term. Dr Bond, in his report on a likely suspect for the Ripper murders, also suggested that others might know the Ripper's identity.

'He is possibly living among respectable persons who have some knowledge of his character and habits and who may have grounds for suspicion that he is not quite right in his mind at times. Such persons would probably be unwilling to communicate suspicions to the police for fear of trouble or notoriety.'

Many advances in criminal profiling have occurred in the many years since the Ripper murders, but even if we look at descriptions of the probable suspect, even a century later, it is incredible how well they match Francis Thompson. This is seen in the 1988 profile of the Ripper that was given by the famed former FBI agent John Douglas. Douglas appeared with a panel of experts in the TV show *The Secret Identity of Jack the Ripper*. A panel of experts were asked to examine the show's five suspects. These did not include Thompson. As well as appearing on the show, ex-special agent Douglas looked at the probabilities and wrote a description of who we should be looking for if we are to find the Ripper. His description almost exactly matches Francis Thompson. Douglas said that the killer might have had a physical abnormality. And Thompson said he was denied entry into the army because of his small chest. His addiction to morphine had made his arms and legs thin and unsightly. Douglas said the killer would be single, like Thompson. He said the Ripper, by the method the women were slain, had an aversion to blood. An aversion to blood is said for Thompson, who gave it as his reason for leaving his medical school. Douglas said that the murderer may have only had relationships with a prostitute and Thompson's only relationship was with a prostitute. Douglas said the murderer was a local, and so was Thompson. Thompson's biographer, John Walsh, said the police might have interviewed Thompson for the murders but let him go; Douglas suggested the same thing for the Ripper. Douglas told that the Ripper had knowledge of anatomy and may have had a job in the medical field. Thompson had trained as a surgeon for six years.

Douglas described how the Ripper was absorbed in the ritual of the crimes. Thompson was recorded as governing his life with ritual down to small detail. This was a trait accentuated by his absorbed interest in the Catholic rites and rituals from his days at his seminary college. A biographer of Thompson, JC Reid, expressed Thompson's love of ritual, 'Certainly he was always fascinated by ritual …ritual is poetry addressed to the eye … he found in ceremonial an end in itself rather than a means, that the rite was at least as important, as perhaps more important than, the creed.' FBI criminal profiler Douglas told of the Ripper's obsession with ritual, 'However, the personal desires and the needs of the subject are expressed in the ritual aspect of the crime. The ritual is something that he must do because it is the acting out of the fantasy.'

Thompson was a loner and kept to himself, as too did the Ripper in Douglas's profile. Douglas said the Ripper would be in his mid to late twenties, as was Thompson who was aged 28 in the autumn of 1888. Douglas said the Ripper would have a dishevelled appearance. Thompson was widely described as appearing dingy and untidy, a man who could not keep his clothes looking clean or new for long. Douglas described the Ripper as nocturnal and known to cover large distances by foot. Thompson was a habitual long-range walker at night. Bridget Boardman, in her 1988 biography on Thompson, said, 'walking was to a lifelong and truly recreational habit.' He would go out walking until the early hours. As a result, he would often sleep in until the late afternoon. Douglas thought the Ripper would not have committed suicide and that he stopped murdering by being confined. In the week after the last murder, Thompson was put in a private sanatorium and then sent to a far-away male-only country priory. He went on to live for 20 more years.

This book's Ripper suspect lived in Spitalfields, only a two-minute walk from the address of the fifth victim, Mary Kelly, where she was killed. He may have even known her. His own letters prove he was then carrying a dissecting knife. Kept concealed under his coat. Most accept that the murderer had some medical skill and Thompson was an ex-medical student with years of experience working in a busy surgery. He lived at Number 50 Crispin Street, Spitalfields, in the immediate vicinity of the crimes. Having been largely homeless for the prior three years, Thompson possessed an intimate knowledge of the streets on which he sought out the prostitute who shocked him by abruptly ending their romance and leaving him.

The books about Thompson all agree that, in the autumn of 1888, Thompson was walking the streets, trying to hunt down this woman, as Jack the Ripper did. She fled Thompson in June 1888, probably to the East End. In an area famed for being thick with prostitutes, she hid herself after finding out that one of Thompson's poems, about essentially murdering prostitutes, was amongst what had been submitted to at least one editor. His horrid poem about a man armed with a knife who hunts down corrupt women and slices their stomachs open. Just like how the Ripper would slice into women's stomachs in the following year.

Several biographers have written that it was very soon after the Ripper's murders, probably on 11th November 1888, that Thompson was confined in a private hospital. From there, at the start of 1889, he was moved to a male-only monastery. It was here, on the first anniversary of the Ripper murders, that Thompson completed his only ever story. It was a confession, by a murderer, who tells how he first made his lover unconscious and stabbed her. This mimics the method of the Ripper. Thompson's story further resembles the Whitechapel murder investigation, by having a murder that escapes justice, just like the Ripper. The murderer, in Thompson's story, gets away with it to become, like Thompson, a celebrated poet.

Of all the famous characters of the Victorian age, only two, Thompson and the Ripper, are so often spoken of remaining unknown to the populace. During the time of the murders, when he was homeless, and afterwards, Thompson knew hardly anyone. The daughter of his agent wrote that, just like the Ripper, 'Francis Thompson must have been known to fewer people than anyone who has achieved so much fame.' The missing prostitute is the only woman he ever had a real relationship with and she was never heard from again.

Wilfrid Meynell, Thompson's protector and benefactor, on the other hand, was a man who had the friendship and respect of prime ministers and cardinals. He was known to speak about his strong fascination for the Jack the Ripper murders. Meynell received Thompson's first poems and rescued him from poverty so that by the end of August 1888, even though still homeless, Thompson could wash away the grime of the street, throw away his ragged clothes and buy himself a new suit. This all happened on the eve of the Ripper murders.

By the start of the Ripper murders, the way Thompson fits as a candidate makes him the perfect killing machine. First, he knew all there was to know about how to kill these women. His intimate relationship with his working prostitute meant that he had learned how they operated. This would include how they do business, appraise and select their customers, where they take them to perform sex, what makes them suspicious and what removes their doubts. Second, he knew the streets. He knew the alleys, archways, hidden corners and shortcuts. Having slept on pavements with the worry that police would move him along with a shout or whack of their nightstick. In the months and years before the Ripper murders, Thompson was dressed in rags and in a laudanum stupor most of the time, yet even then he was able to lure and gain the trust of at least a prostitute. By the eve of the Ripper murders, an articulate Thompson was off laudanum and, thanks to his editor's kindness, dressed to impress with money in his pockets. Photos of Thompson show a young, handsome English gentleman. He would have presented the ideal customer. During the murders, thanks to the press reports that the maniac was some hulking butcher, gang member or foreign sailor, it would never have occurred to a prostitute that this softly spoken man, whose conversation was filled with religion and poetry and the news of becoming a published writer, kept so many secrets, and a knife that he was ready to use. The knife he carried under his new coat was his dissecting scalpel; the one he kept as sharp as a razor, since he also used it to shave with; a scalpel that, most likely, was retained from his hospital days and used countless times to dissect dead bodies. His skill could not be questioned, having been highly trained in all sorts of surgical operations and with years of experience in a busy surgery and a medical college that supplied, thanks to his extra purchases, a virtual assembly-line of cadavers. He had already written about killing and disembowelling women. He had been jilted from a prostitute, and that he was seeking her out to put things on the right track was his reason for moving to Spitalfields. He had a history of mental breakdown, delirium, drug abuse, conflicts with his family and the police, and suicide. Yet the only things preventing Thompson from being the gentle, saintly poet he has long been portrayed as, and beginning a reign of terror, was his state of mind.

There is the weak argument that this 'dawdling', innocent-looking poet could not have possibly hunted down women, made them unconscious and then cut them open; he only wrote about doing it. His poetry and prose is filled with images of corruption and murder. That someone's girlfriend has left them should never trigger a murder spree of prostitutes. Thompson's circumstances were abnormal beyond the fact that his girlfriend was a prostitute and so were all of the Whitechapel victims. This relationship was the only romantic one he would ever have. At the age of 27 she would be his first and last.

It is the height of reason to assume his friend had likely fled to the East End's Whitechapel, where she could hide herself amongst 90,000 other women of her profession. This was the same district Thompson moved to, bringing with him a dissecting scalpel, kept razor sharp. Thompson, nicknamed the Necktie Poet, resided in the same area in which all the women were strangled and killed with a knife; all people were talking about was a knife-wielding prostitute murderer. People were so surprised when, in 1888, Thompson became famous. Before then, he was destitute, prone to mental breakdowns, deliriums, and taking mind-altering drugs. His mind was unhinged enough to attempt suicide in the spring of 1888.

If Thompson had resolved to kill prostitutes in Spitalfields, then he must have been bold indeed. He would have had to draw on his experience in regard to his medical learning, as well as imagining himself an almost soldier, someone who could set aside pity and normal restraint. In his past, in his military essays, and his recreation of famous battles, he had played at it. Once, in his stint in the army, he had marched in uniform and practised at drill. Now, to cross over the threshold from pure imagining and make pretend to concerted action, he must have been able to effectively talk himself into it. This is what the Son-of-Sam serial killer, David Berkowitz, did. He wrote of his transformation into a soldier of death, and his reasoning for killing six people,

'The demons were turning me into a soldier. A soldier can't stop every time he shoots someone and weep ... He simply shoots the enemy. They were people I had to kill. I can't stop and weep over them. You have to be strong and you have to survive.'

Had Thompson, a survivor type, argued the same sort of thing to himself? If so, he probably would have done it in the same vein as the argument of an essay he wrote, around three months after the Ripper murders. His essay, *The Macbeth Controversy*,' first appeared in the *Dublin Review* in July 1889. It was on Shakespeare's famous murder tragedy, in which the villain, Macbeth, is spurred on by witches and kills the King of Scotland. Thompson's essay argued that Macbeth, goaded on by witches, begins his murder spree like a true soldier, without warning or mercy. Was his essay a secret coded message, a cryptogram in which he argues his own decision to take lives? It is more than puzzling that at this essay's start Thompson repeatedly wrote of cryptograms, e.g. 'immortal cryptogram' and 'prefer the cryptogram' and 'finding that the great cryptogram' and 'evidence of the great cryptogram' and 'the cryptogram reveals' and 'the great cryptogram lags'. Thompson's essay finishes with him writing how such a resolute and masterful murderer, like Macbeth, should not be hated but should be admired,

'He proceeds without hesitation and without remorse, "more than an executioner might feel" in a career of bloodshed, stimulated by the witches, by blood, by assassination ... he foresees the necessity for further murders on his part; this belief that he can commit the crime and yet escape its infamy, the necessity of engaging boldly in bloodshed. His natural disposition is that of a soldier, bold, decided, instant in action, accustomed to go straight and openly to his object. Moral scruples cannot restrain him; he has completely set them aside, has resolved to jump the life to come. The murder is done, and he ceases to waver. Not because he has foreseen all the issue of his crime but because the decisive mental conflict once over, the resolution once taken and executed, his nature rebounds like a slackened bow to its natural determined temper. He faces all the sequel of his crime as a commander, once having decided to give battle, accepts and meets all the chances of the battle. Thenceforward he sets his face towards crime as he was accustomed to set it towards fight; and the witches' counsel, the splendid hardihood of the man ... rises to absolute grandeur in the final scenes. It is impossible to withhold admiration ... and admiration swells almost into sympathy.'

In the years after the murders Thompson would pace the room of his one-bedroom lodgings, muttering to himself. After his death his landlady would point out the hole Thompson had worn through his carpet from so many hours of indecision and rumination. Such endless pacing is also very reminiscent of his editor's son's description of Thompson losing his mind after his heartbreak over the Rothschild incident, when the banker gave him such a generous florin tip for the newspaper Thompson had sold him. Everard wrote, in his 1913 biography, of how Thompson's paralysis of indecision finally broke,

'For hours he has stood in one place, or paced one patch of pavement, as if his feet were trapped in the lines between the stones … He is tied to the few slabs of stone that fill the space beneath his archway. It seems dreadfully perilous to move beyond them, and he sways within their territory as if they edged a precipice. And then, he knows not how or why, his weakness has passed, and he is drifting along the streets, not wearily, but with dreadful ease, with no hope of having sufficient resolution to halt.'

Such a description is echoed by Thompson in his murder story *The Final Crowning Work*, his only story. In it Thompson has his hero explain that he had to kill his victim with a knife because, once decided, there was no turning back. The murderer walks about in circles, contemplating if he should act. After pacing the streets in troubled thought, he makes up his mind and sets himself on killing his love. Thompson writes,

'No; the first step includes all sequent steps; when I did my first evil, I did also this evil; years ago had this shaft been launched, though it was but now curving to its mark; years ago had I smitten her, though she was but now staggering to her fall... When at length, after long wandering, I retraced my steps, I had not resolved, I had recognized that I could resolve no longer... I swear I struck not the first blow.'

When deciding upon a suspect for this, the most studied series of murders, experts will often look at other British serial killers to see if, by studying them, they can more closely understand the true nature of the Ripper. Distasteful as such an exercise may be, there is merit in this approach. It should be applied to Francis Thompson, but the problem is that when this is done, Thompson gets in the way. Facts about his life continually coincide with facts about other known serial killers. A remarkable anomaly between Francis Thompson and England's most prolific serial killers is that they all lived where he lived. Of Britain's 936 towns, Francis Thompson's primary areas of habitation feature as their killing grounds. In 1864, when Thompson was aged five, he became lost whilst out shopping with his mother in the market of Ashton-under-Lyne near Manchester. It was an unforgettable moment for Thompson, as the first time that he felt 'world-wide desolation and fear'. In the 1960s a child was kidnapped from Ashton's marketplace. He would be tortured and killed by a couple, Myra Hindley and Ian Brady, in an event to be remembered as the 'Moors murders'. On 31st January 2000, Manchester resident – dubbed by the press as 'The Gentle Murderer' – Dr Harold Shipman was convicted for killing 15 of his elderly female patients through a lethal dose of morphine. He was formally charged at Ashton-under-Lyne's police station. Dr Shipman is believed to have killed a further 150 people, and is considered England's most prolific murderer. It was in Manchester that Thompson, a doctor's son, studied as a surgeon and first began his chronic opium habit gained from the addictive morphine that the drug contained. It was also in Manchester, in 1977, that Peter Sutcliffe, the 'Yorkshire Ripper', picked up a prostitute before killing her in the Southern Cross Cemetery. Preston, Thompson's birthplace, was host to the convicted sex attacker who wanted to become a serial killer but got caught after his second murder. One of the women that Derek Brown killed was a prostitute. The police said this newspaper delivery-driver was trying to emulate Jack the Ripper. In 2008 the jury found Brown guilty of the murders despite the victims' bodies never being found. During the trial Brian Altman QC, for the prosecution, stated in the Old Bailey, 'Both women were street workers and both were soft targets for a predatory killer.' In 1886, while Thompson was homeless, he spent his nights sleeping on the Charing Cross embankment of the Thames River. In the 1980s, before Dr Shipman, there was Dennis Nilsen. Known as England's second most prolific murderer, his victims included tramps found sleeping along the Charing Cross embankment. When Thompson was 14, in 1873, he began studies at Durham. In the same year Mary Ann Cotton, England's third most prolific murderer, was tried in Durham and hanged for the lethal poisoning of 14 males. The youngest victim was aged 14. In 1906 Thompson boarded at a monastery in the town of Crawley in Sussex. He had previously been living in Kensington. In 1949 police captured the multiple murderer George Haigh at his Kensington hotel. Haigh confessed to killing his last victim in Crawley in Sussex.

Francis Thompson's. *The Mistress of Vision*.

'All things by immortal power,

Near or far,   Hiddenly

To each other linked are,

That thou canst not stir a flower

Without troubling of a star;'

Francis Thompson's *Darkest England*.

'You have sown your dragon's teeth, and you shall reap—armed men?

Nay, I tell you, but dragons.

From dragon's teeth, dragons; and from devil's teaching, devils.'

When we examine the lives of these serial killers, we find, not surprisingly, that their lives up till their murderous exploits hold an affinity with what we would think to be for Jack the Ripper. Surprisingly, or not, we also find that their psychology shows an affinity with Francis Thompson. George Haigh is as good example as any other.

In March 1944 George Haigh, who would become known as the 'Acid Bath Vampire' was involved in a car accident and experienced repeating nightmares. Before the end of the year he had committed his first murder. Haigh described his most common one,

'I saw before me a forest of crucifixes, which gradually turned into trees. At first there appeared to be dew, or rain, dripping from the branches, but as I approached I realised it was blood. Suddenly the whole forest began to writhe and the trees, stark and erect, to ooze blood ... A man went to each tree catching the blood ... When the cup was full he approached me. "Drink," he said but I was unable to move.'

Even in a harrowing nightmare image, we would wonder what sort of man desires someone to drink from a tree that drips blood. Francis Thompson seems to be such a man. It was a vision shared by him. In 1891 he was living in the Harrow Road district near to the site of where the Tyburn Tree once stood. This 'tree' was a platform gallows, made with a frame of wood. From 1536 to 1681, during the English Reformation, 100 Roman Catholics were executed upon the tree. Crowds of 200,000 would converge to witness the condemned be beheaded, disembowelled, cut into sections or hung. The hangman was known to amuse the crowd by pushing the hanging corpse or shaking its hand. Thompson, in his poem *To the English Martyrs*, writes of the bloody Tyburn Tree,

'Rain, rain on Tyburn tree,

Red rain-a-falling;

Dew, Dew on Tyburn tree,

And pouring out the eager cup,

How sweeter than bee-haunted dells

The blosmy blood of martyrs smells!

Who did upon the scaffold's bed,

The ceremonial steel between you wed.'

Chapter 7
Fields of the Dead

'How dark it ran, bow deep, how pauseless; how
unruffled by a memory of its ancestral hills!'

Francis Thompson.

A cursory examination of where in the world the Ripper
murders occurred makes it seem like the stage was set
for this type of carnage long ago. Despite what some
must think about Victorian times, London in 1888 was a
modern city in most senses. It had worldwide
communications and efficient transport. Victorians knew
about such things as calculators, film, neon lights,
typewriters, handheld cameras, vending machines and
rubber tyres. There were 20,000 telephones, and postal
deliveries were made seven times a day. In contrast to
this modernity was the East End, although so iconic to
London, particularly the district of Whitechapel. The
East End seems to have always existed in some kind of
alternate reality.

The East End in the time of the Romans was a wet
and marshy area, unchanged since 20,000 years earlier
when, through continental shift, it broke from Europe at

the Rhine. In AD 43, after a local garrison of soldiers were attacked and slaughtered, the Emperor Claudius established the Roman river port city of Londinium. The first Roman inhabitants of the East End were the dead. By the third century AD, fortified Roman Londinium city held 50,000 citizens; the city chose this area, east of the fortified walls, to dispose of their people. Hence, the East End first bore the name the Fields of the Dead. The area became a place for slaughterhouses when, in 1371, the killing and gutting of livestock was banned within the city walls. Violence further afield swelled the population. The French Massacre of St Bartholomew in 1572 and the revoking of the Edict of Nantes in 1685 brought into the East End an influx of French Huguenot refugees. The Huguenots were Protestants fleeing religious persecution by the Catholic majority. Over 15,000 settled in London. The Huguenots comprised mainly of weavers. At first, the weaving work prospered, and with them so did their other trades including bell and clock makers. By the eighteenth century, the weavers' fortunes had brought them three-storied workshops with the third floors serving as the family homes. The bricks of these buildings and walls, still standing during the time of the Ripper, were made partly from ancient human remains. During the early Elizabethan period, historian John Stow, whose records were stored at the Guildhall Library, told of the discovery of an ancient Roman cemetery, upon where Christ Church now stands. Stow detailed the discovery of this vast necropolis that had been covered for one and a half millennia, 'a large field, of old time called Lolesworth, now Spittle Field;

which about the year 1576 was broken up for clay to make brick; in the digging whereof many earthen pots, called 'urnae', were found full of ashes and the burnt bones of men ... Every one of these pots had in them with the ashes of the dead one piece of copper coin, with the inscription of the Emperor then reigning, some of them were of Claudius, some were Vespasian, some of Nero, of Antoninus Pius, of Trajanus and others.'

The 1860s was a decade of grief for the already lapsing fortunes of the East End's weaving economy. The mass production of the industrial age, which brought the underground railway whose lines crisscrossed the Thames, and steam-driven ships of steel, was accompanied with a renewed trade treaty with France. The treaty caused the price for local cloth to plummet and poverty levels to increase. As thousands of families became unemployed, many of the weaving factories and the once well-fitted homes fell into decay.

The massive problem of overcrowding in the East End can be blamed on waves of immigrants who were met with poor planning. Its problems of crime and disease were seeded in 1580. Queen Elizabeth I became concerned about overcrowding in her city and prohibited new building. In consequence, many houses, particularly in lower working-class areas, were subdivided to provide more rooms for a growing population. In Spitalfields, spacious weavers' mansions had partitions built, and courtyards were covered with hastily constructed roofs. Cellars, once used exclusively for storing coal, and attics, built for ventilation, became extra accommodation areas. Existing sewerage systems, drainage and supplies of clean drinking water could not sustain the numbers living in family homes. To access this explosion of subdivision and habitation of illegal and unlicensed dwellings, a series of tangled and ridiculously narrow streets and small courtyards, perpetually in shadow, were constructed. Unsanitary conditions and unchecked crime, in this maze of miniature streets and yards called rookeries, became widespread. Epidemics of cholera and dysentery came in successive waves. To bring things under control new acts were passed by parliament. These acts allowed buildings, designated as unsafe to health, to be torn down. Prime targets for demolition were the habitations in and around Flower and Dean Street. In 1871 Flower and Dean Street had 31 common lodgings, with each housing an average of 29 people. In 1877 a trust purchased seven and a quarter acres around Goulston Street and on the eastern side of Flower and Dean Street. In 1882 the trust pulled down and cleared nearby Upper and Lower Keate streets, Keate Court, Wilson's Place, Sugar Loaf Court, Crown Court, New Court and parts of George Street and George Yard. Some 4,200 people were evicted and many of them were made homeless. Despite demolitions, there were still areas of Whitechapel that the police dared not enter, and criminal gangs could operate without fear of the law. Social worker Henrietta Barnett wrote of Whitechapel's poorer districts and gave an account of the conditions of destitution where in some parts the annual mortality rate was one in 25, and where most children died of sickness and malnutrition before the age of five. She recorded,

'None of these courts had roads. In some the houses were three storeys high and hardly six feet apart. The sanitary accommodation being pits in the cellars; in other courts the houses were lower, wooden and dilapidated, a standpipe at the end providing the only water. Each chamber was the home of a family who sometimes owned their indescribable furniture, but in most cases the rooms were let out furnished for 8d [pennies] a night. In many instances broken windows had been repaired with paper and rags, the banisters had been used for firewood and paper hung from the walls, which were the residence of countless vermin.'

When the inquest into the death of the Ripper's first victim, Mary Ann Nichols, began on 3rd September, it was held in the library of the Whitechapel Working Lads Institute. The building was an unlikely place to hold a murder inquest, but like its makeshift morgues, East Ender's were again forced to compromise.

If you were to leap 300 metres into the air in early September 1888, you would probably have seen yet another grey and cloudy day. Temperatures had been below normal with chilly nights and bleary rain-strewn days. A low, oily, black vapour that rose from coal stacks and chimneys hid most of London itself. From out of this smog, towers, masts, cranes and steeples broke through. Whitechapel consisted of thousands of buildings, two or three storied high, in rows upon rows. Many buildings were tenements housing lower class, menial workers; backing these tenements were hundreds of large four-to-six-storey factories or warehouses.

These buildings were in a confusing maze of thin side streets with narrow footpaths, all clustered at the juncture of Commercial Road and Whitechapel High Street. Many tenements had shop-front windows beside crooked little alleyways that wound around to stone courtyards. Most of the smaller streets had roads, six metres wide, made by bricks encased in dirt, and strewn with rubbish. The footpaths rose five centimetres from the curb and were three metres wide. On the footpath, in intervals, were metal grates beside small locked wooden doors used to deposit coal. The walls flanking the streets had narrow windows and were often three to four stories high. Projecting about a metre from the walls at a height of three metres were gas lamps for lighting open doorways. Running off Commercial Street, with a reputation as one of the worst streets in London, was Dorset Street. This short avenue, of 120 metres in length, held 1,200 people. Facing it at one end was Providence Row, Thompson's residence in November 1888; near the other end was the entrance to Miller's Court, where Mary Kelly would be killed.

The world of the East End during the 1880s can only be touched on in this work. Suffice to say that a massive influx of refugees, misguided planning and crippling poverty were all combined in a comparatively small area. During the reign of the Ripper, London's East End held 900,000 people. This area was almost treated as a foreign land by the rest of the populace. It went by many adages including the 'Empire of Hunger' and the 'Sink of London'. Its inhabitants were denoted by outsiders as the 'Marginal Tribe'. Impressions of the environment are almost uniform in their depiction of poverty and squalor. Toilets in the houses usually consisted of pits in the cellar. During winter, banisters on stairs were torn off and used for firewood. Dock Union Leader Ben Tillett told of the daily procedure practised by those seeking employment at the entrance to the wharfs,

'Coats, flesh and even ears were torn off. The strong literally threw themselves over the heads of their fellows and battled through the kicking, punching, cursing crowds to the rails of the 'cage' which held them like rats - mad rats who saw food in the ticket.' –

A visitor of the Stepney Division School Board recorded the chances of anyone escaping all of this,

'They do not migrate out of the district, but they are constantly changing their lodgings. They are like the circle of the suicides in *Dante's Inferno*, they go round and round within a certain area.'

Magistrate Montagu Williams QC summarised the state of lodging houses in the East End,

'In my humble judgement they are about as unwholesome and unhealthy as well as dangerous to the community as can well be. There are places among them where the police dare not enter and where the criminal hides all day long.'

Reverend FW Newlands, an East-End Missionary, warned on the consequences of the Ripper murders,

'A lurid light has recently been thrown upon the state of walks in some parts of the East End. I do not hesitate to say that in this seething residuum there is a chronic danger to the Commonwealth; we are living at the crater of a volcano which may at any moment overwhelm the community as with a torrent; it needs very little to bring about a crisis and a catastrophe.'

Chapter 8
The Stage is Set

'Pain was well paid which brought me to your sight.'

Francis Thompson.

Francis Thompson's whereabouts on 31st August 1888, the night of the first Ripper murder, is unknown. He has no alibi for this night or any other night in which the murders occurred. His only honest excuse, if he were stopped by an officer and asked what he had been up to, would have been that he was seeking a prostitute whom he had unfinished business with. Ironically, if the Ripper were also an honest man, he would have furnished the same excuse. What we do know is that Thompson had recently moved from the West End to somewhere within the East End's West India docks. The same area where the distracting warehouse fire had been burning, leading officers away from their usual patrols in Whitechapel. Reaching the site of the fire and Buck's Row, where the first murder happened undetected, was easy. The straightest and most covert route was to simply follow the Great Eastern railway line that began at the Thames. The railway cut through streets before plunging beneath

Whitechapel. It passed right under Buck's Row as it headed north. Extremely steep brick walls that would be impossible to climb unassisted flanked most of the railway as it went through the underpass. Here, exiting the line and gaining access to the street above was easy. As are shown in photographs of other bridges from the time, there were probably convenient wooden steps with a guardrail that led up from the tracks to the 1.8-meter-high brick wall that could be climbed over to reach the street. Once someone was on the other side, they would be standing about four feet from where the body was found. After the murderer had found, courted and killed his prey, all he needed to do was take a moment to step up to the wall and descend the steps down to the unlit and empty train tracks to be able to vanish. It was not only the apparent convenience of being able to instantly escape that makes this first murder comparatively easy to commit. The fear of the Ripper had not yet taken hold on the streets, so prostitutes where not specially alarmed or wary. Also, this had not been a typical Saturday night. The nearby dock fires had temporarily drawn away potential clients with other entertainment, so business for Whitechapel's prostitutes would have been slow, but as the fire had been put under control, the crowds would have returned. The fire would have brought strangers, with some making their way to Whitechapel, the known prostitute's haunt, to end a night of revelry. Prostitutes would have expected that they would be serving more than the usual clients. For Thompson to be the killer on that night more than any other night, all that he would have needed was to have some coins, and be wearing good clothes and a smile. Thanks to his new editor's help with money and purchasing a new suit, and some cash from a kind donation by the family friend Father Carroll, Thompson was more than capable of convincing this prostitute to walk with him down Buck's Row. Thompson, with his intimate knowledge of London streets and the ways of prostitutes, could say he was only on the hunt for his missing prostitute, the love of his life. He would have told anyone asking that he wished to find and rescue her for a new life as the wife of a respectable journalist.

From the air, Buck's Row was a place of crooked chimneystacks, adorning sloped roofs covered in terracotta tiles that had been blackened over the years with soot and grime. The street was of narrow cobblestone, six metres wide, with slightly raised footpaths less than a metre in width. Large warehouses and other industrial buildings backed the street and facing it were rows of two-storey residences. A lifetime can see many changes, and this was no less true in the nineteenth century. The two men who found the body of Mary Ann Nichols on their way to work would have had no idea that, a generation ago, where the body lay was almost exactly where there was once a ducking pond.

This pool was used in the eighteenth century to torture suspected witches and extract their confessions. The accused woman would be strapped to a wooden chair at the end of a long wooden lever and this chair and woman would be ceremonially dunked into the water in front of a crowd of onlookers. This form of water torture often proved fatal through drowning. By 1888 such ideas about witchcraft were outdated to most people, but not to Thompson. The primary place in London to find out about this ducking pond was in the Guildhall Library. This was where the bulk of London's old maps were stored, including ones going back to the Medieval period. Thompson, as is known already, spent much time reading there, both to escape the harsh winters and to feed his thirst for knowledge. By the start of 1888 Thompson, once an aspiring doctor, had failed in his hospital career and was now reduced to rags on London's streets. Directly to the south, and less than 100 meters from Buck's Row, where once stood the witch's ducking pond, was the London Hospital. The hospital would, by the time the murderer's work was done, receive a threatening letter by the writer who called himself Jack the Ripper. Directly to the north of Buck's Row, less than 100 meters away, was the Brady Cemetery. This was where most of the Rothschild family had been traditionally buried, including the founder of its English branch. For Thompson, a failed doctor and servant of God, with his destitution exposed by a Rothschild, Buck's Row could not have been any more perfect if he wanted to seek revenge. Even, incredibly, the nickname of the Buck's Row victim, Mary Ann Nichols, can be associated with Thompson. Both this woman, and Francis Thompson's sister, Mary Thompson, were usually referred to as Polly.

When police questioned those living close to where the murder had happened, most said that they knew of nothing out of the ordinary. This pattern of witnesses, appearing surprised a murder had taken place or claiming to have not seen anyone suspect, was one that would run through the entire murder investigation. It is hard to believe they did not see or hear anything, even harder that they had yet dared to feign ignorance. Perhaps simple fear of reprisal kept them quiet. A more plausible explanation is that they may have heard or seen something, but in the appalling conditions that the East End presented they had become immune to most cries of murder, sound of argument or struggle. Shadowy, suspicious characters were simply part of the scenery.

Once the body was taken from where she was found to a makeshift mortuary, the police directed that the footpath be washed clean of the blood. This was 1888; the facts were that, unless there was something obvious such as a clear boot print in it, the average police officer would think the bloodstain was of no practical use in aiding the investigation. Leaving the blood would only have drawn curious onlookers. From such tales as Conan Doyle's *Sherlock Holmes*, we often have formed the image of the Victorian detective as someone who would seek the smallest clues and ensure that the integrity of the crime scene was maintained. We see him as wielding an oversized magnifying glass to scour every centimetre for traces of evidence. He even carries a small case that acts as a miniature chemical laboratory to ascertain and match various found substances. Almost like an art form, he then precisely recreates the culprit from the evidence gathered. Sadly, such a thing was a fantasy. Victorian detectives, like modern ones, were overworked, underpaid and under-resourced to deal with the high volume of cases they were assigned. Their peers would probably have seen any detective who had hoped to adopt such techniques as simply eccentric, even as troublesome. In addition, in 1888, the tools and clues available for forensics were different than today. Most of what we now use, such as fingerprinting and toxicology, was known of but not widely established. Although there were tests to determine if a substance was blood, it could not be then known what type it was or even if were from a human or an animal. What this meant to the investigation was that if a man walked up to the officers, his body splashed in blood and carrying a knife, there would have been no scientific evidence to connect him to the crime. In almost all cases, for the police to catch a criminal, they would need to have actually seen the crime being perpetrated, found a credible witness or hope for a confession. Only 20 years later, discoveries in blood typing, fingerprinting and photography would have caused criminal investigators to be shocked at how the crime scene was so casually cleaned. What needs to be highlighted is a problem with the entire investigation: the methods that had been developed over many years by law enforcement and investigation to enable the capture of culprits were futile when applied to Jack the Ripper. Here was a new species of criminal that defied the usual sequence of a murder investigation. His behaviour is now typified by legions of his type, but in 1888 a serial killer was a new phenomenon. The Ripper thought outside all previous definitions of what a criminal was. His fears and his drives were not like that of others. Being without precedent, motivation could not be comprehended and his actions seemed as meaningless as they were abhorrent. The things that we think of as trivial normal daily life, such as how someone sets their hair or the choice of flower on a lapel, to a serial killer on the hunt, are seen as guideposts that speak to him in signs and omens. The incidental words spoken in a crowd when a bell tolls, or the colour of a horse in relation to the name of its owner are, for the psychopathic, delusionary mind, potent with meaning and triggers for all sorts of thoughts and responses. The established avant-garde art and culture magazine *Rapid Eye*, in their 1992-95 *Creation Books* release, explored coincidence in the realm of magical thinking,

'[Ted] Bundy, for instance, killed over twenty girls in the mid-seventies, usually strangling or battering them to death in an uncontrollable frenzy. He carried out several of these murders in accordance with an astrological timetable. The overall sequence also contained a disproportionate number of "double initial'" victims ... Six out of 20 isn't enough to constitute a pattern, [James] Austin concedes, but it is significantly higher than the distribution of double initials in the population as a whole. Bundy is now known to have had marginal occult connections, as did several of his victims. Was he too caught up, Willy Nilly, in some kind of Twilight Language stratagem? Some of the evidence may fall apart on close examination, but there is a definite residue of data here that cannot be dismissed as "mere" coincidence.'

The question of a reward or pardon that would lead to the murderer's arrest was posed throughout the investigation and was vigorously debated. The Home Office, in 1884, had made the decision to cease offering rewards. This policy was formed when the police discovered a conspiracy to cause an explosion at the German Embassy. The conspirators planned to frame an innocent person so that they could obtain the expected reward. The Secretary of State conferred with police authorities on the matter and it was decided that the practise of offering large rewards in cases of serious crimes was ineffectual and could actually hinder investigations. It was also felt that rewards caused the police to be more lax in their investigations and that the testimony of witnesses would become biased. Since then the Home Office have stood firm with their decision, despite appeals by the public, with other high profile murder investigations.

Chapter 9
The Black Knight

'I have knowledge, not indeed great or wide, but within certain narrow limits more intimate than most men's.'

Francis Thompson.

Francis Thompson, in his *Witch Babies* poem, had imagined himself as a black knight, one who was self-appointed to rid the world of corrupt women. If Thompson was the killer, with delusions of grandeur and bent on some type of lone religious crusade, he could not have found a more suitable nemesis than another knight – Sir Charles Warren. This officer had military experience and, like Thompson, specific knowledge of biblical history. Another trait he shared with Thompson was that he saw himself as a type of poet. Warren's military career began when he joined the Royal Engineers in 1857 and, 10 years later, he was Commander of the Royal Engineers of Saukin and Governor of the Red Sea Littoral. Warren served in Palestine and there carried out archaeological work. He spent the years between 1867 and 1869 authenticating biblical sites under government orders. He explored and mapped places such as the Holy Sepulchre, where he gained the nickname 'Jerusalem Warren'. His efforts, in 1882, in the Sinai desert earned him a knighthood.

When Sir Warren became Commissioner of Police, it was felt that his experience would do a great deal to modernise the force. Unfortunately, it soon seemed apparent that Warren was intent on militarising the police. He was more concerned with uniforms than police grievances. His annual reports, for example, were largely on dress code and ordering the right type of boots and saddles for his mounted forces. Sir Warren also brought in harsh penalties for officers found to be drunk on duty. Drill practice, long ago abolished, was reintroduced. His manner with sections of the press was uncompromising and his response to complaints of police brutality was unforgiving. Resentment for his policies had quickly grown. Added to all this was growing friction between Sir Warren and his police inspectors. Warren found them to be unprofessional and made noises about removing plainclothes inspectors altogether. He saw inspectors as foreign to the militaristic model that he felt the police should follow with each officer in uniform.

Sir Warren showed little tolerance for the public's concerns of their freedoms being suppressed, and the tide of public support had almost turned completely against him. Even more so when, on 13th November 1887, there occurred what became known as 'Bloody Sunday'. This was when homeless protestors refused to disperse from Trafalgar Square. Sir Warren ordered the police to fire into the crowd. Two people died and 150 others were injured. The spate of murders in Whitechapel served to alienate Sir Warren, and the press was quick to couple the failure of the police with a failure of his leadership. An odd trait shown by Warren during this civil unrest was his use of poetry in his drafted orders. One example, upon law and order in Trafalgar Square reads,

'The Commissioner has observed there are signs of wear

On the Landseer Lions in Trafalgar Square.

Unauthorised persons are not to climb

On the Landseer lions at any time.'

Sir Warren was also a member of the Freemasons. This is an exclusive fraternal organisation that most probably began near the end of the fourteenth century. Catholics have been traditionally barred from joining. When most people hear about Jack the Ripper, they often think of the killer as being someone connected to the Freemasons. This stems from author Stephen Knight's 1976 book *Jack the Ripper: The Final Solution*. His book suggested that the murders were because of a conspiracy between Freemasons and the British Royal Family. This theory spawned the 1978 film *Murder by Decree* and the *From Hell* graphic novel which was made into a film in 2001. Freemasons were involved in the Ripper case. Many of those heading the police force and leading the Whitechapel murder investigation were Protestants and members of the Freemasons. These people included the head of the force, Police Commissioner Sir Warren, who as well as being a member, conducted research for the society. Dr Robert Anderson, who upon his return from Switzerland was placed as head of the investigation, was a Freemason. Coroner to the murder inquests Wynne Edwin Baxter was a Freemason of the South Sussex Lodge. Because the Freemasons were so pervasive in the ruling class, they have often been blamed by conspiracy theorists for the Ripper murders. The theory that the very police who investigated these crimes were also responsible for them is as bizarre as its popularity, even though most serious researchers see it as implausible. If anything, the opposite assumption should be investigated. Since senior police were mostly Freemasons, the killer may have not been a member but instead a non-mason with a grudge against this order.

Thompson had a grudge against the Freemasons. He hated them. When it came to these groups, his ready interest in the occult and secret societies was not limited to pure research. Thompson was a conspiracy theorist. He believed that an evil organisation was secretly running the world. To Wilfrid Meynell, Thompson wrote in later February 1906, 'The country is not governed by a ministry, but by permanent administration, whose names nobody hears, who are responsible to no censure, and whose sole political creed is that, whatever Cabinet reigns, still they draw their salaries.' He personally took on the Freemasons. Thompson's enthusiasm was gained by the support he felt he had from the Catholic Church. Pope Leo XIII reflected the view of many Catholics in the nineteenth century on Freemasonry in his 1884 encyclical. His 8,000-word paper named *Humanum Genus* argued against the doctrine of Freemasonry and said in part,

'The race of man, after its miserable fall from God, the Creator and the Giver of heavenly gifts, "through the envy of the devil," separated into two diverse and opposite parts ... one is the kingdom of God ... The other is the kingdom of Satan ... At this period, however, the partisans of evil seem to be combining together and to be struggling with united vehemence, led on or assisted by that strongly organised and widespread association called the Freemasons. No longer making any secret of their purposes, they are now boldly rising up against God Himself ... it is Our office to point out the danger, to mark who are the adversaries and to the best of Our power to make head against their plans and devices ... the sect of Freemasons grew with a rapidity beyond conception in the course of a century and a half, until it came to be able, by means of fraud or of audacity, to gain such entrance into every rank of the State as to seem to be almost its ruling power ... For these reasons We no sooner came to the helm of the Church than We clearly saw and felt it to be Our duty to use Our authority to the very utmost against so vast an evil.'

As a hard-line opponent of Freemasons himself, Thompson, in his later years, began to gather data in his aim to expose what he saw as 'a history of hidden evil' that had 'left its ruthless fingerprints on the wrist of history'. Although his notes and a manuscript for a book he hoped to publish are believed to have been destroyed by his editor, we do know some things about it. This comes through an associate of Thompson's editor, Elizabeth Blackburn. Of Thompson's Freemasonry research, Blackburn wrote,

'As to the Freemasonry notes, I imagine that could be collated and disentangled to prove at least more than interesting. His plan, often discussed, was to begin with the Gnostics, go down through the Templars and other military orders – till reaching the Reformation period and the Rosicrucians, with the French revolution, modern Masonry in its mischievous continental attitude stood clearly revealed. How much or how little he wrote, I of course don't know. At first I took slight notice, but as he went on he showed a wonderful appreciation of what lawyers call "evidence" – and it was surprising to see how he fitted in the pieces – more puzzling than any jig-saw – to make a perfect picture.'

Seeing that so many of those whose task to capture the killer were Freemasons, and Thompson had a loathing of that order, it is sound to think that if he was the Ripper, he had no hesitation in eluding and taunting the police. Warren, with his Freemasonry membership, knowledge of biblical history, military prowess, and pretentions to be a poet would have ideally suited Thompson.

The failure of Sir Charles Warren to capture Jack the Ripper is blamed for his resignation and the ruin of his police career. On Thursday 8th November, the day before the murder of Mary Kelly, Warren tendered his resignation to the Henry Matthews the Home Secretary. In his letter to Matthews, Warren's resignation blamed the murderer when he wrote that his department's failure to capture the ripper was due to 'the extraordinary cunning and secrecy which characterize the commission of the crimes.'

That Warren and the thousands of police officers under his command could not catch a single murderer in a quarter-square-mile of London's East End, may have led to Warren's bizarre behaviour many years later when he triggered, arguably, one of the worst disasters in military history. It appears that, frustrated by his failure in 1888, Sir Warren tried recreating the crimes 10 years later, and used a battlefield as the setting for a strange experiment where he replicated some of the key elements of the Ripper murders. Removing speculation about the Ripper crimes leaves us with a man who, all within in a half-square kilometre, went on a killing spree. The Ripper attacked always at night, working under time pressure and ready, at any moment, for a policeman's lamp that would give away his position.

After the Ripper murders, in a remote battlefield in South Africa, Warren commanded the British in the Battle of Spion Kop. Military historians view this battle as one of the worst military disasters in modern history. Warren's strategy was to have a select group of men fight on a half-square kilometre plateau of a small hill. He had the men armed only with knives, fighting at night and under time pressure. He had ordered his men to sneak into the area; he then waved his lamp from the safety of his camp and revealed their position to the enemy Boars who machined-gunned them, killing hundreds.

It was during the second Boer war fought between Great Britain and the Afrikaner republics of Transvaal and the Orange Free State. Sir Warren had been given orders to capture Spion Kop. The soldiers were told that it was considered a key strategic site, though not long after the battle the victorious Boar army abandoned it. Sir Warren's troops had assembled 11 kilometres from the hill. His plan was to capture Spion Kop under the cover of darkness. He gave orders forbidding the men to smoke in case the Boers saw them. Sir Warren was in command of 22,000 troops, collectively designated as the fifth division. Sir Warren ordered 20,000 men to wait and ordered 2,000 men, mainly from the Lancashire Fusiliers, into battle.

It just so happened that the Lancashire poet Francis Thompson, this book's Ripper suspect, had his own views on the Boer war. Retrieved as fragments from his notebook was one poem, *A Ballad of the Boer(ing) War*, which mocked the fate of the British troops,

'Alas! Poor Wight, he has to fight

In lee of stones and banks,

Upon his stomach, till you'd think,

To look upon such pranks,

Frogs, banished from commissioned breasts,

Had crawled into the ranks.

...

And then such clouds of Khaki dirt

Food, water, mouth encrust,

It seems the curse that's laid on him

Is like the Serpent's, just –

For all his days to go on upon

His belly, and eat dust.

Against Warren's 2,000 soldiers, the enemy Boers at first numbered 600 troops. A delay of 26 hours, in which Sir Warren supervised the transport of his personal baggage across the Tugela River, allowed a further 6,000 more foes to gather. His men were told that each would be given a sandbag to fill and use for protection. They were told that food and water supplies would be available along the way. They were told that two guides would meet them at the base of the hill. They were also told that digging tools would be waiting. As dusk fell, his men began the long march to the base of the hill. The sandbags were not given out. The food and water did not arrive. One of the guides fled and the other became paralysed with fear. The digging tools had vanished. After travelling across rough ground and fording watercourses for 11 kilometres, Sir Warren's 2,000 soldiers reached the base of Spion Kop and began the 490-meter upward trek. They were placed under the command of General Woodgate who, at 55, had to be carried. Exhaustion had already caused many men to fall down asleep. As the soldiers climbed, sometimes on their hands and knees, it began to rain. Their path consisted of old goat trails that rapidly churned to mud. The men, who moved in darkness in concordance with Sir Warren's orders to gain an element of surprise, were dismayed to see that ex-policeman Warren's hurricane lamp could be seen shining from his wagon at Three Tree Hill down on the plains below, giving away their presence to the enemy Boers. There had been no previous recognisance of Spion Kop.

At 3.30am, the men, who had been ordered to unload their magazines at the main camp and fight only with fixed bayonets, were relieved to find that the steep hill gave way to a flat plateau. It held a small dugout and 200 Boer troops. The Boers fled, wounding three soldiers. Believing that they had reached the summit of Spion Kop, the men, under gathering fog, began to dig in and wait for daylight. As the sun rose and the fog lifted, they found that they were not actually at the top of the hill at all but a third of the way down, on an exposed plain measuring a half-square kilometre, with knives their only weapons. The trenches they had built had walls of loose earth measuring a height of 36 centimetres. Combined enemy fire, which included five field guns, rained down from the Boers above, killing 1,700 of the 2,000 British. Ants attacked the remaining men who cowered in ditches under the now blistering heat.

The almost surreal events became only more fantastic when, as the day wore on, wounded stragglers fled down the hill to be met by Winston Churchill, the future WWII Prime Minister. Then a young lieutenant, Churchill, whose mother was good friends with Thompson's editor Wilfrid Meynell, had broken ranks from Warren's larger idle force of 20,000 and ascended on foot. Winston Churchill had already come to know the wife of Thompson's editor, Alice Meynell, through weekly tea parties held at Stafford House, the home of her friend the Duchess of Sutherland. Churchill, ignoring the orders of his commanding officers, began to rally the routed British forces. Warren, who 10 years earlier had failed to capture Jack the Ripper, ordered Churchill's arrest. As the carnage continued, the dead and wounded were carried away by stretcher-bearers under the command of Mohandas Gandhi, the future Indian Prime Minister, who was living in London during the Ripper murders in 1888. The Battle of Spion Kop has now become infamous for being one of the bloodiest battles in Boer history. Eventually the British took the hill and then, since it was strategically worthless, they soon abandoned it.

Chapter 10
Down on Whores

'You have made a thing of innocence as shameful as a sin, I shall never feel a girl's soft arms without horror of the skin.'

Francis Thompson.

Ever since the Whitechapel murders, amateurs and experts have written on possible solutions to the case. Some, like this one, have concentrated on a particular suspect. Others have explored theories as to the type of person to look for. In the quest to uncover the name of the killer, almost every possible angle has been explored and every fact, of which there seem to be very few, has been exploited and questioned. We are now in an age of research and speculation where nothing is sacred. Books exist by reputable researchers who have dismantled everything about the case that was once certain. In an attempt to have history fit a particular agenda there are books which assure the reader that none of the witnesses can be trusted and that they all lied for the sake of publicity or money. These books conveniently forget that during the murders the fear for one's life of every inhabitant was palpable. Everybody has been made a suspect. Those who found the body were fingered for the crimes simply by being in the wrong place at the wrong time, for example carman George Cross who discovered the first Ripper victim, Ann Nichols. Even the victims themselves have been accused of killing the other women and changing their identities. Every statement on the murders is now argued with, including the number of victims by the hand of the murderer. For many years, it was generally assumed that there were five victims, starting with Mary Nichols on 31st August and ending with Mary Kelly on 9th November 1888. The 'Canonical Five', as they have been known, has been so diluted by countless theorists that to say the Ripper killed five women is met with derision by many Ripperologists. In its most extreme form there are now some theorists that have declared with confidence that none of the murders were connected and that Jack the Ripper did not even exist.

There can be no clearer single example of this desperate historical revisionism than the changed view of the veracity of the Jack the Ripper letters. When, during the height of the Whitechapel murders, these letters were sent to the press and people involved in the case, the police and newspapers were convinced the hand of the murderer, or someone with intimate knowledge of the crimes, wrote them. The police made facsimiles of them and had them posted on the front of stations and reproduced in the papers in the hope that someone might recognise the handwriting and come forward with information. Now, despite that the very name 'Jack the Ripper' originated from these letters, many books on the Ripper do not even bother to cite them, the assumption being that police were fools, and that the common sense of the populace is what should be suspected. This book may be the only one that assumes that given the right suspect, every witness was telling the truth, and that what happened during the Autumn of 1888 is exactly as those investigating the case assumed. Of course, it may be that any exploration of the Ripper letters, as crucial to solving the case, could be because they so perfectly fit Francis Thompson as a suspect.

On 19th April 1905 the writer Arthur Conan Doyle, the creator of the greatest fictional detective, Sherlock Holmes, was in the East End investigating the Whitechapel murder case. In 1892 Conan Doyle, once a doctor in Portsmouth, had visited the Scotland Yard's Black Museum, which displayed a photo of the mutilated Mary Kelly and the original *Dear Boss* letter. In 1894 Doyle told an American journalist his views of the Ripper, expressed as, 'a man accustomed to the use of a pen. Having determined that much, we cannot avoid the inference that there must be somewhere letters which this man has written over his own name, or documents or accounts that could readily be traced to him. Oddly enough, the police did not, as far as I know, think of that and so they failed to accomplish anything.'

A man accustomed to the use of a pen? A man much accustomed to the pen was Thompson, who wrote, 'expert in concealment, not expression, of myself. Expression I reserved for my pen. My tongue was tenaciously disciplined in silence.' Regardless of the veracity of the handwriting of the writer of the infamous *Dear Boss* letter, both the Ripper and Thompson wrote in English copperplate style. More important is that both were written in the style of Francis Thompson. The recipients of these Ripper letters included the police, press and other professionals such as doctors.

Here is the infamous letter, in full, sent, some say, by the 'murderer uncaught',

'September 25th

Dear Boss,

I keep on hearing that the police have caught me but they wont fix me just yet. I have laughed when they look so clever and talk about being on the right track. That joke about Leather Apron gave me real fits. I am down on whores and I shant quit ripping them till I do get buckled. Grand work the last job was. I gave the lady no time to squeal. How can they catch me now. I love my work and want to start again. You will soon hear of me with my funny little games. I saved some of the proper red stuff in a ginger beer bottle over the last job to write with but it went thick like glue and I can't use it. Red ink is fit enough I hope <u>Ha ha</u>. The next job I do I shall clip the ladys ears off and send to the police officers just for jolly wouldn't you. Keep this letter back till I do a bit more work, then give it out straight. My knife's so nice and sharp I want to get to work right away if I get the chance. Good Luck

Yours truly

Jack the Ripper don't mind me giving the trade name

PS Wasnt good enough to post this before I got all the red ink off my hands curse it No luck yet. They say I'm a doctor now. <u>ha ha</u>'

The history of the *Dear Boss* letter is that on Thursday 27th September 1888, it arrived at the Central News Agency in New Bridge Street, London. The Central News was the centre of news distribution in London. A female mail sorter first opened the letter, before calling journalist Thomas John Bulling to look at it. The letter bore an East London postmark dated 27th September. It had a one-penny Inland Revenue stamp, and it was addressed to 'The Boss'. Jack the Ripper is remembered as the murderer of a cluster of five women in the East End. The press widely reported that the wanted man was some of sexual lust murderer. The papers published somewhat conflicting articles upon the serial murders, saying that the police thought the murders were the work of a butcher, and also that the killer's skill in anatomy meant it might even be a doctor. The criminal would usually kill his victims with great speed. He would first strangle them. Then, once the heart had stopped pumping blood, the killer would lay his victims down on the ground, further reducing blood flow. He quickly cut into them with a long sharp blade. The writer of the letter claimed to be the person who had already killed at least two women. Pressman Bulling was unsure what to make of this letter. He first thought it was probably a kind of sick joke, till it dawned on the busy journalist that possibly the prostitute murderer, then dubbed 'Leather Apron' by the press, had given himself a new name. At the time the *Dear Boss* letter was received by the Central News Agency, *The Star* newspaper was furiously reporting events in the most sensationalistic way. Their report echoed what many letter writers and other papers were suggesting. The paper believed the murderer was a man, probably a butcher, suffering some severe brain disorder. In essence, a 'Leather Apron' suspect who was suffering fits. Either that or someone like Thompson the Catholic zealot, who had been to medical school and was prone to deliriums and nervous breakdowns,

'The theory of madness is enormously strengthened ... everything points to some epileptic outbreak of homicidal mania. A slaughterer or butcher who has been in a lunatic asylum, a mad medical student with a bad history behind him or a tendency to religious mania…'

One might wonder, if Thompson had chanced to read this popular paper with its suspect so much resembling his own self and his particular background, what his response would have been. Would it have been with dark menacing humour, like shown with his knight, who laughs a 'Ha Ha' from his *Witch Babies* poem? Would his pride have brought him to mock the press reports with a clever play on words?

Thompson's outlook can be summed up by his favourite motto, which said that under extreme conditions, we are bound to fail.

'Every scope by immoderate use turns to restraint.'

In the *Dear Boss* letter, the writer said the same in cruder form. 'I shant quit ripping them till I do get buckled'

At the very time that the *Dear Boss* letter was sent, Thompson had his first essays published. Included with his submission to his publishing editor was his *Nightmare of the Witch Babies* poem, the one about the jolly knight who constantly laughs, 'Ha Ha',

'… A lusty knight,

Ha! Ha!…

A rotten mist,

Ha! Ha!…

No one life there,

Ha! Ha!…

'Swiftly he followed her

Ha! Ha!…

Into the fogginess

Ha! Ha!…

Into the fogginess

Ha! Ha!

Lo, she corrupted

Ho! Ho!

Comes there a Death ...'

In the *Dear Boss* letter, the writer made the same laughter his habit. 'Red ink is fit enough I hope Ha ha.'

When Thompson sent his poem, he was a failed doctor. The *Dear Boss* letter has the writer express surprise and repeated laughter in response to the news reports that the killer must be a doctor. 'They say I'm a doctor now. ha ha'.

Thompson had just found work as a pressman. As Everard Meynell, in his biography on Thompson, recorded, 'The streets, somehow, had nurtured a poet and trained a journalist. He had gone down into poverty ... and now emerged a pressman.' {Life p93}. The Ripper letter was sent to the Central News Agency, which drew on news submissions from pressmen. To a London journalist, such as Thompson was, this agency was like a news chief. It would not have been out of place, for Thompson, to begin a letter, to the editor of the agency, with the words, 'Dear Boss'.

After three years of destitution, doing odd jobs or having not a coin, Thompson had finally gotten a job as a journalist, even though he refused to leave the streets until he found the prostitute who had fled him. Thompson must have been eager to find his prostitute and start his literary career. He might have said, as the writer of the *Dear Boss* letter did, 'I want to get to work right away if I get the chance.'

Everard Meynell detailed the final conversation between Thompson and his, since vanished, prostitute. Everard Meynell told of her growing resemblance to Thompson's dead mother and dead sister:

'After his first interview with my father he had taken her his news, "They will not understand our friendship," She said and then, "I always knew you were a genius." And so she strangled the opportunity; she killed again the child, the sister; the mother had come to life within her.'

Thompson wrote of his hatred of prostitutes,

'These girls whose Practice is a putrid ulceration of love, venting foul and purulent discharge – for their very utterance is a hideous blasphemy against the sacrosanctity [sacred ways] of lover's language!' {LIFE p77}

If we were to describe Thompson's sentiment, on the subject of prostitutes, in only a few words, we could not do better than the writer of the *Dear Boss* letter, who said, 'I am down on whores'.

The *Dear Boss* letter's style has been analysed more than any other historical letter and the conclusion of most experts is that the writer deliberately wrote to appear less literate than he was. This was a trait also known to Thompson, who sometimes dumbed down his writing, shown here by this example,

'Onurd Sir,

I see. Now, wot I ave to say is, as I 'ave no personal animosity … I 'ave 'im set this food while, bein' a man of critical taste as keeps a oservant eye on his fellow-litteratures; and I size 'im up as agent of some littery ability, take my tip, and look at me … I don't take much stock of potes as writers of Bleedin ... I sign myself by a name-de-plum. Fly-by-night.'

The writer, of the *Dear Boss* letter, who signed his name as Jack the Ripper, was, like Thompson, happy to use a nom de plume. 'Dont mind me giving the trade name'.

Thompson liked the colour red because it reminded him of blood. He wrote of it,

'Red has come to be a colour feared; it ought rather to be the colour loved. For it is ours. The colour is ours and what it symbolises is ours. Red in all its grades ... to that imperial colour we call purple, the tinge of clotted blood ... proudly lineal; a prince of the Blood indeed.'

The author of the *Dear Boss* letter also had a thing about the colour red. As seen when he wrote, 'Red ink is fit enough I hope'.

Everard Meynell also wrote on the way Thompson sent postcards in the mail,

'he sitting in grey lodgings, who crowded into the chilly ten minutes before 3 am, the writing of a long letter to be posted, after anxieties over address and gum [glue] of which we know nothing and a stumbling-journey down dark stairs, in a pillar-box still black with threatening dawn.'

Despite the boldness, exhibited in the *Dear Boss* letter, it's writer shared the same level of anxiety as Thompson when it came to trying to write it first in blood, 'but it went thick like glue and I cant use it' and in delivering the letter without a problem, 'Wasnt good enough to post this before I got all the red ink off my hands curse it'.

When the *Dear Boss* letter was sent, boasting of the East-End murders, Thompson was using the Salvation Army refuge in nearby Limehouse. The shelter had narrow wooden boxes for the men to sleep. Each man was given a leather apron to cover the boxes for protection. Thompson joked about the leather apron, which had to fit just right to keep out the rats. His black humour was that such an apron was a fashion accessory, for those keeping up appearances, rather than someone that had to have it really fit to keep the vermin at bay. Everard remembered this in his 1913 biography on Thompson. Everard, includes in this memory, how Thompson's group of homeless men, who sometimes gathered together, was a wanted murderer, like Jack the Ripper. Everard Meynell, however, does not say if the wanted murderer was, in fact, Thompson.

'In a common lodging-house he met and had talk with the man who was supposed by the group about the fire to be a murderer uncaught. And when it was not in a common lodging-house, it was at a Shelter or Refuge that he would lie in one of the oblong boxes without lids, containing a mattress and a leathern apron or coverlet, that are the fashion, he says, in all Refuges.'

The ever-playful *Dear Boss* author wrote, 'That joke about Leather Apron gave me real fits'.

Was Francis Thompson behind the writing of the *Dear Boss* letter? Perhaps, though there may be a twist to this tale. Importantly, what must be understood is that, apart for an egomaniacal urge to boast of his crimes, there is no sound reason for the killer, whether it was Thompson or not, to have written it. By the fact that the killer eluded the police through five murders, we must assume that the murderer did not want to be captured. A letter sent to the authorities would have been a huge risk to his freedom. Neither the Ripper nor Thompson would have had an understandable motive to write or send the letter, but his editor, the journalist Wilfrid Meynell, did. On 23rd February 1887 a homeless Thompson let fall a crumpled parcel into his future publisher's letterbox. The parcel held *Nightmare of the Witch Babies* with its 'Ha Ha' verses, as well as an essay and two other poems. This was before the Ripper murders had begun. Wilfrid Meynell did not open this parcel for almost half a year. When he did, Thompson was still lost on the streets, and his publisher assumed he was dead through exposure to the elements or suicide. In April 1888, Meynell, thinking Thompson was dead, placed one of his poems from the set Thompson submitted in his magazine *Merry England*. It is claimed that Meynell did so to alert Thompson, who he had not been able to find, that he had read and accepted his submission, which of course contained his poem on ripping into women. It seems Meynell had no qualms in using the press to get Thompson's attention. All the possible allusions in the *Dear Boss* letter – the 'down on whores', the 'joke about leather', and the phrase 'they say I'm a doctor now', are also facts about Thompson, relating his circumstances at the same time the Dear Boss letter was written. that Meynell, even with his limited knowledge of Thompson, could have known.

The canonical Ripper murders began at the end of August 1888. By the time the *Dear Boss* letter was sent to the Central News in September, Thompson had returned to the streets to seek his prostitute and Meynell had lost contact with him. Thompson did not return for many months. Meynell was a London journalist with many years of experience. The *Dear Boss* letter was received by the Central News on 27th September. Dr Robert Anderson, of the Whitechapel murder investigation, when answering whom he believed had written the *Dear Boss* letter, said,

'The "Jack the Ripper" letter is the creation of an enterprising London journalist ... I am almost tempted to disclose the identity of the murderer and the pressman who wrote the letter.'

Taking his words as literal truth then Anderson is not speaking of one, but two people. He says the letter is the creation of a London journalist (perhaps Wilfrid Meynell?) and his murderer and pressman. This meant that first there was the murderer (Thompson?), whose circumstances were recorded in the letter, and second the pressman (Meynell?), who actually wrote it. One of the most vocal advocates for the letter being a hoax, faked and not written by the killer, was first promoted by the journalist George Sims. This was when he wrote in the *Referee* on Sunday 7th October 1888 about the *Dear Boss* letter,

'Jack the Ripper is the hero of the hour. A gruesome wag, a grim practical joker, has succeeded in getting an enormous amount of fun out of a postcard which he sent to the Central News. The fun is all his own, and nobody shares in it, but he must be gloating demonically at the present moment at the state of perturbation in which he has flung the public mind. Grave journals have reproduced the sorry jest, and have attempted to seriously argue that the awful Whitechapel fiend is the idle and mischievous idiot who sends blood-stained postcards to the news agency. Of course the whole business is a farce.'

Why Sims might have been so keen to downplay the letter could have been to protect his very close friend, the journalist Wilfrid Meynell. They corresponded with each other, and Sims and Meynell collaborated on a book along with Meynell's son. If Thompson was the Ripper, then Meynell may have come to connect Thompson to these crimes. By now this editor had become hopelessly tangled up with Thompson, having already published his work and having received the poem *Nightmare of the Witch Babies*, which was about hunting down and killing women with a knife. He had even paid Thompson to buy a new suit, so that he would appear more decent and attractive to the victims. Meynell, who was a keen follower of the Ripper case, searched the streets for Thompson but failed to find him. It is more than possible that Meynell felt he could not afford the scandal and possible conviction if he approached the police. (No offer of pardon to accomplices had yet been given by the government.) Meynell might have run out of options. Maybe Meynell, being an enterprising journalist, had arranged that the letter be written and sent to flush Thompson out. Meynell, who had already once been willing to publish Thompson's poem *The Passion of Mary* to bring Thompson to heel, may have created the *Dear Boss* letter, with its hints about Thompson's unique circumstances, to make him too fearful to kill more women, and lure him out of hiding. Only Thompson and the Meynell knew about Thompson's murder poem and the circumstances of his relationship with the prostitute. Only both knew that there was a trained surgeon on the streets with a scalpel looking for a prostitute. When the *Dear Boss* letter was released to the public, Thompson could have seen veiled references to him and recognised the 'Ha Ha' in it (which was underlined). He may have seen that it was from Meynell to him, showing that his game was up. We could speculate that Thompson did not take the bait, and went on to kill further women, bringing Meynell to become only more deeply involved with Thompson and the Ripper crimes. When Thompson returned to Meynell, exhausted, in what would have been probably mid-November, Meynell might have had no choice to but continue to keep his suspicions secret

187

and send Thompson to the country monastery, the one that had attack dogs, high walls and a room for him on the top floor.

Just because Thompson may not have written the *Dear Boss* letter, it does not mean he did not write others. It can happen that when one mystery is solved, serendipity can help answer another. We might not only have determined whom Jack the Ripper was but we also might have discovered the eventual fate of Thompson's vanished prostitute lover. Thompson told that in June of 1888, his girlfriend, who worked as a prostitute, left him after a dispute. He said it ended with her threatening to leave him because he was now too well-known. He claimed he needed to stay on the streets looking for her; he gave up searching for her in October. In the same month the remains of a woman were found buried along the London embankment. Although not as well-known as the Whitechapel crimes, what became known as the Whitehall Torso Mystery was also striking in both its macabre nature and its apparent lack of motive.

The remains, found on the building site of New Scotland, was a decayed human torso, wrapped in possibly a petticoat and tied with string. It had been hidden there for not more than three days. An interesting feature of the crime was that the style of the killer in this case mimicked that of Thompson who hated the sight of flowing blood. An autopsy determined that after death the killer had tied tourniquets before removing the victim's limbs to stem the blood flow. This has led researchers to remark that someone with medical skill had killed her. The limb's sites of amputation were packed with newspapers from 24th August. The coroner found that the woman, who was aged about 24, died of suffocation. Her uterus had been removed. The coroner concluded that the woman, with fair skin and dark hair, was not someone who was used to manual labour and that she had been killed in late July. This was the same month that Thompson's prostitute lover left him. Could this torso have been what was left of her? It might explain why it was in October, the month that the Torso was found, that Thompson is said to have accepted that his prostitute would not return to him. Although the torso was thought by some to be yet another Ripper murder, the identity of the woman, like Thompson's prostitute, was never discovered.

Surprisingly, the Ripper himself is believed to have written to the police about this very crime. Perhaps not surprisingly, the contents of the letter show a bizarre resemblance to, not only Thompson's style of writing, but also the same rare knowledge of biblical history and leaning to religious extremism. This is made apparent when Francis Thompson, who had trained as a priest and a surgeon, gave a review of London under the pen name of Tancred. The name came from an early Medieval eastern crusading knight. It was not the first time Thompson depicted himself as a crusading knight, as was seen with his April 1888 poem *Nightmare of the Witch Babies,* with his knight hunting down and disembowelling women, and laughing as he tears babies out from their stomachs.

In response to the police's discovery of the Whitehall torso, it appears the assailant, normally glad to claim his guilt, said that if he killed this prostitute it was only because God had forced his hand. He wrote to them three days after the torso had been found,

'Central News Agency' on October 5,

'Dear Friend In the name of God hear me I swear I did not Kill the female whose body was found in Whitehall. If she was an honest woman I will hunt down and destroy her murderer. If she was a whore God will bless the hand that slew her, for the woman of Moab [place of human sacrifice] and Median [worshipers of pagan Gods] shall die and their blood shall mingle with the dust. I never harm any others or the Divine power that protects and helps me in my grand work would quit forever. Do as I do and the light of my glory shall shine upon you. I must get to work tomorrow treble event this time yes yes three must be ripped I will send you a bit of face by post I promise this dear old Boss. The police now reckon my work a practical joke ha ha ha Keep this back till three are wiped out and you can show the cold meat.   Yours truly Jack the Ripper.'

By any measure, the Ripper murders were the product of a sick and twisted mind. It is true, also, that Thompson was not a normal personality by any stretch of the imagination. Thompson's review, called *Catholics in Darkest England*, was published in the January 1891 edition of *Merry England*. This was a Catholic literary magazine owned by his editor, Wilfrid Meynell. The review was written as a reply to the book *In Darkest*

England, by General Booth, head and founder of the Salvation Army. Thompson's view was that Catholics should take up and accentuate the militarism of the salvationists. It is written in the same style as the October Ripper letter and like the letter, it contained themes of Old Testament religion, prostitution and human sacrifice,

'I see upon my right hand a land of lanes and hedgerows, I look upon my left hand and I see another region – is it not rather another universe? A region whose hedgerows have set to brick, whose soil is chilled to stone; where flowers are sold and women, where the men wither and the stars; whose streets to me on the most glittering day are black. For I unveil their secret meanings. I read their human hieroglyphs. I diagnose from a hundred occult signs the disease that perturbs their populous pulses. Misery cries out to me from the kerb-stone, despair passes me by in the ways; I discern limbs laden with fetters impalpable, but not imponderable; I hear the shaking of invisible lashes, I see men dabbled with their own oozing life ... This contrast rises before me; and I ask myself whether there be indeed an Ormuzd [a god of light] and an Ahriman [a destructive spirit of darkness], and whether Ahriman be the stronger of the twain. They are brought up in sin from their cradles ... the boys are ruffians and profligates, the girls harlots in the mother's womb ... Here, too, has the Assassin left us a weapon which but needs a little practice to adapt it to the necessity of the day? Even so our army is in the midst of us, enrolled under the banner of the Stigmata. Far better your children were cast from the bridges of London than they should become as one of those little ones.'

Today, many people argue whether any of the letters were actually sent by the murderer, but there is one that most agree is authentic. This is because it came with what looked to be a body part from one of the victims. Called the *Lusk Letter* or the *From Hell Letter*, it came in the form of a most gruesome parcel that was delivered on 16th October to the home of George Lusk. This man was the Chairman of the Whitechapel Vigilance Committee. It consisted of local traders who had come together to do their bit to rid Whitechapel of the killer. These businessmen were concerned that having a murderer at large was bad for business. The letter said,

'Mr Lusk

Sor

I send you half the

Kidne I took from one women

prasarved it for you tother pirce

I fried and ate it was very nise I

may send you the bloody knif that

took it out if you only wate a whil

longer.

signed

Catch me when

you Can

Mishter Lusk'

The letter was written in very bad English. For ease of reading, here it is with corrections

'From Hell – Mr Lusk. Sir – I send you half a kidney. I took from one woman, preserved it for you, the other piece I fried it and ate; it was very nice. I may send you the bloody knife that took it out if you only wait a little longer. Catch me when you can, Mr Lusk.'

The letter included a cardboard box, about nine centimetres in height and wrapped in paper. It arrived at around 5pm and bore a 15th October, London postmark. When Lusk opened this carton, he found inside a piece of adult human kidney that had been kept in wine. Catherine Eddowes, who had been killed in Mitre Square, had her left kidney taken away by the killer.

Did Thompson write the *Lusk Letter*? There are strong reasons why he might have disliked Mr Lusk. Lusk was a member of the Freemasons. Thompson hated Freemasons and was a hard-line opponent of them. Lusk's business was building music halls. Thompson hated music halls. In his essay *Paganism Old And New*, Thompson wrote how modern theatres were blights on society. To him, it was far better that people returned to the traditional Greek open-air theatres. He saw it as an evil that forest timber would be sacrificed, to build roofed buildings simply so the public could laugh at vaudeville comedians. Thompson wrote,

'The theatre unroofed to the smokeless sky … contrast the condition of to-day … the dryadless woods regarded chiefly as potential timber … the temple to the reigning goddess Gelasma, (personification of laughter) which mocks the name of theatre …'

Lusk was an Anglican churchwarden. Thompson had reason to dislike Anglican churchwardens. Thompson was fired and forced onto the streets by one. John McMaster, who, in 1886, had briefly hired Thompson to work his shoe repair shoe shop, took to firing him after he did little work and injured a customer. This forced Thompson back into vagrancy. Biographers, even those who have tried to paint Thompson as a nice guy, have confessed that Thompson harboured a deep grievance over this episode. The *Lusk Letter* kidney preserved in a box was found to be damaged by Bright's disease, which was the same disease that Catherine Eddowes suffered from. Thompson, who was a trained doctor, and Catholic priest, believed that preserving bodily organs was a good thing to do. He said it removed diseases. In his essay *Sanctity and Song,* he praised the methods of the Ancient Egyptians, who mummified their dead by removing the organs of the body and reserving them in a jar. Thompson said,

'The purifying power of suffering was known even to the heathen. In the Egyptian obsequies, the removal of the most perishable parts of the body, the preservation of the rest by steeping and burning nitre, signified the cleansing of the human being by pain; and the symbolism was emphasised by the words spoken over the embalmed corpse, "Thou art pure, Osiris, thou art pure".'

The *Lusk Letter* is noted for its seeming intentional spelling errors, as if someone were making a point of appearing less literate. This is a trait in writing that Thompson has been known to do. The dumbing down of the letter, and the theme of preserving a body parts, match Thompson's style. In addition, Thompson held reasons to hate George Lusk, a Freemason, churchwarden and a builder of music halls.

Chapter 11
The Dread Rite

'You have but to direct my sight, and the intentness of
my gaze will discover the rest.'

Francis Thompson.

The idea that a religious extremist committed the Ripper
crimes is strengthened by the discovery, made by city
Police Constable Alfred Long. Some see it as the most
important yet enigmatic piece of evidence that the
Ripper ever left behind. On the night of the double
murders, at 2.55am in Goulston Street a police
constable's lantern illuminated a piece of bloodied white
apron that was found at the entrance to a doorway. It
matched the apron of Catherine Eddowes, the fourth
victim and the second one found that night. Her body lay
horribly mutilated in Mitre Square, 350 metres northeast
of the doorway. Written, in a doorway beside where the
apron was found, was the graffito,

'The Juwes are the men that will not be blamed for
nothing.'

This section of Whitechapel was the Jewish heartland. It was home to thousands of newly arrived immigrant families who were escaping persecution from Russia, Poland and Germany. More than 80 percent of those people in Goulston Street were Jewish. The same applied to neighbouring Flower and Dean Street, Hanbury Street, Old Montague and Thrawl Street. There had been a long history of conflict and distrust between Christians and Jews, and many non-Jews were outspoken of their outrage that so many Jews had congregated in the East End.

With these series of murders in the East End the public, eager to find a culprit, allowed old superstitions and prejudices to come to the fore. As was highlighted in a rise of anti-Semitism the *East London Observer* contained an article remarking on happenings,

'On Saturday in several quarters of East London the crowd, who assembled in the streets began a very threatening attitude towards the Hebrew population. It was repeatedly asserted that no Englishman could have perpetrated such a horrible crime and it must have been done by a Jew.'

Anti-Semantic hysteria was a feature of the reaction of the mainstream press to these murders. This was widespread, so it was easy to think that almost anybody could have been responsible for attaching blame to Jews, simply to vent anger and create further discord. A close examination of events earlier that night, involving Elizabeth Stride, reveals a possible motive behind the Ripper scrawling this missive next to the blood-soaked piece of apron. It seems that the killer was reacting to when his game of 'cat and mouse' was almost spoiled by an innocent Jewish man who happened to be passing by while the murderer had begun stalking Elizabeth Stride.

Typically, serial killers follow several key phases as they make preparations to kill. Physiologists call the first step the 'aura phase'. This is when the killer withdraws from reality. Because this step is physiological and internalised, others are usually unaware of the subject's changing perception of time, which appears to slow down, or changes in how colours and sounds become more vivid and intense. The serial killer also becomes antisocial and quiet as they withdraw from normalcy and distance themselves from usual patterns of morality or feelings of empathy to fellow humans.

Not long before the double murders, when a Jew inadvertently may have provoked the Ripper, the killer had already entered the second phase, the 'trolling phase'. This is when the killer begins the hunt for his victim. He frequents those places where the type of victim he desires would be found. With these murders, all the victims being prostitutes, the Ripper haunted localities where these women plied their trade and sought clients – places like common lodging houses and pubs. In the trolling phase the serial killer will lie in wait, while trying to blend in with the crowd. They select their victim as they wait. They observe their prey, learning their movements while keeping an eye out for any threats that may mean their capture or detection.

The number of witnesses who claimed to have seen the Ripper discredits the idea that he moved through the streets as a phantom without being spotted. This is reflected by the account of Israel Schwartz, a Jewish Whitechapel resident. Schwartz reported being chased by a man who may well have been the Ripper, and, judging by his appearance and behaviour, also Francis Thompson.

It was after midnight on 30th September 1888 when Israel Schwartz, a Hungarian Jew who worked as an actor, walked the corner off the main thoroughfare of Commercial Road into Berner Street. This was the street where the Ripper's third victim, Elizabeth Stride, would be murdered less than an hour later. Schwartz had walked almost a block south when he saw a man come out of a hotel in front of him. This man approached Stride and started arguing with her. The man began to handle Stride roughly and pulled her to the ground. Stride yelled out three times. Schwartz then saw a second man leave the same hotel and cross to the opposite side of the street to stand watching. The second man has now become known as the 'Pipeman'. In most respects, he resembles Francis Thompson. This other man was aged about 35. Thompson was only a few years younger, aged 28, though his years of hardship through homelessness would have probably made him appear older. Schwartz described the Pipeman as being five foot, 11 inches in height, while Thompson was perhaps only an inch shorter. The rest of Schwartz's description of the Pipeman exactly describes Thompson. His complexion was fair with light brown hair and moustache. This is the same for Thompson. Pipeman was said to have worn an old black wide-brimmed felt hat and dark overcoat. Thompson wore this. Pipeman gained his label because he smoked a long clay pipe, and was seen to be continually spending time and many matches in trying to light it. Thompson was well-known for his habit of smoking from long clay pipes. Thompson's pattern of using around 14 matches to light his pipes brought Viola Meynell, a daughter of his editor, to remark on the time he took to do so, 'He misspent his powers and wasted his minutes as he wasted matches.' The writer Katherine Tynan, when she gave a description of Thompson, could not neglect mentioning his pipe smoking, '... the unfailing pipe, a pipe of the grimiest, clutched in his finger when it was not between his lips.'

When the rejected man, who fought with Stride, crossed the road, he walked passed Pipeman and yelled out to him, 'Lipski!' This was intended as an anti-Semitic insult. In July the previous year, a 23-year-old Polish Jew named Israel Lipski had been found guilty and hanged for the murder of a woman, whom he killed by pouring nitric acid down her throat. The name of 'Lipski', thereafter, had become a slang name for any men, particularly those of Jewish descent, who were of suspicious character. It was evident that the man, a gentile, who pushed Stride yelled out to Pipeman thinking he was a Jew and that the insult of 'Lipski' would unsettle him. Schwartz, who was Jewish, on the other hand, may have perceived things differently. Pipeman was dressed in the manner of a Jew but although Schwartz saw that the man was foreign to the area, he did not say that he was a Jew. The man, who had fought with Stride and yelled the Lipski insult, did not seem to be aware of this.

Pipeman spotted Schwartz watching him. Schwartz began to walk away. He then heard footsteps behind him. Pipeman had begun chasing him and Schwartz ran, fearing for his life. As Schwartz ran south down Berner Street he felt for a moment that the man chasing him might also be running away. Schwartz was tempted to stop and wait for his pursuer to catch up, but he continued to run past several streets. His pursuer gave up the chase when Schwartz reached the arches of an overhead railway a few blocks south. Pipeman's strange behaviour can be explained. Pipeman could have well known that he appeared Jewish, and in an area that had a large Jewish population, he would have blended. He could have otherwise been able to walk the streets without attracting attention. Although the murders had set everyone's nerve on edge, the Hebrew population, that lived essentially separately from gentiles, saw the crimes as something that concerned outsiders. Many Jews, already upset at the media's portrayal of 'Leather Apron' as a repulsive Jew, tried not to be involved. Hence they were not as active in keeping a watch out for the Ripper, for even if they did spot anyone they felt was suspicious it was thought that they would not be taken seriously. This explains why, even though Schwartz reported what happened to the police, he was not called as a witness to the inquest. It was also highly likely that if a Jew came forward with a story involving a gentile suspect, they may have risked reprisals from those who were anti-Semitic. Furthermore, if Schwartz had given testimony and it had led to a conviction, the murderer would have surely been put to death. This would have gone against Jewish law and what is commonly known as the 'Two Witnesses Rule'. The Old Testament's Deuteronomy 17:6 states, 'On the testimony of two or three witnesses a person is to be put to death, but no one is to be put to death on the testimony of only one witness.'

Because of the dress of Pipeman, being so out of the ordinary of most nineteenth-century Englishman, it is likely that he knew that he may appear Jewish to an Englishman, and been discounted as being just one of the Jews from the area. This would have suited his purposes of going about unnoticed. Schwartz and Thompson had something in common. Schwartz was an actor, and would have been used to how clever use of costume could be employed for disguise. Thompson had a strong love of the theatre. He developed this early on, when, in his youth, he was a member of Ashton's amateur theatre company. When Pipeman saw Schwartz observing him, he may have realised that his obvious English appearance, with his light-coloured hair and fair complexion, still visible beneath his wide-brimmed hat, betrayed him. It may have showed to Schwartz he was really a gentile. Pipeman may have realised that Schwartz had seen through his ruse and would rightly ask himself why was he loitering in Berner Street and watching Stride. He appeared conspicuous to Schwartz who inevitably might remember him after his planned murder. This may well have been why he followed Schwartz; primarily to scare him off. The Pipeman was, after all, the only out-of-place person in this incident and hence the most likely suspect for the eventual murder of Stride.

The fact that the Pipeman chased Schwartz, moments after the first man had the altercation with Stride, has led many to speculate that the man fighting Stride and the Pipeman were in cahoots and working as a team, with Pipeman acting as a lookout – even though this idea flies in the face that the Ripper worked alone, as do the far majority of serial killers. Many people also assume that the man who fought with Stride was the Ripper, but this goes against what we now know about serial killers. Such an overt display of public aggression is not in keeping with serial killers, who instead prefer to remain inconspicuous as they engage in the trolling phase, when they prefer to remain in the background to wait and watch.

Many people find the reason why the Ripper placed the mysterious writing on the wall to be inexplicable, but maybe not to Francis Thompson. It just so happened that the entranceway where the writing was placed was the new Wentworth model buildings. These were built primarily from the efforts and money of the Rothschild family, the same family whose high-standing banker had inadvertently taunted Thompson with the florin tip and sent him spiralling into his long delirium. This is the second Rothschild connection to the murders, the first being that the 31st August murder happened near to the Brady Cemetery, where the Rothschild family is traditionally buried. The message of the writing on the wall, with its misspelling of Jews as 'Juwes', and its meaning has ever since been much debated. It is relevant to note that in the 17th century, 'Juwes' was a common way to spell the name of these people while Thompson is described as writing poetry that mimicked the style of the 17th century. Not long after finding the writing on the wall, Sir Charles Warren, concerned that the message, coupled with the rising anti-Semitic attitude on the streets and in the media, had it removed. His action was met with disbelief from most quarters. Many saw it as a vital clue that had been needlessly destroyed. It was not photographed, because of the poor light, which meant the handwriting couldn't be studied and compared with suspects. From then until now the meaning of this riddled writing has remained one of the enduring mysteries of the case. When we turn our attention to Thompson, however, answers may be found. In his poem *From the Night of Forboeing* Thompson references Daniel, a wise Jewish man from the Old Testament and the *Book of Daniel*. One story in it, known as *The Writing on the Wall*, relates how Daniel was asked by King Belshazzar to assist in interpreting a message. An anonymous hand had scrawled it with a candlestick upon the plaster of the wall of the King's palace. The King, like the head of police Sir Warren, was afraid it might be seditious and cause unrest. None of his people had so far been able to understand it. Daniel's interpretation pleased Belshazzar, bringing Daniel to prominence in the royal court.

Thompson's poem has him ask if a wise Jew would understand what he once scribbled on a wall, that to him symbolises death and sacrifice. He describes his particular wall as being a palimpsest. This is a surface, much like a blackboard, on which writing can be erased, and is similar to the black stucco wall on which, with white chalk, the 'Juwes are the men' graffito was found written in 'neat schoolboy hand'. Thompson concluded that no famed Jew would appear to solve his riddled writing, as is given in these lines from the poem,

'The struggling wall will scantily grow,

And through with the dread rite of sacrifice

Ordained for during edifice,

How long, how long ago!

Into that wall which will not thrive

I build myself alive,

Ah who shall tell me, will the wall uprise?

Thou wilt not tell me, who dost only know!

The stars still write their golden purposes

On heavens high palimpsest

Nor any therein Daniel, I do hear.'

Dr Robert Anderson was, in 1888, Junior Assistant Commissioner at Scotland Yard. In 1907, after his retirement, Anderson spoke to the *Daily Chronicle* of evidence attained on the Ripper crimes. Here he seems to be referencing both the Goulston-Street graffito and the Pipeman who he also connects with the murder of Mary Kelly, the fifth Ripper victim, and the fireplace in her Miller's courtroom,

'In two cases of that terrible series there were distinct clues destroyed ... In one case it was a clay pipe. Before we could get to the scene of the murder the doctor had taken it up, thrown it into the fireplace and smashed it beyond recognition. In another case there was writing on the wall – a most valuable clue; handwriting that might have been at once recognised as belonging to a certain individual. But before we could get a copy, or get it protected, it had been entirely obliterated.'

Chapter 12
The Deepening Mystery

'And the moral is—no, the reader shall have a pleasure
denied to him in his outraged childhood. He that hath
understanding, let him understand.'

Francis Thompson.

Another witness came forward who, like Schwartz, also
claimed to have seen Elizabeth Stride, the third Ripper
victim, with someone who may have been the Ripper.
This second man's testimony seemed to only add to the
mystery of who the killer was and his purpose. Matthew
Packer was a fruiterer who owned a fruit and vegetable
store on the intersection of Berner Street. It was just after
11pm when Stride and a male companion approached
him, as he was just about to shut his shop. The man
wanted to buy grapes from him. Packer said the stranger
with Stride was dressed like the Pipeman, with a long
black coat and a soft wide-brimmed hawker's hat. The
man asked him for the price of his grapes. 'I say, old
man, how do you sell your grapes?' the stranger asked of
Packer.

'Sixpence a pound the black 'uns, sir, and four pence a pound the white 'uns.' Packer answered.

The stranger turned to Stride and asked of her, 'Which will you have, my dear, black or white? You shall have whichever you like best.'

Stride indicated the black grapes.

'Give us half a pound of the black ones, then,' said the stranger. Packer thought the stranger spoke in an educated voice that was quick and rough, and Packer felt as if he had been treated in a sharp, commanding manner.

After the man bought half a pound of black grapes, he and Stride walked off and stopped before a school. Packer noticed that it had begun raining but saw that, peculiarly, the man and woman did not seek shelter. He observed to his wife, 'What fools those people are to be standing in the rain like that!' Of the East-End fruiterer's statement, Inspector Walter Dew, who was involved in the Whitechapel murder investigation, wrote,

'I am puzzled. Frankly, I cannot reconcile the buying of those grapes in the company of the woman he was about to kill and his reappearance a few days later in the same street ... I used to feel at times that the fates were conspiring against us and doing everything to assist the man behind the problem which was daily deepening in mystery.'

It certainly seems inconsistent that a murderer would treat his victim to grapes, the stuff of wine, before killing her, and we might wonder what motive there might be.

Packer's description of this Ripper suspect, with his coat and wide-brimmed felt hat, is once again consistent with that of Francis Thompson. Today we would categorise the Ripper as a ritualised sex-murder. To such a criminal even the most mundane-seeming actions before the kill would be loaded with meaning and figure as significant to the fantasy created in their minds. Even the simple act of sharing of grapes with a victim would be part of a dream-scheme that was invisible to outsiders. By examining Thompson's writing and knowing some of his personal history, the grape episode and its mystery are suddenly resolved.

A central teaching of the Catholic Church is that of transubstantiation. This is the change of wine, during the service of Mass, into the blood of Christ. Thompson, having trained as a Roman Catholic priest and spending many years as an altar boy would have often partook in this sacred ritual, which is considered holy. Tragically, Thompson was judged as unfit to partake in this ritual as an ordained priest. What seemed a promising life in the Church was dashed after seven fruitless years in a seminary, when the priests who were, as he said, 'against him', failed him. He must have keenly felt this rejection, more so as an outcast living rough on the streets of the East End. We can only guess as to his thoughts, but it is true that, after his rescue, he never set foot in a church again. It is hard to imagine a killer would think that eating grapes in the rain, with their victim, before killing them a prerequisite to the murder. It is perplexing that Elizabeth Stride and the man who probably killed her were observed sharing grapes standing in the rain.

Though it seems that did, for half an hour before heading to where music and song could be heard coming from a meeting hall across the road. Could Thompson, stripped of his church vestments, have dared to pervert the Mass where the juice of grapes was made to mingle with blood? It would appear that he might well have if we are to take the verses of his poem *The Poppy* to heart and recall that Thompson himself revealed that his poems were diaries recording his own life. In his poem *The Poppy*, he describes blood-red wine flowing in the gutters of London's East End. He ended his poem with a prophecy. It was that his greatest secret will only be discovered some time after his death. Considering that only in our day people might think of him as the being the Ripper, he might have been right. His poem talks of slaughter in showers of red wine, with its true meaning being known in a future time, after many deaths,

'With burnt mouth, red like a lion's, it drank

The blood of the sun as he slaughtered sank,

And dipped its cup in purpurate [crimson] shine

When the Eastern conduits ran with wine ...

And drowsed in sleepy savageries,

I hang 'mid men my needless head

And my fruit is dreams, as theirs is bread,

The goodly men and the sun-hazed sleeper

Time shall reap, but after the reaper

The world shall glean [know] of me, me the sleeper.'

Most critics say he failed as a great poet because he was too obscure, and it is true that sometimes reading him is like reading the quatrains of a deranged prophet. A telling example of how we might interpret Thompson's poetry of more sinister allusions to the murders of autumn of 1888 can be found in his poem *A Corymbus for Autumn*. In great detail, this poem asks that we think of it as written by the god of grapes and wine. As is common to much of Thompson's verse, even the most devout fans of poetry can be forgiven for throwing up their hands in frustration when trying to understand its meaning. This obscurity has distanced Thompson from readers and often hidden the true meaning of much of his work. His *Autumn* poem is typical in its archaic wording and obtuse phrasing. If it did not contain perhaps clues to the most horrific of murders and hold the sealed confession of the greatest criminal known to man we would be tempted to leave it to the experts. To assist readers, here is given an outline of the poem in plain English, as well as passages of the original work.

The poem confesses to be more about spurting blood than wine, a type that gushes over a bunched-up woman's dress. The writer tells us that the poem is set in autumn in October. The night of the double murders is said to have occurred on 30th September but in actuality the women were killed after midnight on 1st October. In Thompson's poem, he begins by describing a female, while thinking if the blood in her body is ripe for taking. He details how she will bleed. He describes the woman falling while he, the god of grapes, releases his stranglehold on her. He blends images of black grapes with her collapsing body. He describes how, in a wild frenzy and with a knife, he almost severs her head from her neck. He describes doing this while looking at her dying through the reflection of the knife blade resting in the palm of his feverish hand. He pictures himself as a priestly knight kneeling before a body in the East End, as a church bell rings. Thompson leaves his poem with some final decorative speech on the victim's blood, as wine, flowed from her. He ends by explaining how her body was simply there to make wine that night. Those who wish to read further poetry on Thompson will find it instructive how he might be possibly describing all of the murders, by using rhyme and metaphor to both boast of his deeds and, like the Ripper, hide them in plain sight. Thompson's poem begins with him telling that his song is like that sung by a high priest of the Bacchante, the Greek god of wine and revelry,

'Hearken my chant, 'tis As a Bacchante's, A grape-spurt, a vine-splash, a tossed tress, flown vaunt 'tis! Suffer my singing ... Totty [drunk] with thine October tankard ... maiden!'

Thompson depicts his female subject as fully drunk, as Elizabeth Stride often was. In the two years before 1888, Stride had been convicted at least eight times at the Thames Magistrate Court on charges of public drunkenness. Her partner often resorted to padlocking her into their lodgings to prevent her drinking sprees. The second victim Catherine Eddowes, on the night of the double murders, had previously been detained in

Aldgate by the city police for being drunk and disorderly. When she had sobered up enough she was let go and, not long after, killed by the Ripper. Thompson begins his poem by describing this woman as being drunk, relaying how he desires the blood that courses through her veins and how he admires the way it flows and spurts out of her down her body to her feet. This was much like the way the blood flowed down from the Ripper victim Elizabeth Stride's slit throat.

'With cheeks like apples russet [dark reddish brown] ... How are the veins of thee, Autumn, laden? ... And pulped oozes Pappy [mushy] out of the cherry-bruises Froth the veins of thee, wild, wild maiden! In tumbling clusters, like swarthy [black] grapes, of the feet whereunto it falleth down.'

While it is believed that the Ripper first throttled his victims to prevent them crying out and rendering them unconscious, Thompson describes how, in a fevered state, he loses his grip on his 'October Maiden', and he begins cutting with his blade,

'His Bacchic fingers disentwine ... His reveling fingers disentwine and let them fall with a sword to sheer, poised in the palm of thy fervid hand ... Shed, curling as dead.'

Thompson pictures himself performing this mutilation, as a priest, working under time constraint at night,

'See how there the cowled [hooded] night kneels on the Eastern sanctuary-stair. An inarticulate prayer, But

213

there is one hour scant ... Of this grave ending chant ... Then died before the coming of the moon.'

By the time the poem ends, Thompson tells how the wine that once flowed blood-like through this woman has been spilled from her body, staining her clothing and being left to pool at her feet,

'Till the gold wine spurted over her dress, till the gold wine gushed out round her feet; Spouted over her stained wear, And bubbled in golden froth at her feet ... Her too in Autumn turned a vintager; [winemaker] And, laden with its lamped cluster's bright, The fiery- fruited vineyard of this night.'

Of course, not all of Thompson's poems can be said to reference the murders, but there are others. There is his *Ode to the Setting Sun* with its references to his liking for death and dying, where other connections might be made. In this poem, for example, he writes of rain, ferns, roses and death,

'The fairest things in life are Death and Birth,

And of these two the fairer thing is Death.

Mystical twins of Time inseparable,

Who made the splendid rose

Saturate [wet] with purple glows? ...

For birth hath in itself the germ of death,

But death hath in itself the germ of birth.

The falling rain that bears the greenery,

The fern-plants moulder when the ferns arise.

For there is nothing lives but something dies,

And there is nothing dies but something lives ...

Are Birth and Death inseparable on earth;

For they are twain yet one, and Death is Birth.'

On Sunday 30th September 1888, at 1am, in Berner Street, Whitechapel, as the rain lessened, Elizabeth Stride, having feasted on grapes with her killer, walked to her death. As she did so, her black jacket sported a solitary red rose and a maidenhair fern. It is also fitting, if Thompson is the Ripper, that the last sighting of Stride was from William Marshall, who lived at Number 64 Berner Street. He was drawn onto the street by the music that played in the upstairs Jewish socialist meeting hall. Marshall saw Stride near the entrance of Dutfield's Yard, where her body would be found moments later. He saw the man –who was with her, –kiss and tell her, 'You would say anything but your prayers.'

Chapter 13
Dead Men Tell Tales

'But woe's me, and woe's me, for the secrets of her
eyes! In my visions fearfully, they are ever shown to be,
as fringed pools, whereof each lies pallid-dark beneath
the skies of a night that is but one blear necropolis.'

Francis Thompson.

That the killer was able to elude a prepared police force
with extra personnel and kill two women, in one night,
without being caught is remarkable. His bravado and
luck has brought the public to imbue him with almost
magical abilities. That the Ripper was an invisible agent,
though, is just another myth that encircles these murders.
As well as Schwartz and Packer, with their sightings
concerning Elizabeth Stride and her possible assailant,
there is also a sighting of who might have been the
Ripper, from a member of the police. In the case of
Sergeant Stephen White, dead men do tell tales.

White is believed to have encountered the Ripper
just after the second of the double murders was
committed. It happens to be a perfect description for
Francis Thompson. This portrayal of the Ripper was

given in an article that appeared in the *People's Journal* after the turn of the century, from a Scotland-Yard man. It told of a meeting between Dr Robert Anderson and Detective Sergeant Stephen White (born 1854, died 1919, warrant number 59442). It is said that White's report may have led Dr Anderson to suspect that others knew the identity of the killer. Dr Anderson, later Sir Anderson, was the Assistant Commissioner of the Metropolitan Police and in charge of the Whitechapel murder investigation from 6th October 6th until the file was closed in 1892. Of the Whitechapel murderer, Anderson wrote,

'One did not need to be a Sherlock Holmes to discover that the criminal was a sexual maniac of a virulent type; that he was living in the immediate vicinity of the scene of the murders; and that, if he was not living absolutely alone, his people knew of his guilt, and refused to give him up to justice.'

Detective White had been assigned to the recently formed Special Branch. White's duties involved the detection of political terrorists. The *People's Journal* tells that at approximately 1:45am on 30th September 1888, Detective Sergeant Stephen, aged 34, stood in wait for the killer.

It was Detective White's normal duties in this maze of slums to capture members of political organisations such as the Anarchists, Fenians, and Dynamitards. The Special Branch being involved indicates how important the Whitechapel murder investigation had become. His being assigned indicates the pressing need to catch the killer. It seems that White had been placed on duty because of suspicions that terrorists were behind the Ripper murders. Some in Scotland Yard proposed that the killings were done with the aim to weaken the English establishment and government.

Evidently, Detective White had been assigned a covert operation, overseeing with two other officers, in what was probably Mitre Square. This area in Whitechapel was where the Imperial Club premises were located. The club was a place where suspected terrorists were said to gather. White lay in watch in a district patrolled by the city police and consequently not in his jurisdiction. He could not afford to expose himself and his men unless he was certain that he would capture the killer.

White's magazine account, published in 1919, just over a week after his death, had him tell of his close encounter of the murdering kind. This encounter probably happened on 30th September, the night of the double murders. This can be assumed because it is known that Sergeant Inspector Abberline sent White to Berner Street to enquire house after house about the 30th September murder of Elizabeth Stride.

Detective White was working in special branch with other officers, outside his jurisdiction. Essentially, he and his men were spying on supposed terrorists. These operations were considered so secretive that even researchers are denied access to files from 1888. Although White would not have been able to reveal details such as a location or date of his duties, he could give a perfect description of his suspect. Here is Detective Stephen White's account of his meeting with who may have been Jack the Ripper. It is so instructive in also describing Francis Thompson, our Crispin Street resident, that it is given in full,

'For five nights we had been watching a certain alleyway just behind the Whitechapel Road. It could only be entered from where we had two men posted in hiding, and persons entering the alley were under observation by the two men. It was a bitter cold night when I arrived at the scene to take the report of the two men in hiding. I was turning away when I saw a man coming out of the alley. He was walking quickly but noiselessly, apparently wearing rubber shoes which were rather rare in those days.'

Thompson was an ex-medical student and would have been issued with protective clothing for his studies in the operating theatre and infirmary in Manchester. This would have included the new form of protective rubber soles. White's description of his encounter told that his suspect also wore rubber-soled shoes. To further strengthen the validity of White's account, in the days following the double event the papers relayed that the police now believed the killer wore silent rubber-soled shoes, shoes like those worn in hospitals, and described for Sergeant White's suspect. Subsequently the police requested that these shoes be issued to them so that they could be heard while they made their patrols, though the request was denied.

White's description of the Ripper continues to resemble our Spitalfields suspect, Francis Thompson. A turn of good fortune had presented itself to Thompson when, just prior to August, he had been able to rid himself of the ragged clothes of a homeless man and buy fresh clothes, including a coat. This was thanks to his editor giving him payment for his poem and an essay. He had also been given money out of charity from Cannon Carroll. By 30th September, Francis Thompson's new outfit, because he refused to leave the streets for his search for his prostitute friend, would have become scruffy. Thompson's height has never been officially recorded, though the one group picture of him with his medical-college classmates shows him to be slightly shorter than his peers. Accounts given of him are that he was shorter than the average man. He was probably around 170cm in height, though his habit of walking slightly hunched may have made him appear a bit shorter. Sergeant White's description of his Ripper encounter continues,

'I stood aside to let the man pass, and as he came under the wall lamp I got a good look at him. He was about 5 feet 10 inches in height, [167cm], and was dressed rather shabbily though it was obvious that the material of his clothes was good. Evidently a man who had seen better days, I thought, but men who have seen better days are common enough down east, and that of itself was not sufficient to justify me in stopping him.'

His deprivation, in the years previous, had meant he was underweight. People described him as having a narrow face, as well as a narrow nose with a slight upturn. Thompson's sister, Mary, described the colour of his hair as, 'very dark brown, so dark as to appear almost black at first sight.' She also said, 'His complexion was sallow rather than pale.' {Life}

The Detective continues his description,

'His face was long and thin, nostrils rather delicate and his hair was jet black. His complexion was inclined to be sallow'

Thompson's sister told that the most pronounced feature about her brother's face was his eyes, which were brought to prominence by his complexion. She said,

'A dark grey with a bluish shade in them – something like the shade one sees in mountain lakes. Full of intelligence and light … His complexion was sallow rather than pale, drawing further attention to his eyes.' {Life}

Detective White told about his suspect's most obvious feature,

'The most striking thing about him, however, was the extraordinary appearance of his eyes. They looked like two luminous glow worms coming through the darkness.'

A school prefect, Canon Henry Gillow, who was in charge of Thompson during his seminary days, described Thompson and how he stood and walked with a bent posture, causing his coat to slip forwards, 'Every now and then he would hitch up the collar of his coat as though it were slipping off his none too thickly covered shoulder blades.' Thompson was, in September 1888, aged 28, but again the hardships of homelessness may have taken its toll. A man like Thompson, whose plaster casts of his hands show them to be delicate with long tapering fingers, was not used to hard work. Instead, he had meant to be a professional man, such as a doctor or priest.

Detective White's description of his Ripper encounter continues,

The man was slightly bent at the shoulders, though he was obviously quite young – about 33 at the most – and gave one the idea of having been a student or professional man. His hands were snow white, and the fingers long and tapering. As he passed me at the lamp I had an uneasy feeling that there was something more than usually sinister about him, and I was strongly moved to find some pretext for detaining him; but the more I thought it over, the more I was forced to the conclusion that it was not in keeping with British police methods that I should do so. My only excuse for interfering with the passage of this man would have been his association with the man we were looking for, and I had no grounds for connecting him with the murder. It is true that I had a sort of intuition that the man was not quite right. Still, if one acted on intuition in the police force, there would be more frequent outcries about interference with the liberty of the subject, and at that time the police were criticised enough to make it undesirable to take risks.'

A work associate of Thompson, Mr Wilfred Whitten, described how Thompson spoke, 'When he opened his lips he spoke as a gentleman and a scholar.' Thompson's sister also described how he spoke and the sound of his voice. When compared to those sailors, butchers and street-reared, uneducated Spitalfields locals that Thompson now found himself with, his foreign voice would have been the easiest thing to spot him as not from to these parts. His sister said, 'When he opened his lips he spoke as a gentleman and a scholar ... His low voice had a peculiar quaver, a slight wobble in tone, that empathised its curiously measured cadence.'

The Detective's surprise at finding such a man in the tough surroundings of Spitalfields was made more so when he chanced to exchange a few words with him,

'The man stumbled a few feet away from me, and I made that an excuse for engaging him in conversation. He turned sharply at the sound of my voice, and scowled at me in surly fashion, but he said 'Goodnight' and agreed with me that it was cold. His voice was a surprise to me. It was soft and musical, with just a tinge of melancholy in it, and it was the voice of a man of culture – a voice altogether out of keeping with the squalid surroundings of the East End. As he turned away, one of the police officers came out of the house he had been in, and walked a few paces into the darkness of the alley. "Hello! What is this?" he cried, and then called in startled tones for me to come along. In the East End we are used to shocking sights but the sight I saw made the blood in my veins turn to ice. At the end of the cul-de-sac huddled against the wall, there was the body of a woman, and a pool of blood was streaming along the gutter from her body. It was clearly another of those terrible murders. I remembered the man I had seen, and I started after him as fast as I could run, but he was lost to sight in the dark labyrinth of East-End mean streets.'

White's thorough description is usually discredited because he was not called as a witness to any murder enquiry. Since he was on secret duties, this may have not been possible. It is also because people believe he incorrectly stated the murder site was a cul-de-sac, but to vehicular transport, with only one wide entrance, this is what it was. None-the-less, for pedestrians, none of the two 30th September murder sites, apart from possibly the gateway where Stride's body was found, were dead ends. This error may have been intentional to protect Scotland Yard and the identities of the two other officers who worked with him that night. Mitre Square was the only murder site that had an alley leading out from it. It could not be described as a cul-de-sac having more than one exit, unless one happened to be the murderer. Mitre Square, where Eddowes' body was found, had three exits. There was Mitre passage, leading west to Mitre Street, another dark covered passage that led north to St James' Place. The third exit, leading east, was a passage to Duke Street. The only safe escape route was Duke Street. Mitre Passage and the passage to Duke Street were both on the route of patrolling police officers. Each officer would return to Mitre Square every quarter of an hour or so, carrying a lamp. The two officers had different routes that overlapped at Mitre Square at different times. The murderer, who may have reconnoitred the site earlier, observing their beats, would have seen that Duke Street to the north wasn't patrolled. This book's Ripper suspect may have known these routes that officers made at night on these streets, because he had slept mostly around there for almost three years. As he told, he was used to being moved along by police who found him sleeping in doorways. The writer JC Reid; in his biography on Thompson, told of the vagrant poet's problems with the law, 'While he was homeless, he had consistent run ins with the police.' He tried to climb out of homelessness by working as a bootblack but was moved from the corner he had set up his shoeshine stand by the police. He tried to use the Guildhall Library but was removed by the police. He would try to sleep under archways and doorways only to be 'kicked and frequently moved on by the police'. Francis Thompson had reached his nadir.

To keep out of the way of patrolling constables, Thompson would have been practised in knowing the beats of officers before deciding the step or pavement on which he was to sleep. Thompson may have already planned to take the north exit, thinking it was empty. One could only imagine his surprise to find a man in plainclothes, lurking in the dark. He would have been equally surprised that this policeman did not arrest him but offered some kind words and let him walk on his way. Thompson's small notebooks, which he kept during his time on the streets, were in the form of little jottings. Sometimes he simply wrote brief phrases to record moments that he thought were important to remember.

Although undated, but written perhaps on the night of the double murder, is one page from his notebook with three short phrases, 'My Two Ladies' -- 'Only once a policeman aided me' -- 'Murder'.

Three sightings on the night of the double murder bear similarities to Francis Thompson. Taking a woman's life, when police had strengthened their numbers and were on heightened alert, and with armed vigilantes patrolling the streets, was difficult enough. Killing a second woman so soon after was the risky in the extreme. The murderer's usual skill at eluding detection and avoiding suspicion would have been sorely tested. This may explain why three sightings on the night of the double murder bear similarities to Francis Thompson. These are not the only witness descriptions to match Thompson. There would be more. There is another description of the murderer that is so detailed that modern Ripperologists dismiss it. This description, like Detective White's, is also out of keeping, with the stereotypical East Ender Which is why many people do not think it is possible. The description comes from George Hutchinson.

He is believed to be the last person to see the Ripper's final victim, Mary Kelly, alive. Hutchinson followed a man who was with Kelly for three city blocks and had a good look at him under a pub's lamplight. Kelly had been drinking at various pubs in Spitalfields. This included the Horn of Plenty at Number 5 Crispin Street, the same street that Thompson's night refuge, where he was staying, was located. Hutchinson saw

Kelly walk down the passageway to her room with a man that looked like Thompson. Hutchinson said that the man was no older than 35. Thompson was 28, but even with a new suit, his years living in destitution had worn him down. The man with Kelly was about 167cm. Thompson was about the same height. Thompson matches Hutchinson's description of the man having dark hair and a heavy moustache.

In the 10 weeks from the first murder on 31st August and 9th November, Thompson's appearance changed. Due to the help of his editor, in the weeks before, Thompson was no longer emaciated, dressed in rags, barefoot, and in an opium stupor. By 31st August he was clean-shaven and in good clothes. To the streetwalker he would have looked as if he had resembled an office clerk who had just stepped out for a coffee. We know from Thompson's letters, in the beginning of the New Year, that he had already grown a full beard. During the time of the murders Thompson would have first grown a slight moustache and possibly a goatee, but by November he would have already sported a beard and whiskers, like that shown in the first photos of him after the murders. In the passing weeks, from September until November, Thompson's attire would have become worn as he sought out his prostitute. Thompson could never keep a set of new clothes looking good for long. It took him little time for any of his outfits to become grungy. Mr Wilfred Whitten, an associate of Thompson's, who knew him 10 years after the murders, reflected this in a description of him. Whitten and Thompson both worked for the magazine *The Academy*. Whitten's description of

Thompson was typical of how most people viewed him. By then, Thompson, who had gotten off laudanum, by the autumn of 1888, was after a year break, back to becoming a heavy user. Whitten conveyed,

'A stranger figure than Thompson's was not to be seen in London. Gentle in looks, half-wild in externals, his face worn by pain and the fierce reactions of laudanum, his hair and straggling beard neglected … his disastrous hat … No money could keep him in a decent suit of clothes for long. Yet he was never "seedy". From a newness too dazzling to last, and seldom achieved at that, he passed at once into a picturesque nondescript garb that was all his own and made him resemble some weird pedlar or packman in an etching by Ostade. [The artist Ostade depicted his pedlars wearing large felt hats.] This impression of him was helped by the strange object his fish-basket, we called it which he wore slung round his shoulders by a strap.'

From description, photos and sketches of Thompson, he is shown to have the same attire as Hutchinson's suspect. This included the dark felt hat, a long dark coat, light waistcoat and dark trousers. Both Thompson and Hutchinson's man carried a small parcel with a kind of strap around it. Descriptions of Thompson and the man are of respectable appearance, though somewhat dingy. Hutchinson described his man as 'shabby genteel'. Thompson and Hutchinson's man are both described as walking very sharp though softly. Hutchinson said that he believed his man lived in the area and he had seen him a few days earlier in Wentworth Street, which was a stone's throw from Crispin Street, where Thompson then lived. Hutchinson even described how the man he followed walking with Kelly wore a thick gold chain, while Thompson, a practising Catholic, never removed his consecrated chain and medal. This chain was usually kept hidden, with his knife, under his coat and shirt.

People claimed to have seen the murderer many months and even years after the murders took place. Some sightings may have been likely, while others are hard to believe. The most strange and intriguing involves an encounter between a well-known clairvoyant and stranger on a London bus. The urge to solve the Ripper crimes was never the domain of the police alone. Many people from all occupations have been compelled to do so. Amateur detectives, writers, doctors and even psychics have tried their hand at unmasking the murderer. One famed clairvoyant, Robert James Lees, was active in his attempts to solve the case. In 1888, during the investigation, Lees tried more than once to assist the police and Scotland Yard in finding the murderer. Lees had sensed details and seen visions of the killer and he felt he should share his feelings with them. The authorities, however, declined his offer. In 1895 the *Chicago Sunday Times-Herald* wrote a feature story about Lees. The paper told that Lees suffered a physical collapse during the Whitechapel murder investigation. His medic ordered him to take an extended holiday to the continent where he stayed in France and Italy.

Some years later, upon returning to London the clairvoyant and his wife were on board an omnibus at

Notting Hill. The bus stopped to pick up passengers and Lees began to feel uneasy. A man got on the bus and sat down. Lees whispered to his wife, 'That is Jack the Ripper.' His wife laughed and told him that he was a fool. Lee hushed her, 'I am not mistaken, I feel it,' Lees insisted. The omnibus rode along Edgware Road. As it turned right into Oxford Street, Lees' suspect got off the bus. Lees and his wife also got off and followed the man until he waved down a cab that he climbed into and was then lost from sight. The strange narrow escape, occurred in a very different part of the city from where the murders occurred. Although Lees, who had just returned from the continent, strongly felt that this man was the prostitute murderer, his Edgware Road omnibus suspect appears to be inattentive to who sat so near to him. Lees' failure to act may have been his unwillingness to accept that this passenger, who appeared to be just an innocent Londoner, was evil personified.

Could this stranger on the bus have been Francis Thompson? We may never know, but buried in Everard Meynell's *Life of Francis Thompson* is an oddly coincidental reference to Thompson and Edgware Road, and how an inattentive poet saw it as one of the grand continental streets of Europe. He also eerily described how on an Edgware omnibus he would often be too distracted by his private thoughts to be aware of those who sat with him,

'Edgware Road was his Rambla, his Via dei Palazzi his Reu de Rivoli ... His inattention in the Edgware Road was out and out... inattention in the Edgware Road made the place as blank as a railway tunnel ... Riding in an omnibus he would not know whether Mlle. Polair [a Moulin Rouge dancer known for her licentious immorality] or a Sister of Charity [the order of nuns who ran the Spitalfields Providence Row refuge] were at his side.'

Chapter 14
The Row

'I am your child, you may not shut me out!'

Francis Thompson.

The good Sisters of Mercy, who still run Providence Row, tell us that record of attendance in 1888 was not kept; but that he did stay in this building is confirmed by several sources. These include Thompson's own admission, and credible historians and biographers. Thompson praised the Providence Row night refuge in his last essay, written on St Ignatius in 1907, the year of his death. The sisters, who presently run the Row, tell us that records of who attended their shelter have gone missing, but it is generally accepted that Thompson used it.

Historian and Thompson's biographer John Walsh verified, in his 1967 book *Strange Harp, Strange Symphony - The Life of Francis Thompson,* that Thompson used Providence Row. Walsh, the respected historian had unprecedented access to Thompson's papers. As well as those kept in the Burns Library, Walsh examined many sources and held many interviews, gained from journeying to England. These included sources kept at Greatham Cottage, the Meynell family home. Here he examined Thompson's notebooks from his time on the streets, between the years 1886-1888. Walsh also did further research in Chichester, London, Storrington, Sussex, Ashton-upon-Lyne, Manchester, Pantasaph, Ushaw College, Crawley, Owens College, Manchester, Preston, the Guildhall Library and the British Reading Room. It was the depth of his research that made Walsh one of America's most distinguished historians and why the staff at the Burns Library Special Collections in Boston College, Massachusetts – that houses the world's most extensive collection of Francis Thompson's papers and letters – see his book as the best biography on the poet.

Other Francis Thompson biographers agree that Thompson stayed at Providence Row. This includes, Paul Van K Thomson, who also wrote that he stayed there. In November 1888 Thompson possibly hinted he was there in one of his notebooks that he kept at that time. He wrote, 'Mont. Williams workhouse.' There was no workhouse by that name but it may have been the adage for Providence Row's most vocal supporter, Mr Montague Williams. This East-End magistrate, who was involved in the Ripper case, said of Providence Row, 'There is no more excellent institution … The place is beautifully clean … This institution, which is not nearly so well-known as it deserves to be, is in the heart of Spitalfields.' {Leaves}

As well as being a shelter known for its exemplary treatment of its residents, Providence Row may have been unique as a shelter for having the policy of not locking residents in at night and therefore allowing them to leave at all hours. This may have been because the Row encouraged its inmates to find work and many professionals seeking employment used this shelter as a home while they looked for work, including professions such as lamplighters, matchbox sellers or those who worked in the markets; those who, necessarily, worked odd hours. If the Ripper slept at a refuge, this policy would have made Providence Row perfectly suited to his nightly forays.

John Walsh, in his book on Thompson, wrote on what biographers consider being the one of the most fascinating and important episodes in Thompson's life,

'When neither food nor bed was available, he would, along with the other derelicts, often gravitate to one of the recently established Salvation Army shelters, or the Catholic Refuge in Providence Row. It was of the later place that Thompson supplied, evidently from his own experience, a harrowing picture.' {Walsh. p50}

Walsh then quoted Thompson's description of the Providence Row shelter that was situated opposite the entrance to Dorset Street, which held Miller's Court where the last victim lived and was killed. Thompson spoke of the 'nightly crowd of haggard men', who, with 'sickening suspense and fear' waited to be admitted. Thompson's account of his experiences in the Row was featured in the manuscript for his essay *Catholics in*

Darkest England, but before it was published, his editor Wilfrid Meynell removed all references to him staying there.

This refuge only opened in the colder months, from November until May, with guests given a six-week stay. A guest could not enter unless two conditions were met: they had to be respectably dressed and they had to provide a reference. In all the time Thompson was homeless, between 1885-1888, only in November 1888 could he fulfil these conditions. For most of Thompson's vagrancy, he was dressed in rags and could not have provided this crucial reference, having lost contact with family and friends.

Thompson being well dressed would have come from money donated to him by the family friend Cannon Carroll. He had done so when he saw Thompson had his poems published in the *Merry England* magazine. It was payments from the magazine's editor, Wilfrid Meynell, during the summer of 1888 that provided more money for Thompson. The editor, in giving him his fee, had instructed Thompson to buy respectable clothes. In the years before the November 1888 refuge opening, despite Thompson wishing to, staying there for any proper length of time would have been impossible. Only when it opened its doors in November 1888 could Thompson fulfil the second condition of entry. This was the submission of the reference. All through the previous years in London, Thompson, who had fled home, had cut ties with family and friends. The only time he had full-time work was when the shoemaker had hired him, but

McMaster had already organised lodgings for him and McMaster's shop was on the other side of London. Only when the refuge reopened in November 1888 could Thompson have provided the needed reference. Before the Row's November 1888 opening, Thompson was an unemployed bum on drugs, without any prospects. In November, however, Thompson could show the admittance officer that he was gainfully employed to the editor of a Catholic literary magazine and friend to the London Catholic cardinal. Although founded as a non-sectarian charity, Providence Row was still a Catholic-run organisation. The refuge would have accepted his reference without hesitation. By November Thompson could also cheerfully relate to the refuge's managers that he was an ex-seminary student. The manager would have been impressed by his connections to Catholic priests, who were friends of the family.

When he attended the Row can be traced by the fact that he was shipped off to Storrington Priory before the year's end, after having spent the Christmas of 1888 in London. We also know that after his editor lost contact with him in August, Thompson returned 'many days later' suffering from exhaustion. From what he was exhausted by has never been fully explained. From July onwards both Meynell and Cannon Carroll had helped Thompson with money, clothes and food. He no longer needed to beg, and surely if he needed extra money, now that he had become a published poet, he could have turned to either men for further assistance. Thompson was not pressured to write further; his earlier submission to Meynell, with its essay and poems, had freed his time.

The only thing that was taking Thompson's energy was that he was searching the streets for the prostitute who had abandoned him, during the time that the Ripper was seeking out prostitutes. Thompson, however, did return to Meynell severely fatigued. In response, Meynell had him placed in the private hospital. The name of the hospital is still unknown, as well as the dates that he was admitted. When he was put into the hospital, though, can be deduced from the pencilled note that Wilfrid Meynell wrote into the margins of the manuscript of his son Everard Meynell's 1913 biography on the poet. His father wrote of 'Six weeks my son!' We know from his editor that about four days after being released from the hospital, Thompson again tried to return to a life on the streets, and by the New Year's Day of 1889, he was in the country monastery, just outside the town of Storrington in Sussex.

The Row opened for the cold seasons on the first Monday of the November, which would have been 5th November. Thompson would have been allowed, initially, to stay for six weeks. This would have been reduced to only two weeks because we must allow for his six-week stay at the private hospital and the four days between his release and being sent to Storrington before the year's end. Using the 1888 calendar as our guide he would have entered the Row on 5th and left by Thursday 15th.

The Row did allow entry for a short period of time (five days) while the reference was being verified, so he could have been admitted earlier. However, any reference that Thompson might have given before the November opening in 1888 would have been an act of deception by Thompson, and although there is plenty of evidence to show Thompson was secretive, and even a liar by his omission of facts, there is nothing of his character to show that he would have deliberately provided a false reference. Thompson wrote of his experience as a resident of Providence Row in his article published in the *Merry England*. This was a highly respected Catholic magazine. It is doubtful that he would have submitted his article or that his editor would have published it, if he had stayed at the Row under false pretences. It is possible that Thompson did stay at the Row before 1888, but unlikely.

Interestingly, if it could be shown that he stayed at this shelter earlier than 1888, in the years 1885 to 1887, it would only serve to increase the history of his association with Spitalfields and the likelihood that he may have formed associations with the murdered prostitutes.

Providence Row, the abode of Francis Thompson, is also where Mary Kelly is thought to have once stayed. Apparently, prostitutes were used to pretending that they wished to reform, to get a bed for a couple of nights at the Row. This comes from a 1973 BBC interview with an elderly nun. She related how, when she worked at the refuge, another elderly nun told her that Kelly had begun using the Row in 1884. The nun said that she trained there as a domestic servant.

That Francis Thompson possibly also knew Mary Kelly comes from the English writer Robert Thurston Hopkins (1884-1958). He wrote that a friend of his, who was a poet, was also Kelly's friend and that the friend, like Thompson, dressed and looked the same as the man that George Hutchinson claimed was with Mary Kelly on the night that she was murdered. Hopkins never revealed the name of his friend, and this had led to much speculation, but there are enough links between Hopkins and Thompson to rightly assume it was Thompson.

The historian John Walsh, in his 1967 biography on Thompson, *Strange Harp, Strange Symphony the Life of Francis Thompson,* informs us that, in 1927, Hopkins visited people and places associated with Thompson. Hopkins preserved his findings in his 1927 book *This London - Its Taverns, Haunts and Memories.* For his book, Hopkins went to Panton Street in London's Haymarket District. There he spoke with John McMaster, the shoemaker who took Thompson off the streets to work in his shoe shop in 1886.

To protect his friend, or those who knew his friend, from any scandal, Hopkins used a made-up name for his friend when he wrote about him in his 1935 book *Life and Death at the Old Bailey.* The Bailey was the name of London's courthouse that had trials for capital criminal offences such as murder. Hopkins compiled his book using the experiences of a knowledgeable police officer who worked there. This officer knew much about the Ripper crimes. Hopkins said that the officer, who he also did not name, was 'on duty in the East End throughout the whole run of the murders.' Using information supplied by the officer, Hopkins gave an accurate account of the Ripper crimes, as well as looking at several suspects. Hopkins pressed the idea that the Ripper may have been a religionist who had lost his mind and that he had surgical skill. His book also suggests that the body found on the site of New Scotland Yard was another Ripper victim.

Because Hopkins would not reveal his friend's name, he used the nickname 'Mr Moring'. That name might seem meaningless, but not if he was suggesting Francis Thompson. Almost all of Thompson's poetry and prose that were published, before Hopkins' 1935 book, were simply decorated, just having had rings printed on the covers. After Thompson died in 1907, on his head stone was carved 'more rings', with two entwined as a vesica piscis. In his book Hopkins remarked that his poet's appearance was the same as the man seen by George Hutchinson as he stood outside Miller's Court watching him with Mary Kelly. As has been shown it fits very well the description for Francis Thompson. We know already that all Hutchinson had to do, when he was watching Mary and her man, was turn his head to also see Thompson's Providence Row lodgings and the window to Thompson's room. Here is a section of Hopkins's chapter on the Ripper, detailing the poet and his friendship with Kelly,

'One of Mary Kelly's friends was a poor devil-driven poet who often haunted the taverns around the East End. I will call him "Mr. Moring", but of course that was not his real name. Moring would often walk about all night and I had many long talks with him as together we paced the gloomy courts and alleys ... He had black, lank hair and a moustache, and the long, dark face of the typical bard ... Moring, who knew every opium den in the East End – although at that time they were not counted in with the sights of London – often gave himself up to long spells of opium smoking. "Alcohol for fools; opium for poets was a phrase which recurred constantly in his talk. "To-morrow one dies," was his motto, and he would sometimes add "and who cares – will it stop the traffic on London Bridge?" After reading the above statement [George Hutchinson's inquest testimony] I looked back on my memories of the wandering poet and curiously enough that description fitted him down to the ground! But I could not connect a man of such extraordinary gentleness committing such a dreadful series of outrages.'

Before this book, Ripperologists have tried to answer who Hopkins' friend may have been. The poet Ernest Dowson (1867-1900) has been suggested; though Dowson, unlike his poet friend, was not an opium addict. While Hopkins said his friend would say, 'Alcohol for fools; opium for poets'. Dowson was a heavy drinker. He avoided opium and died of alcohol poisoning. Thompson, on the other hand, was a heavy opium user who died of the drug. Hopkins was only 16 when Dowson died in 1900, so there is little chance they could have been friends, but he was 23 when Thompson died. It is far more likely that Hopkins had time to strike up a friendship with Thompson, rather than with Dowson.

Limehouse, where Dowson lived, was kilometres away from Kelly's home, while Thompson lived only a few yards up the street from her. An interesting side note is that both Dowson and Thompson sat side by side at a meeting of the 'Rhymers Club'. This was a group of poets that held regular meetings at each other's homes, but more often at the Cheshire Cheese tavern in Fleet Street.

The fifth and final murder of Mary Kelly, within hearing distance of the Row, happened on 9th November. It coincided with Lord Mayor's Day. This was an annual celebration and a street parade in which the Lord Mayor on a cavalcade held a street procession that wound itself through the city. On this day the police, who normally contended with keeping law and order and crowd control, had the added duties of controlling the crowd that had gathered around Miller's Court where the body was found, and cordoning off the area. In the weeks preceding, suggestions in the press and opinions by experts that the murderer had surgical knowledge had been a distraction to medical students and their lecturers. There was suspicion on both sides. Some students felt it was one of their own thumbing their nose at the medical establishment. On hearing about the double murder, medical students already fired up with drink and celebrating the Mayor's festival took to the streets and raced past bewildered officers whose police caps had been knocked off. The street parade ended at the Guildhall Library, which lay about a kilometre and a half from the murder scene. This was the same library that Thompson used to visit and read in when he was homeless in the winters. Of the many thousands who gave good cheer and waved to the passing Mayor, Thompson was not one of them. His essay *Paganism Old and New*, that he submitted to the *Merry England* magazine showed his derision of this tradition. He complained that it was a lifeless extravagance, an unchristian celebration calculated to distract the people from the social evils that encumbered the city, 'The cold formalities of a Lord Mayor's Show ... dead songs on dead themes ... everything most polished ... Vice carefully drained out of sight ... a most shining Paganism indeed – as putrescence also shines.' The 9th November was the third anniversary of Thompson fleeing his father's home after his heated arguments over his future stepmother's demand that he find a job or leave. November, which saw the murder of Mary Kelly, also witnessed the release of Thompson's essay *Bunyan in the Light of Modern Criticism* in the *Merry England*. In this essay, the up-and-coming journalist, reverted to the terminology of his days as a medical student when he compared a good writer to someone skilled in the use of a knife on a corpse,

'He had better seek some critic who will lay his subject on the table, nick out every nerve of thought, every vessel of emotion, every muscle of expression with light, cool, fastidious scalpel and then call on him to admire the "neat dissection".'

Chapter 15
Method and Madness

'The fairest things in life are Death and Birth, and of
these two the fairer thing is Death.'

Francis Thompson.

Just to summarise things: In 1888 and specifically when
a murder was being carried out Thompson was living in
Providence Row refuge, less than 100 yards from where
the victim, Mary Kelly, lived. He was carrying a razor-
sharp dissecting knife and his only reason for roaming
the streets of Spitalfields at night was to find a prostitute.
He also carried in his coat pocket a poem he wrote about
hunting down prostitutes and killing them with a knife,
and disembowelling them so he could find and kill their
foetuses too.

The belief that the murderer had medical knowledge
was a theme that ran through the entire investigation.
That the killer understood human anatomy and possessed
great skill in surgical operations was arrived at by the
testimonies of many experts, including those of the legal
profession. In summing up the evidence the coroner,

Wynne Edwin Baxter, for the inquest of the second murder victim, Annie Chapman, said,

'The injuries had been made by someone who had considerable anatomical skill and knowledge. There were no meaningless cuts. The organ had been taken by one who knew where to find it, what difficulties he would have to contend against, and how he should use his knife so as to abstract the organ without injury to it.'

The medical profession agreed that the killer had surgical skill. Dr George Bagster Phillips, the police surgeon who had examined Annie Chapman, concluded that the wounds were made by someone with knowledge of anatomy and a bladed tool for dissection. Dr Chapman said under oath, 'such an instrument as a medical man used for post-mortem purposes … the mode in which the knife had been used seemed to indicate great anatomical knowledge.'

Dr Frederick Gordon Brown also believed the Ripper had anatomical skill. He performed the post-mortem for the third murder victim, Catherine Eddowes, and said,

'I believe the perpetrator of the act must have had considerable knowledge of the positions of the organs in the abdominal cavity and the way of removing them. The parts removed would be of no use for any professional purpose. It required a great deal of medical knowledge to have removed the kidney and to know where it was placed.'

The press concurred with these opinions. The most respected paper, *The Times*, also reported,

'The injuries had been made by someone who had considerable anatomical skill and knowledge … There were no meaningless cuts. The organ had been taken by one who knew where to find it, what difficulties he would have to contend against and how he should use his knife so as to abstract the organ without injury to it. No unskilled person could have known were to find it or have recognised it when found. For instance no slaughter of animals could have carried out these operations. It must have been some one accustomed to the post-mortem room.'

The police believed the same thing. Sir Robert Anderson, Commissioner to the CID from 31st August 1888 onwards, wrote of the Ripper,

'One thing is certain, namely, the elusive assassin whoever he was, possessed anatomical knowledge. This, therefore, leads one pretty surely to the conclusion that he was a medical man, or one who had formerly been a medical student.'

Despite much discussion, during and immediately after the murders, that the Ripper was a doctor or medical student, today many consider that the final word on the matter rests with Dr Thomas Bond. He was the esteemed doctor who examined the last Ripper victim, Mary Kelly. He quashed the medical-student hypothesis when he wrote,

'In each case the mutilation was inflicted by a person who had no scientific nor anatomical knowledge. In my opinion he does not even possess the technical knowledge of a butcher or horse slaughterer or any person accustomed to cut up dead animals.'

In 1888 Dr Thomas bond, at the age of 47, was considered an authority on the medical aspects for homicides. His decision was based on what seemed unorthodox cuts and the unaccountable removal of the organs from the Ripper's victims. Today pathologists routinely remove the organs from cadavers, but when the expert Dr Bond trained at London's King's College Hospital, between 1860 and 1865, this was unheard of. Although it is now the standard procedure in medicine today, when Bond was a medical student it was not the practice to remove organs. It was the pioneering work of the German pathologist Rudolf Virchow that saw organ removal become part of modern pathology, but when in 1888 the Ripper was taking away kidneys and uteruses, the practice taught to do this had not yet extended beyond Manchester's Owens College. It was here that Thompson had been taught. It was his lecturer of pathology and his infirmary director, Doctor Julius Dreschfeld, who had first begun to teach, in England, the idea that determining cause of death was better accomplished by not treating the body as a whole but by the examination of individual organs. This theory is now standard practice but at the time it was a new and radical idea. Francis Thompson, when he studied from 1878 till 1884, would have been the first to learn about treating each organ as separate entities. It was only in 1880, a few short years before the murders and well after Bond had finished studying, that Virchow first published, in Philadelphia, an English translation of his German book on post-mortem technique, *Post-Mortem Examination with especial reference to medical-legal practice*.

Although available to Thompson, this 145-page textbook, complete with illustrations, would not have been found on the shelves of Dr Bond's college library when he was a medical student 20 years earlier. If Bond had read it he would have seen how it accords with his own findings on the mutilations of Mary Kelly. Virchow wrote in his book on how a good student should remove the heart,

'To bring the heart into the right position for the dissection, when the incisions for the right side are to be made, I extend firmly the forefinger of the left hand, and push it under the heart, and keep it against the base, so that the ventricular portion hangs down over the forefinger, which is as a fulcrum to it.'

To perform this heart removal, the pericardium, which was the layer holding it in place, had first to be cut through. When Dr Bond wrote, in his post-mortem of Mary Kelly, 'The pericardium was open below and the heart absent', he described a procedure straight out of Virchow's manual. Bond's own medical training would have brought him to the uniformed but logical conclusion that such an act had nothing to do with any profession; not slaughter-men and certainly not doctors.

Although the removal of body organs was a feature of the Ripper murders, as well as the heralded new Virchow technique, there were deviations. If the Ripper, like Thompson, had been taught Virchow, this could be explained by the strange circumstances in which the technique was performed. Having to alter how the organs were collected by different incisions was not only *allowed* in Virchow's teaching, but also *actively encouraged*. In his book Virchow wrote,

'It is scarcely necessary to point out that there are many cases in which deviations from this method are not merely allowable, but also absolutely necessary. The individuality of the case must often determine the plan of the examination.'

Francis Thompson, aged 28 at the time of the murders, had received not just the training of one doctor, but because he delayed leaving medical school by four more years, he had gained the training of three. The Ripper performed cuts that removed internal organs on three of the five prostitutes – with only one knife, in the dark and under time constraint. Such a feat with a dissecting scalpel, for Thompson, would have been difficult but not impossible. That a single knife was used for all cuts was the opinion of most of the medical experts involved in the Ripper case. Use of just one knife was something Virchow himself praised. In his medical textbook on what Thompson was taught, the German pathologist wrote of its merit, 'A good pathological anatomist is perfectly able to dissect all the viscera of one subject, or even of two, with one knife.'

All the other doctors who examined the victims were aged in their forties to sixties and, like Bond, would have been untrained in Virchow. To them the use of one knife and nature of the mutilations would have appeared insensible. They would see no reason to remove a heart, for example. Most people, and most murderers, would never contemplate doing so, but the Ripper did. Thompson did. In his poem *The House of Sorrows*, he writes.

'The life-gashed heart, the assassin's healing poniard [knife] draw.

The remedy of steel has gone home to her sick heart.

Her breast, dishabited,

Revealed her heart above,

A little blot of red.'

Thompson himself said his poems were not made up, but were as much diaries of his daily life. He was taught, for several years, a rare surgical technique that might also be found in the mutilations made by the Ripper. Even from this, how could one argue a reasonable doubt that Thompson was the Ripper?

Chapter 16
Confessions

'But I never meant to write all this.'

Francis Thompson.

Thompson, in July 1889, published his poem *Non Pax-Expectatio* (Latin for *A pause in Battle*). Within the poem, which was written very soon after his reaching the priory at the start of 1889, are these words,

'Hush! 'tis the gap between two lightnings ...

Behold I hardly know if I outlast

The minute underneath whose heel I lie;

Yet I endure, have stayed the minute passed ...

Who knows, who knows?'

From Providence Row, Thompson was placed in a private hospital. Four days after his release, he was shipped off to the priory in Storrington. In his first correspondence, from the priory, the born again pressman poet wrote from the top floor of the three-storey building. This religious retreat was run by French monks – French was a language he was fluent in – and surrounded by high walls. The grounds were patrolled by a guard dog that attacked him when he tried to set foot on the grounds. In his first letter to his editor, Thompson expressed his needs and was straight to the point,

'And I want to make a request which looks rather a luxury, but which I believe to be a necessity in my present position. Can you send me a razor? I shall have to shave myself here, I think; & it would of course be saving of expense in the long run. Any kind of razor would do for me, I have shaved with a dissecting scalpel before now. I would solve the difficulty by not shaving at all, if it were possible for me to grow a beard, but repeated experiment has convinced me that the only result of such action is to make me look like an escaped convict … I know this is a very perfunctory letter … there is no cause for uneasiness on that account.' {Letters p25}

Being homeless for the previous three years meant Thompson was forced to carry everything he owned on his person. When he was homeless, being able to shave was not just something one did out of hygiene or to keep fashionable, it prevented arrest. To some police officers, a homeless man with a long, unkempt beard was a sign that a vagrant was trying to hide his face like a wanted criminal might do. It also showed everyone else that such a bearded man had been homeless for a long stretch of time and probably knew no one. This would make them an easy target to anyone who wanted to do harm. Thompson kept his dissecting scalpel under his coat razor sharp, not only because it was something he liked to do, but because it was something he had to do. Fortunately, we will probably never know just how dangerous life on the streets was back then. Thompson lived out in the open on the ground floor of this huge metropolis. Every other day someone was being killed here, or ending their own lives. Thompson, with his suicide attempt, is just one example. We can read in daily papers of people jumping off bridges and towers or walking purposely into oncoming tram cars and trains. The number of dead fished from the Thames each year was 100 times more than what the Ripper killed. In 1887, 18,004 people were reported missing; 9,203 of them were found and 85 were declared suicides, leaving 8,716 unaccounted for. Precisely, how many murders were taking place in London was unknown. In 1882, for example, 544 bodies were found in the river, with 277 cases returning an open verdict. Even discounting the Ripper murders, crime was rampant. The homeless were seen particularly as second-class citizens or criminal types. Under those conditions Thompson, who was not a fighter, would have required his scalpel as his first line of defence. That he survived three winters with the criminals he was known to associate, and came out without a scratch, is amazing. It was by more than using harsh words that he protected himself.

Apart from all the inferences surrounding his personal circumstances that point to Thompson being the knife murderer, he pretty much wrote that he was. Some examination of his published works and research into his unpublished prose, verse and private correspondence informs us that Francis Thompson's desire to communicate images of murder and horror is pathological in its frequency. Undoubtedly some of Thompson's writing was inspired by the works of other gothic crime writers and from his own visceral experiences as a medical student, but the depth and detail points to another inspiration. That being the exploits of the killer who people say roamed the very streets he did. Often Thompson's written work is a fusion of his experiences of the operating theatre, his own dark musings and a sinister third element.

Another example of that is his only written story; his *Finis Coronat Opus* (Latin for both *Final Crowning Work* and *The End Crowns the Work*). The story was written from the monastery that he had been sent to, at the start of 1889. He completed it in the autumn of 1889, on the first anniversary of the Whitechapel murders. It is set in a future kingdom, during autumn. A poet, named Florentian, narrates it. The poet, wanting to be crowned the city's chief poet, holds a pagan sacrifice. He does a deal with Satan and kills his female lover with a knife. This too aptly parallels the writer himself, who, having sacrificed his relationship with his missing prostitute, was now being welcomed as one of London's new poets. The story starts with the writer explaining this story is the only way he can confess to murder, without being discovered by the authorities.

With Francis Thompson having been a Catholic student-priest for several years, the confessional would have held profound importance. In this small booth the Sacrament of Penance is performed. Here the faithful make their **confessions of sins**. Here, even murder can be confessed, but only if the killer is repentant. At the start of Thompson's story, the killer explains how this piece of writing was the only way he could tell anyone of his deeds and escape capture by the police,

'If confession indeed give ease, I who am deprived of all other confession, may yet find some appeasement in confessing to this paper. With the scourge of inexorable recollection, I will tear open my scars. With the cuts of pitiless analysis, I make the post-mortem examine of my crime.'

For a Catholic to seek confession was a sacred duty, but only once is Thompson known to have done so. Francis Thompson was a self-professed Catholic so the question arises, if he was the Ripper, did he confess this to a priest. Francis Thompson, after his 1888 rescue by the Meynells, visited Cardinal Manning. This English Roman-Catholic Archbishop of Westminster was a long-time friend of Wilfrid Meynell, Thompson's editor. Katharine Tynan discussed just how interested Meynell was in the Ripper case in a book. Tynan was an Irish writer, and friend of the editor and his poet wife Alice. In her biography *Twenty-Five Years: Reminiscences* Tynan wrote about a meeting she was present at. The meeting was between Meynell and Cardinal Manning. Here the Ripper was discussed. The meeting occurred early in the autumn of 1889. On 10th September a female torso was discovered in the East End, not far from Commercial Road. This was a short distance from Berner Street, where Elizabeth Stride had been killed a year earlier. Thompson was by now out of the picture, 70 kilometres away in the Storrington monastery. The new Police Commissioner, James Monro, considered the modus operandi to be different to that of Jack the Ripper and ruled this woman out as one of his victims. The press, though, saw enough similarities to the Ripper murders to think it was a continuation of his exploits. As Meynell and Tynan travelled to Manning's residence, they passed newsstands that had broadsheets declaring that the Ripper had returned. Of the meeting, Tynan told in her memoirs,

'I paid my last visit to the Cardinal just before I left for home at the end of September. The visit was made in the early forenoon, and as we walked along from Victoria Station, the newsboys were shouting the latest Jack-the-Ripper murder. We were the first to carry the intelligence to the Cardinal, who received us in the little inner room off his big room, where he sat by the fire wearing his warm quilted overcoat. I suppose there was an autumnal nip in the air, though I did not feel it. He looked very old and frail as he sat there; and now and again, he hummed to himself in a way, that spoke painfully of old age. I dare say the business of the dock strike had wearied him, for he looked a very tired old saint that day. When Wilfred Meynell told him of the murder, he closed his eyes and the strangest look came into his face, "careful for a whole world of sin and pain." … I was quite angry when Wilfred set out to demonstrate to me that the Jack-the-Ripper murders were the work of an Irishman.'

In 1891 Manning, perhaps noting that Thompson had been taken off the very streets the Ripper roamed, asked Meynell if Thompson would make his confession personally to him. When Thompson, with great reluctance, visited and entered the room, the cardinal was already waiting, hidden behind a black curtain that divided them. Did Thompson confess to the Cardinal of Westminster that he killed a series of women? Whatever he told Manning was just between both of them and God, but we do know that it left the good cardinal wondering if the extent of Thompson's sins could have been even possible. Thompson never confessed to another priest again.

When, a year later, the cardinal died, Thompson was obliged to write a tribute. His poem *To the Dead Cardinal of Westminster* advised the deceased cardinal what he should do next in the afterlife, where an all-knowing God would be able to verify Thompson's confession. Thompson viewed his meeting with Manning as a frightening ordeal. In an 1892 letter to Alice Meynell, his editor's wife, Thompson divulged how he was certain he was going to go to hell,

'You must know this thing of me already, having read the Manning verses, which I do not like to read again. You know that I believe in eternal punishment: you know that, when my dark hour is on me, this individual terror is the most monstrous of all that haunt me.'

Here is an excerpt from Thompson's poem on the dead cardinal,

'So ask; and if they tell

The secret terrible

Good friend.

Tell!

Lest my feet walk hell'

Biographers have thought it odd that a poem dedicated to such a fine man was less on Manning's life and more about Thompson. Alice Meynell told that this poem was, '… rather on himself than on the dead, an all but despairing presage of his own decease, which, when sixteen years later it came, brought no despair.'

Apart from this one confession, Thompson preferred to keep his sins to himself. It was only when he wrote, that he revealed his secrets. We would hardly ever assume that just because someone wrote about committing murder, they were actually a murderer. It is surely a bizarre way to make a confession, but Thompson tells us that with him we should assume his writing was about actual events. He admitted, more than once, that his written work reflected happenings in his own life. In a private letter to his editor, Thompson told of his fears that his writings would display more than art. Thompson warned Wilfrid Meynell that what he wrote was indeed a confession of sins,

'I am painfully conscious that they display me, in every respect, at my morally weakest ... often verse written as I write it is nothing less than a confessional, a confessional far more intimate than the sacerdotal [religious] one. That touches only your sins ... if I wrote further in poetry, I should write down my own fame.' {Letters p29}

When examining his *Crowning Work* murder story, we should pause on the similarity between Thompson's real-life medical training, at the Manchester infirmary, and the story's details. At the infirmary, where Thompson trained, he would wait by the shared fire, near to a hanging bell. He was used to hearing the bell's ringing; it alerted him to get to practical work with his knife. The biographer Bridget M Boardman had this to say about Thompson's medical training and the environment in which he worked,

'Outside there was a constant flow of traffic with patients arriving on stretchers or in carriage-like ambulances drawn by police horses ... In the main hall a huge bell was continually clanging, twice for medical aid and three times when surgery was needed. In the Accident Room staff and students waiting to be called for their services gathered round the fire ... There were two operating theatres with wooden tables, to which were attached leather straps for controlling those whose fear led to violent protest.'

Thompson's story has his narrator confuse the sound of bells, chiming the hour, with a ringing that commands him to action. Jack the Ripper is said to have rendered his victims unconscious before slicing their throats. He likely did this, too, to Mary Kelly before slaughtering her in her room, where a fire was burning in the grate. In Thompson's story his 'hero' describes how a ringing bell called him to begin slicing into his unconscious female victim before a fire. The district of Whitechapel, where the Ripper worked, is famous for its bell foundry, and its high concentration of churches and ringing bell towers, like Christ Church Spitalfields that had bells installed in 1730. This landmark church, with its tall bell tower, was about 50 meters from where Mary Kelly was killed. The area's profusion of tolling bells is reflected in the names of pubs such as the 'Ten Bells,' one of the pubs Kelly was said have been drinking in on the night she died. Here is a section, from Thompson's story, when the killer claims his victim,

'At that moment, with a deadly voice, the accomplice-hour gave forth its sinister command. I swear I struck not the first blow, Some violence seized my hand, and I drove the poniard down. Whereat she cried; and I, frenzied, dreading detection, dreading, above all, her wakening, struck again...There was a buzzing in my brain as if a bell had ceased to toll. How long had it ceased to toll? I know not. Has any bell been tolling? I know not ... Or—was it the cathedral bell? ... Silence now, at least; abysmal silence; except the sound (or is the sound in me?), the sound of dripping blood; except that the flame upon the altar sputters, and hisses.'

Thompson's story is not, as some have speculated, an inspired and out-of-the-ordinary take on the Ripper murders or just the hallucinations of an opium addict. Long before the murders Thompson wrote at least a dozen half-completed, never-published poems of the same gory nature. Of that which has not been burnt by his executors are the motivations, concerns and excuses of a knife murderer, clearly worded. Subsequent to Thompson's murder story's narrator's committal of murder, he worries that the law will catch up with him. Thompson, the author of the famous *The Hound of Heaven* poem described his anguish of being pursued by God. In his murder story Thompson uses a similar metaphor for his relief that he has escaped justice, and pursuing bloodhounds that have lost his scent,

'I know you and myself. I have what I have. I work for the present. Now, relief unspeakable! That vindictive sleuth-hound of my sin has at last lagged from the trail.'

In his 1888 *The Hound of Heaven* poem Thompson told how, after trying to evade capture, he fell exhausted like a criminal awaiting capture,

'I fled Him, down the nights and down the days;

I fled Him, down the labyrinthine ways …

'So it was done ...

I was heavy with the even,

I pleaded, outlaw-wise

Round the day's dead sanctities.

In the rash lustihead of my young powers,

I shook the pillaring hours.'

Thompson, in his poem, seems to reference Samson, a biblical figure known for his supernatural strength. Samson destroyed a temple by pushing down the pillars on which he was chained. Oddly, one poem supposedly sent to the police, during the Ripper murders and signed Jack the Ripper, also seemed to reference Samson.

'I've no time to tell you how

I came to be a killer.

But you should know, as time will show,

That I'm society's pillar.'

Another better-known subject of the Ripper investigation was the attempt by the police to bring in bloodhounds to find the murderer. Before 1888 there had been cases of bloodhounds being used to track down killers by means of detecting the trail of their scent. Many papers had discussed the possibility of using these animals to catch the assassin in Whitechapel. Since the double murders of 30th September, Commissioner Warren had been actively seeking suitable bloodhounds. He hoped to deploy them, if another murder occurred. Dogs were found, and Sir Warren personally tested their skills in Hyde Park, but although he was satisfied with the results, the dogs were already booked for a country show and he was not able to use them in the field.

Thompson's story was written a year after the last Ripper murder. Perhaps not coincidently, Thompson has his murderer confess a year after his last slaying, of his wonderment of his coming fame. He also wonders how the rest of the world will react to being subjected to such a crime without the discovery of the culprit's identity,

'I have had a year of respite, of release from all torments but those native to my breast; in four days I shall receive the solemn gift of what I already virtually hold; and now, surely, I exult in fruition …What crime can be interred so cunningly, but it will toss in its grave, and tumble the sleeked earth above it?'

The narrator is dumbfounded that he can kill in a city full of people, and be able to boast about it in his writing, right under the nose of everyone. He finds it difficult to believe that he has gotten away with murder, and gained immanent fame as a poet. Once again he conjures up bloodhounds, and imagines that they have sought him out. When Thompson's killer finds that he has, indeed, escaped detection and suspicion by being clothed in the camouflage of innocence, he is quick to show that he has no remorse,

'Or some hidden witness may have beheld me, or the prudently-kept imprudence of this writing may have encountered some unsuspected eyes. In any case the issue is the same; the hour which struck down her will also strike down me. I shall perish on the scaffold or at the stake unaided by my occult powers; for I serve a master who is the prince of cowards, and can fight only from ambush... I can fly no farther, I fall exhausted, the fanged hour fastens on my throat, they will break into the room, my guilt will burst its grave and point at me; I shall be seized, I shall be condemned, I shall be executed... I am at watch, wide-eyed, vigilant, alert ... I am all a waiting and a fear … Nothing happened; absolutely nothing … I do not repent, it is a thing for inconsequent weaklings ... To shake a tree and then not gather fruit – a fool's act.'

When Thompson wrote about killing women, he did not limit it to stories and poems, but, ever versatile, he also wrote a play on the same subject. His only ever completed play held this as its central theme. His unpublished 1900 drama *Napoleon Judges* is about how the French dictator assumes the role of court judge to prosecute one of his generals for falling for a prostitute. He orders the general's execution but there is a twist in which the prostitute is instead slain with a sword. Before she expires, Napoleon vents his rage upon her, telling her that her very being is a thing worse than death,

'Aye, the harlot's mercy he shall have! Habitation of lust and death! He had better have stroked the sabre's edge than you, kissed the musket's mouth than yours! The sword sometimes spares, the musket sometimes misses; the harlot never! Fair Destruction! He has clasped you a thought too close to his breast!'

If Thompson was not writing poems, play and stories about killing women or of his sheer delight at swinging various edged weapons about their person, he delighted in reading about it. His editor's son, Everard Meynell, had the unique position of knowing Thompson from his early childhood. This close association to the poet enabled him, under the ever-watchful eye of his father, to write a concise biography on Thompson. It was remarked upon in *The Nation* on 18th December 1913 when the book was first released, 'As the son of that house and intimate friend of Thompson, the writer of this biography has had opportunities that no one else could have enjoyed.' Apart from his biography, Everard is better remembered for the popularity of his store in Westbourne Grove, London. Named the 'Serendipity Shop,' it sold used and old books. Serendipity crops up continually if one reads Everard's biography on Thompson, with eyes that suspect the poet of being, secretly, a knife murderer. Francis Joseph Thompson entered the dictionary in 1913 when the British novelist Thomas Hardy, liking Thompson's work, wrote, 'You may be sure I am a Thompsonian.' Thompson, in return, liked Hardy's work; Everard, in his biography, told what piece in particular gave him the most enjoyment, 'I remember him to have often spoken with particular admiration – that in which Sergeant Troy enthrals a woman by sword-play and the swinging of his flashing steel round and round her person.' The scene that Everard noted comes from Hardy's novel *Far from the Maddening Crowd*. It is the part in which a soldier, with a flair for bladed weapons, acts to seduce a woman by sword-play and the suggestion that he is going to stab her. The scene, which thrilled Thompson, reads,

'The point and the blade of the sword were darting with a gleam towards her left side, just above the hip; then of their reappearance on her right side, emerging as it were from between her ribs, having apparently passed through her body. All was as quick as electricity. "Oh!" she cried with a fright, pressing her hand to her side. "Have you run me through? -- no you have not!

Whatever have you done!" "I have not touched you."
said Troy, quietly. "It was mere slight of hand." ... "Is
the sword very sharp?" "O no – only stand as still as a
statue..." That outer loose lock of hair wants "tidying",
he said, before she had moved or spoken. "Wait, I'll do
it for you." ... It appeared that a caterpillar had come
from the fern and chosen the front of her bodice as his
resting place. She saw the point glistening towards her
bosom and seemingly enter it.'

Chapter 17
Fleshly Ruin

'The other day, as I was walking outside my lodgings,
steeped in ominous thoughts, a tiny child began to sing
beside me in her baby voice, over and over repeating:
"danger, danger, danger is coming near!" My heart sank,
and I almost trembled with fear.'

Francis Thompson.

By March 1890, Francis Thompson, who had returned to
London, found lodgings. Over the years to come, the
routine of living in cheap lodgings and sporadically
being shipped off away to country religious retreats was
his course of life. His editor, who already had some
association with the landladies who managed these
premises, arranged Thompson's accommodation. One of
the landladies, for example, was the wife of Meynell's
printer. Meynell kept close tabs on Thompson and the
landladies were asked to write and report to him if
Thompson said or did anything out of the ordinary.
Pretty much for the rest of his life, Thompson inhabited
various lodgings clustered about the Queen's Park area
of northwest London, and most of his time was spent in

faraway monasteries. When Thompson first returned to London he set himself to work in earnest, keeping himself busy in the composition of poetry and writing critical reviews of the works of other writers. It was all part of the reinvention of Thompson as the 'journalist and literary figure' rather than the 'street urchin and opium user'. His editor had asked Thompson to report to him if he felt he was returning to his old ways. Meynell had good grounds to suspect this. Thompson wrote to him, on a Sunday in September 1890, of how, instead of walking the short distance to Meynell's new place of work, the offices of Burns & Oates (B&O) in Orchard Street, Westminster, he fell into a daze and instead headed in the direction of Whitechapel. Thompson, instead, walked several kilometres further eastwards. He only became aware of his surroundings when he reached Smithfield market. This East End market was the largest in London, and many honest-working Whitechapel residents worked there. Its walking distance to the crime scenes explains why many of the witnesses called to the inquests either worked at or near it. In the year of his return to London, despite being housed in west-London Lodgings, on the other side of the city and close to his editor's home and place of work, Thompson was finding himself again drawn to the East End. In September 1890, Thompson wrote to Wilfrid Meynell,

'Dear Mr. Meynell

I called at Palace Court on Friday, and finding you were gone, started to follow you to B&O's. Unfortunately I fell into composition on the way; and when I next became conscious of matters sublunary, found myself wandering somewhere in the region of Smithfield Market, and the time late in the afternoon … I thought I had disciplined myself out of these aberrations, which makes me all the more vexed on the matter.' {Letters p51}

Strangely, the Ripper murders stopped while Thompson was absent from London, but upon his return, there were further outrages in the East End. Some said it was the work of the Ripper starting up again. For instance, another East-End murder occurred on February 13th 1891. The police briefly arrested a man named Thomas who was acquitted when a man, also named Thomas, testified for him. Although the woman, Frances Coles, lay dying, when found by PC Thompson, nobody was convicted for her murder. Francis Thompson, our wandering poet, was in a typically dark mood with life around this time, when he wrote to Wilfrid Meynell, 'If you see in tomorrow's paper anything about a body being recovered from the Thames, perhaps you will kindly call and identify it?'

Wilfrid and Alice Meynell had many children, mostly girls. When this husband and wife first had dealings with Thompson, in 1888, and invited him into their home, the children were absent. They had arranged for the children's governor to take them away on a seaside vacation. When Thompson returned to London, after his stay at the Storrington monastery, he was delighted to be able to spend time with the children, particularly the little girls. The children, on their part, had no urge to spend time with him. The Meynell youngsters' attitude towards the poet was rather more down-to-earth than his to them. In his poems, he always idealised them as elfish embodiments of joy and innocence; and he believed that they were especially devoted to him. Yet, in later life, Viola wrote,

'He was not the visitor at the sound of whose special knock the Palace Court children raced down the stairs to be the first to open the door; his is not remembered as ever being sought by them or causing the smallest stir of expectation which children easily feel.'

The children ignored, tolerated or avoided him. One daughter, Madeleine Meynell, spoke for her siblings when she remarked of Thompson that, 'We rather despised him.'

This is probably because Francis Thompson held an unhealthy attraction to little girls. On 19th July 1900 he wrote to Wilfrid Meynell. The content of the letter was his delight in snapping up the opportunity to feel a child's hair. That he was then a man of 40, while his glee revolved around a girl who had just reached puberty, is worrying, even if we do not assume that he had already killed and ripped apart five women. Thompson wrote, in his letter to his editor,

'We had a carnival hereabouts ... The only sport ... was for girls to dab you in the face with a peacock's feather ... Only the children made amends for their elders ... I cheerfully submitted my neck to be tickled on my cheek, by the feathery weapons of the kids ... One charming child of 13 or 15 had a veritable impromptu game of 'tick' with me … at last she allowed me to 'tick' her and then, feeling my hand among her bright tresses … I fell in love with her at first sight for she was delightful: of antelope-lightness, fair complexion and long glittering hair … I retained my old attraction for children…Any way, not even the chicks tempted me forth among the crowd on Friday.'

In 1885, the age of consent was raised to 16. When, in 1900, Thompson wrote about this girl, to marry her was already a felony. Thompson struggled to reconcile his love for small girls, not because he felt guilt but because puberty forced them out of his age range. These lines are from Thompson's 1890 poem *Sister Songs*. It was written to two of the Meynell daughters who were aged 10 and under,

'But still within the little children's eyes

Seems something, something that replies,

THEY at least are for me, surely for me!

I turned me to them very wistfully;

But just as their young eyes grew sudden fair

With dawning answers there,

Their angel plucked them from me by the hair.'

The children of the Meynell's became a special attraction to Thompson and his fantasies bled into letters written to them. In one letter written in 1894 to 14-year-old Monica Meynell, Thompson hinted of how he wished he could emulate with her the Greek myth known as *Leda and the Swan*. This story is of how the god Zeus turns himself into a swan and rapes Leda, the wife of a king. Over the ages, poems written about this rape often depict the beak penetrating Leda's vagina. In his letter, to young Monica, Thompson quipped.

'you will have to lift me up in your arms to kiss you … do you still put your thumb in your mouth … It was such lovely weather for bathing. I wished I were a duck with nothing on but feathers. Or perhaps a swan - that would be more poetical' {Letters p116}

It seems that the younger the girl, the stronger Thompson's attraction to her. In another letter to his editor, in September 1890, he told of a girl who he met in Queen's Park. It was located within a few blocks of his lodgings in Third Avenue. In his letter, he again shows sorrow that one day puberty will come to steal her away from him too,

'The dearest child has made friends with me in the park; & we have fallen in love with each other … I rather fancy she thinks me one of the most admirable of mortals … And now I am in fever lest … her kinsfolk should steal her from me. Result – I haven't slept for two nights … Of course in some ways she is sure to vanish …' {Letters p51}

In John Walsh's biography *Strange Harp, Strange Symphony. The Life of Francis Thompson* we are told that the child of which he confessed having sleepless nights over was no more than six years old.

Francis Thompson's relationship with Alice Meynell, his editor's wife, after her husband and she took him in, was at first one of mutual admiration. Thompson had been a long-time admirer of Alice's poetry. It often featured in her husband's magazine *Merry England*. Alice supported his literary growth and tried to overlook his gruesome poem *Nightmare of the Witch Babies*, about the laughing knight that kills and cuts women open. It was a poem that she thought she despised. Then, at the start of September 1892, their relationship soured. Some realisation caused Alice to see Thompson in a new light. She grew cold and distant. She refused to speak with him and generally ignored him. Thompson's reaction was one of anxiety and fear as to what she might do. Here are excerpts from his letters that he wrote at this time, while living in London. They record his warped perception of his editor's wife and his worry that she no longer trusted him,

'To Alice Meynell

Dear Mrs. Meynell. It is a small matter and hardly, I suppose, worth taking a second thought about in your mind. Yet it seems I have offended you. [Thompson then writes a page on how they had arranged to meet at her house to discuss his poetry but she kept her distance] … I felt convinced that you shrank from it for some reason … I felt sharply wounded … I saw you were so cold and estranged from me, that going through the poem would have been a constrained affair, painful for both of us. So I left. It seems that the more I strive to please you and serve you … the more I alienate you from me … I am unhappy when I am out of your sight and would pass every hour, if I could, in your exquisite presence … I know how it must tax you to endure me …'

Three day later Thompson found out that Alice had shared the contents of his letter with her husband. He wrote again to the wife of his editor and future literary heir,

'… I had somehow fallen out of touch with you after the first moment. And I was miserable for it … I had slept little last night, eaten nothing in the morning, and was able to eat little last night. So that I felt utterly spent and unable to stand the strain of emotions …'

Alice and Wilfrid wrote to him telling him, in effect, to leave her alone. Two days later he wrote to her again,

'…. this morning I get your terrible letter … withdrawing from me your love … I feel blinded and paralysed … if you knew all as I know it, you would feel that never man had more claim on you for patience than I have … I am indeed more sinned against than sinning … Henceforth I will only come to your house when business calls me there … I will draw back into the hermit and leave your lives free from me and perhaps when the curse of me is removed from the house it will settle back into its ordinary condition …'

Thompson would not write to Alice again until a full year had passed and he had been sent to a monastery in Pantasaph. Even then it was only on the topic of editing his poems and having them published. Never again would their friendship fully recover.

When writing of a long-dead murder suspect, the fair charge, often laid against the writer, is that suspects are unable to defend themselves. Fortunately for Thompson he spent all his life building his defence. Of his trespasses and sins, Everard Meynell wrote, 'Francis construed his own defence into a hundred aphorisms. These two are signed with his initials,

'Where I find nothing done by me, much may have been done in me,' and 'For the things to-day done in you, will be done by you to-morrow many things.'

It should be difficult to write a character assassination on a poet, whose associates have described him as, 'the most innocent of men.' He has been described as someone who is said to, 'have never killed a fly.' As it turns out, it is an easy task to portray this poor suffering poet as not a nice guy. To show the true face of this Ripper suspect, all we need do is read what he wrote. The following are extracts from his private letters. A London writer's career is made or broken by the pool of fans and how he engenders their respect. This is what he thought of those who appreciated his verse, and his London audience and the England's capital,

'The public has an odd kind of prejudice that poems are written for its benefit … that infectious web of sewer rats called London ... the villainous blubber brained public ...We lament the smoke of London – it were nothing without the fumes of congregated evil, the herded effluence from millions of festering souls. At times I am merely sick of it ... Nothing but the vocabulary of the hospital, images of corruption and fleshly ruin ... The very streets weigh upon me. These horrible streets with their gangrenous multitudes, blackening ever into lower mortifications [shame] of humanity! The brute men; these lads who have almost lost the faculty of human speech, who howl & growl like animals, or use a tongue which in itself a cancerous disintegration of speech ... Seamed & fissured with scarred streets under the heat of the vaporous London sun, the whole blackened organism corrupts into foul humanity, seething & rustling through its tissues.'

Although Wilfrid Meynell's support of Thompson got his career as a writer off the ground, it received a big boost when the famed poet Robert Browning wrote to his friend Meynell, recommending Thompson's verse. Browning died in Italy soon after. Thompson described his effect on the deceased poet, 'as though one stirred a fusty rag in a London alley and met the eyes of a cobra scintillating under the yellow gas lamps.' Thompson's perspective on the big picture could be summed up when he wrote, 'The world-the Universe-is a fallen world.' Of a sunset, Thompson wrote, 'As a burst and blood-blown insect cleaves to the wall it dies on, the smeared sun doth clot upon a heaven without horizon.'

Normal is not the word that could ever be applied to the person who killed at least five women. Francis Thompson was anything but normal. We cannot be sure that he was ever in a relationship. He could not hold a steady job. He suffered from deliriums, hallucinations and mental breakdowns. He tried to commit suicide. He had a disquieting like for small girls. He was a drug addict who was disowned by his family. He has a history of arson. Much of his poetry shows a fixation on death and dying. The only story he wrote was about a man who stabs a woman to death. His only play was about the killing of a woman because she was a prostitute. He was a conspiracy theorist who was fascinated with the occult. He was homeless by his own doing. He mingled with murderers. He claimed to be a magician and to have prophetic powers.

Most people who dealt with Thompson on a daily basis simply accepted that he was not quite right in his mind. His landlady gave the typical impression of him as a lunatic, 'Many a time I've asked him to have his bit of lunch in with me and the other 'mental' – oh yes, she's a mental case, as I may have told you.' The murders happened more than 120 years ago and from that time on all manner of cutthroats, thieves and madmen have been dug up, and presented to the world as the name of the Ripper, though none can be so completely fleshed out in body and soul as Thompson. There has been a waiting game, that has lasted longer than any lifetime, for the hidden evil one to come to light. Will one day a secret police file be released that explains everything, or is Thompson as good as it is ever going to get?

Chapter 18
Good Bye Boss

'Dangerous inventions, postcards! They are like
revolvers, too handy for the vent of momentary spleen!'

Francis Thompson.

After 1888, the years passed and the deluge of letters
after the *Dear Boss*, missive, both copycat and possibly
genuine, slowed down and stopped altogether. This was
until, a writer, calling himself the Ripper wrote again to
the police in 1896. Although sent long after the crimes,
the police considered it one of the few that were genuine.
What triggered this possible update from the killer of
women, and possibly from Francis Thompson? As it
turns out, there may be many reasons. Primarily, it could
have been that another woman whom he admired, like
his prostitute, soon before the 1888 murders, rejected
him. Some ask, that if Thompson were the Ripper, why
did he not try to kill more women. This is partly
explained by his being placed in a male-only priory on
the outskirts of the country village of Storrington. His
publisher and literary heir, Wilfrid Meynell, sent
Thompson there. He was the editor of the *Merry*

England magazine where Thompson's essays and poems were first published. Thompson lived there behind high walls and under the watch of Franciscan monks, from around late December 1888 until March 1890. When he returned to London, he lodged near Meynell who instructed the landlord to keep in contact with him and keep him updated on Thompson. Thompson was asked to visit several times a week.

Thompson's contact with women was limited, with his only previous relationship being his year-long affair with a prostitute who went missing in early June 1888. This changed, when in May 1894, Thompson, during one of his visits to the Meynells, met the young writer Katie King. She was a secretary to the Meynells. He first met her while she was playing with the Meynell children. Thompson had already known Katie through her stories that she had published in the Meynells' magazine. Thompson and Katie liked each other immediately and he became a regular visitor at the Cavendish Square flat that Katie and her mother were renting. The Kings had not planned to be in London long and they were soon to return to their country home in Hale End, Essex. There was a mutual admiration between both writers, but Thompson's visits to her home were cut short when Wilfrid Meynell abruptly organised that Thompson visit the writer Coventry Patmore at his country home for a few days. Thompson and Patmore connected well with their shared interest in religious history, and Thompson felt he could share with Patmore his knowledge of occult history. Thompson could not say no to the invitation, but he planned to see Katie on the morning of his return to London.

In June, when Thompson returned, he was about to take the train to see Katie when Meynell intervened again, telling him to leave immediately for Wales where he was to stay at a male-only monastery in Pantasaph. Francis knew that his enforced departure was to prevent him seeing Katie again and he was angry that Meynell had been the cause of it. With Thompson now far away in Wales, Katie and Thompson became pen pals and he started writing poems for her. At the end of October, while Thompson was in Pantasaph, 'so completely cut off from the world,' he discovered that Wilfrid had written to Katie's mother telling her that Thompson was a 'danger' to Katie and that she should have nothing to do with him. With Thompson removed from the scene all he could do was watch hopelessly.

On 26th November, his good friend, the writer Patmore, died. He had suffered a double blow in only a few months – the death of a friend he could confide in and the destruction of his romantic involvement with Miss King by Wilfrid Meynell. In March 1985 another distressing blow occurred when Father John Carroll died. He was the friend of Thompson's family who had helped him get off the streets in 1888.

Less than two weeks later, though, Katie got back into contact with him to tell him that, despite the interference of others, she wished to renew their relationship. He replied with caution that they should, but this time hinting that their tryst be kept secret from the Meynells and her mother. Thompson once again began hoping that their relationship would become more, but in September 1895, while on holiday, Katie met another man, a vicar from Staffordshire named Godfrey Burr.

Thompson's poetry grew dark and obsessive. To Wilfrid Meynell at Creccas Cottage on Monday 11th May 1896, Thompson wrote in a letter that he had to stop writing verse, in case they betrayed his thoughts, 'It is time that I was silent … and if I wrote further in poetry, I should write down my own fame.' {Letters p 150}. King and Burr became engaged the following spring and married at the end of June 1896. The shock of the news sent Thompson into a downward spiral. He ceased writing poetry and did little work. What he did write hinted at Thompson's dark thoughts when, in the same month, 11th June, Thompson wrote on tragic literature, 'pathos gains on you imperceptibly as a mist and you are unaware of it until it grips you by the throat.' {Letters p173}. Thompson was feeling nostalgic when he praised the writer WE Henley,

'He still takes us by the throat of old. He still takes us by the throat, but his grip is not compulsive. Yet now and again the old mastery thrills us and we remember. It is good to remember.'

Thompson wrote to Meynell telling him of his distress, so Meynell hit upon the idea that Thompson should write a journal of his experiences. Meynell told him to concentrate on his homeless years between 1885 to 1888. Thompson plunged into the writing of this autobiographical essay. He gave a frank confession of his activities throughout 1888, including the months of the Ripper crimes. The purpose of this account was primarily to keep from thinking about Katie King. Thompson had already returned to the habit of walking the alleys and streets at night and seeking opium for comfort. Katie was the second woman to have rejected him. The first was the prostitute in 1888, just before the Ripper murders began. Thompson was in the middle of writing, his confessions of 1888, when the police received another letter signed Jack the Ripper. It was addressed to Whitechapel's H Division Police. The writer reminded the police of his 1888 exploits and revealed how difficult it was for him to recover from the brutal murder of the last victim Mary Kelly. This letter, written eight years after the last, suggested that Jack the Ripper was thinking fondly of repeating his past performance when he wrote, again in red ink, on 14th October 1896,

'Dear Boss You will be surprised to find that this comes from yours as of old Jack-the-Ripper. Ha Ha. If my old friend Mr Warren is dead you can read it. You might remember me if you try to think a little Ha Ha. The last job was a bad one and no mistake nearly buckled and meant it to be best of the lot curse it, Ha Ha Im alive yet and you'll soon find it out. I mean to go on again when I get the chance wont it be nice dear old Boss to have the good old times once again. You never caught me and you never will. Ha Ha. You police are a smart lot, the lot of you couldnt catch one man Where have I been Dear Boss youd like to know. Abroad, if you would like to know and just come back. Ready to go with my work and stop when you catch me. Well good bye Boss wish me luck. Winters coming "The Jewes are people that are blamed for nothing" Ha Ha have you heard this before

Yours truly

Jack the Ripper.'

Did Thompson write this letter? Was he planning his next victim to be Katie King? In February 1897 Thompson finished what was an 'essay unashamedly based on his street-life experiences'. He sent the manuscript to Meynell. Bridget Boardman, Thompson's biographer, told what Meynell did with it,

'Yet the manuscript, the most valuable witness to what had taken place was not only never printed but was almost certainly destroyed.'

The Meynells never told anyone of it and Thompson never mentioned it again. Boardman said that Meynell did this to protect himself because, 'The only possible explanation is that it was too revealing, too dangerous to his reputation.' It was not until the summer of 1901, during the time that Katie King died, that Thompson pulled himself out of his slump, and his urge to write literary reviews returned. Meynell sought to control Thompson and prevent his contact with women. He sent him to men-only institutions and stepped in and stopped his relationship with Katie King. He urged Thompson to write about his time on the streets, to redirect his urges, and then burnt Thompson's 'confessions' so that they remained secret to protect his reputation.

In 1906, the image built up by the Meynells of the simple, spotless poet began to show cracks. It may have been a reaction to the Meynell's constant praise of Thompson, who had competed for survival with the worst types on the London streets for three years, yet was trumped by the Meynells who insisted that, 'his spirit rose from the penal waters fresh as Botticelli's Venus.' Such idealised image-making caused at least one critic to warn the Meynells, 'The way in which you have compared the coming of Frank Thompson to the Messiah is approaching the profane.'

That Thompson was not the wholesome victim of the streets first came from a student, Charles L O'Donnell, and his essay *Francis Thompson*. O'Donnell's had won the Prize essay English Medal at his Notre Dame University in the State of Indiana. He would one day become a well-known American poet in his own right. The university's student newspaper, the *Notre Dame Scholastic* serialised the essay in its summer weekly editions. The essay began to question the truth behind Thompson's poetry and the persistent claims of his perpetual goodness. Everard Meynell wrote that the essay suggested, 'that the streets had put a worse slur than hunger, nakedness, and loneliness upon him.' The essay told of Thompson,

'The idea of seeking a livelihood, of useful employment of any kind, never seemed to occur to him ... No optimism of intent can overlook the fact of his having fallen, and no euphemism of expression need endeavour to cloak it. Down those terrible years he let himself go with the winds of fancy, and threw himself on the swelling wave of every passion. He said, "I will eat of all the fruits in the garden of life," and in the very satisfaction of his desire found its insatiableness.' Similarly, a Professor of Romance Languages at Columbia University announced, 'Thompson is the poet of sin.'

When we read about Thompson's life, we are asked to be believe incredulous things, such as his encounter with a ghost that saved his life, but it seems that fantastic tales surround this suspect. One of these happened when, in the last months of his life, Thompson stayed at the country home of the writer and friend of the Meynells, Wilfrid Scawen Blunt. One day they were having lunch in the garden and the wasps, which were numerous every summer, buzzed about them. At last, one landed in Thompson's wine. Thompson asked Blunt for assistance, saying, 'Will you please kill this wasp for me? I cannot do it, I have never killed anything in my life.' This echoes Alice Meynell once saying that Thompson never hurt a fly. Oddly, Thompson's response when a lone wasp finally bit him was to cast a curse upon all the wasps in the area. The result was recorded by Blunt, 'It has remained a legend here, but I do not vouch for its authenticity as a miracle, though it is fact that for three years after this there were no wasps in the garden.' The typical wasp nest holds 5,000 wasps. True or not, we can turn to Blunt's private diary on this wasp-genocide, 'Sir, to leave things out in a book merely because people tell you they will not be believed, is meanness.'

It was apparent that in the short years subsequent to his death, as a literary force Thompson was spent. Thompson had returned to opium usage with a vengeance. When he was not reading obscure ancient texts on the occult and mysticism, he was in a drug-induced stupor, barely communicating, or ceaselessly pacing the confines of his single-room lodgings. His greatest popularity would occur decades after he died. To those around him Thompson merely existed. The Meynell family however was keeping busy. Wilfrid Meynell was caught up in several projects; Alice Meynell was making a career for herself as a cherished poet and activist for women's rights. The children had all grown up and had lives of their own to lead. Only Everard Meynell gave his time to answer Thompson's letters or allow Thompson to waste his hours in his Serendipity bookshop. Thompson was no longer producing any work of quality and it had become the fashion to criticise the obscurity of his writing and his archaic choice of words. Now the criticism was extending to the man himself, with rumours and suggestions that his homeless years and his relationship with his prostitute were not fitting for a Catholic poet. The bind of the connections that the respectable Meynell had with their genius had become problematic and it needed a final solution.

In 1907 an apparently healthy Thompson was tricked into entering a hospital situated about two kilometres from his lodgings. What happened was that one of the Meynell daughters faked an illness and her father requested that Thompson visit her. Upon entering the Catholic-run hospital of St John and St Elizabeth, Meynell had Thompson placed in an isolation ward. Within a week, on Tuesday 12th November, he was dead. It is perhaps a poignant irony that the oldest Ripper victim, Annie Chapman, was aged 47 years, which was Thompson's age at his death.

Chapter 19
The Collector

'Feeling the infinite must be best said by triviality, and while she feels the heavens lie bare, she only talks about her hair.'

Francis Thompson.

Thompson died of Morphomania – the nineteenth-century's equivalent for a drug overdose. Francis Thompson had only just, hours before dying, signed his will. By then, he was well under the influence of the copious amounts of laudanum that had been prescribed to him by the hospital doctor. Thompson's barely scrawled signature left all rights to Meynell. A fellow patient witnessed the will, who Thompson had never met before. The first priest refused to give Thompson last rights and so a second priest was called in, but the priest could not be sure of the dying man's identity. This may be because a by-now heavily sedated Thompson was not sure. Our poet often went by different names. Works of his were signed by him as Francis Phillimore, Francis Tancred and Philip Hemans. He had nicknames including Tommy, Frank, Our Soldier. Elastic Legs and Necktie Poet.

The manner of Thompson's death is full of unanswered questions. Was it hastened by nefarious means? Was he essentially involuntarily euthanized? The lawyer who was present in his last days at the hospital isolation ward and who wrote the will was the husband of Meynell's daughter, Monica. In 1907 the same lawyer rose to become a vocal member of the leading turn-of-the-century eugenicists, the precursor to the emerging advocates for euthanasia and now-outlawed uses of it in some Axis nations in WW2. The Meynells wrote that his condition was aggravated by tuberculosis. This disease is typified by symptoms of constant fever, fatigue, wheezing, sweating and the coughing up of mucus mixed with blood, all of which Thompson showed no sign of. When, before Thompson died, when Meynell alluded to others that Thompson had a serious lung condition, Thompson refuted it, saying, 'It is all baseless nonsense.' Even though he always wrote he was forever dying, Thompson twice rejected suggestions that his lungs were poor.

No autopsy was recorded and this would not have been allowed without police consent. A day before Thompson's death, people outside the Meynell family had no idea that Thompson had a serious illness. Wilfrid Meynell assured others that Thompson was doing fine. He wrote to his Brondesbury Road landlady telling her that Thompson was recovering and asked her to make sure nobody else touched Thompson's papers. The landlady, Mrs Randle, wrote to Meynell in reply on 11th November,

'I am very pleased to hear that Mr Thompson is better and that he will be spared to reflect on his past that his future may have a brighter aspect ... I will take great care of all Mr Thompson's papers, books and memoranda.'

Biographer of Thompson, John Walsh, wrote in his book on the poet, that the Meynell's advocated that Thompson died through lung problems to steer the public away from thinking it was drug related. Walsh writes, 'on the day of his death the attempt to affect a drug cure had proved fatal.' In other words, they killed him through an overdose of opium. The Meynells subsequently talked up his lung problems to avoid a scandal. A friend of the Meynell family, the writer Wilfrid Blunt, in his diary dated 14th November, wrote, 'It was so arranged that nothing was known of Thompson's death till mine and a number more articles about him were ready to print.' {BLUNT p190}

The Meynells essentially kept Thompson's death a secret from the public and press until they had all got their stories straight. As Thompson's biographer Walsh states that all obituaries were 'released simultaneously ... that they largely emanated from the same source is evident in a similarity of phrasing'. The Meynells hardly suffered monetarily by befriending Thompson. Within a couple of years of Thompson's death, between 1909 and1910, the Meynells sold 18,000 volumes of Thompson's poetry and used the money to buy a seventeenth-century Sussex farmhouse and neighbouring buildings, on a large estate.

As already indicated, the *Dear Boss* Ripper letter holds many parallels to Thompson and could well have been written by him. However, apart from boasting to satisfy attention seeking, he would have had no real reason. If we were to select a more valid writer for the *Dear Boss* letter, we have Wilfrid because he may have suspected Thompson of wrongdoing, and might have written it to scare him to come in from the cold. Even if it were true that Meynell had written it, there was not much Thompson could do about it. If Thompson thought to go to the police and show Meynell's knowledge of the murders, it would have come to no good. The police would have been well satisfied that they finally had their elusive Ripper. They most likely would have concluded that Thompson had written the letter as well, and made no further investigation. Any threat, by Thompson to Meynell, that he would do such a thing would have been pointless. Today a few forensic handwriting experts could be engaged to settle the matter, but in 1888 the police did not use them. There was yet no precedence in the courts where handwriting comparisons had been used to gain a conviction.

This would not happen until 1907. In August of that year occurred the first successful use of handwriting as evidence in a murder trial. The trial was for a carpenter named Richard Brinkley over the supposed poisoning murder of Maria Louisa Blume. She was 77 years old when she and Brinkley met. Brinkley drew up a will leaving him her house and money. Brinkley then tricked her into signing it. Two days later Brinkley poisoned her. Brinkley's trial, at Guilford Assize Court, was the first to introduce forensic evidence of handwriting. The inks used for the will's signature were compared with ink Brinkley owned, and experts examined the handwriting. It was found to match Brinkley's. On 31st August 1907, on the anniversary of the night of the Ripper's first murder and 19 years since the Ripper wrote, 'Red ink is fit enough I hope Ha ha.' Brinkley was hung in Wandsworth prison. The affair of this murder trial was just one of many things that occurred in London that year. These proceedings should not have held any particular interest to Thompson, but they did. After Thompson was buried deep in London's Kensal Green cemetery, Meynell headed to Thompson's room on Brondesbury Road. All of Thompson's few possessions were held in a tin box. Inside the box, with some old clay pipes, Meynell found a newspaper article cut from the *Daily Mail*. The article that had been kept along with just a handful of items was titled, *Maria Blume's Will*. For some reason Thompson thought Brinkley's trial for murder and its feature topic of the will, in which handwriting was used as evidence, was important. Why, is anybody's guess. We could speculate that Thompson was pondering, not long before his untimely death, the possibility of engaging his own handwriting expert. Had Thompson found a way to authenticate the origin of the *Dear Boss* letter and implicate Meynell?

Another object found in Thompson's tin box was a cardboard theatre. Its marionette puppets may hold a way to determine, without a doubt, if Thompson was Jack the Ripper. When Thompson was a boy he constructed a toy theatre. It was made from folding a sheet of cardboard, which had images stamped on it. Either he took it with him when he left Manchester in 1885 or he retrieved it on one of the two times that he returned. This would have been during the Christmas of 1886 or for his father's funeral in 1896. When Meynell went through his items, which Thompson's quickly-drawn-and-signed will now meant Meynell owned. he found that Thompson had methodically replaced the theatre's puppet strings with hair from each of the Meynell daughters. How Thompson had gotten these souvenirs is uncertain. He could have cut them from their heads while they were sleeping. Perhaps he selected choice strands from their hairbrushes. However they were gained, Thompson had carefully strung them to the theatre's puppets. He then tagged each of the puppets with the girls' names. Thompson's plans on each girl were found in one of his notebooks. For example, 'Sylvia's hairs shall work the figures.' Jack the Ripper was a collector too. These included worthless rings wrenched from dead fingers and internal bodily organs, such as a kidney or a heart. We could do worse than retrieving this theatre and examining the hair on all of these puppets for their DNA. They might then be compared to the Ripper victims, or even their living descendants. We may find only that the hair belongs to the Meynell daughters, Monica, Viola, and Sylvia. We might find some of those strands belong to Anne,

Elizabeth, Catherine and two Marys – the Ripper's victims.

In Victorian times, making plaster life casts, from people, was popular. They performed the same role as today's 3D imaging. A life cast was taken of Thompson's face and hands. It very likely that Thompson's plaster life cast of his hand has imprints of his fingerprints. These may match the ink thumbprint on the envelope of the *Dear Boss* letter.

Solving the Ripper case has never been a matter of luck. It's simply inevitable. You will meet Ripperologists who will tell you the crimes can never be solved, and that for the sake of the mysterious fun of it all, they should never be. Giving a face to the Ripper would force everyone to see the murders only though their eyes. If Thompson turns out to be the culprit, those who have spent their lives following another suspect or refuting any possibility that we can lend Jack the Ripper a name, will be left pondering why.

People will tell you that there are so very many other suspects. Ask them if their suspect had a knife. They will answer that knives were everywhere, but could their suspect know how to use it? Ask them if their suspect had a grudge against prostitutes. They will answer, what motive does someone need if they have the urge to kill, as if killing is easy? Ask them if their suspect was near the murders. They will answer that Spitalfields could be reached from anywhere in London in half an hour, but they will not explain why anyone would take the trip

when prostitutes could be found on almost every street
corner of the city.

Chapter 20
Versatile Genius

'Lo, Behold me sick, fevered, unhealed, dying! My flesh
grows old, my flesh grows old in pain. There is no rest at
all from ills. There is no space from sorrow. There is no
pause from pain!'

Francis Thompson.

It was pretty much immediately after Thompson's death
that the drive by the Meynells to rehabilitate the image
of Francis Thompson was in full swing. Thompson had
the skill, weapon and opportunity to kill all the
Spitalfields victims. To prevent anyone thinking he had
the ability, two myths came into being: the first that he
was just too weak to have done it, the second that he was
too distracted and absent-minded to have planned it.

Positioning an audience to think he was too weak
was easy. It took little rephrasing and forgetting of
certain facts to create three occasions to support the
premise that he was simply physically unable to have
subdued and killed anyone. These occurrences were his
illness in 1879, his hospitalisation in 1888, just days
after the last murder, and his final hospital-admittance

days before his death. The Meynells propagated the idea that Thompson having tuberculosis exacerbated these events, but there is nothing to substantiate these claims. Of his illness in 1879, all we know is that Thompson suffered from some fever, but nothing more. During his 1888 hospitalisation, the opinion of researchers is that he did not have this disease then either. In John Walsh's 1967 biography on Thompson, he has this to say about it in the appendix,

'It has never been made quite clear whether he was also being treated for tuberculosis at this time. It would appear, however, that he was not. Brompton Hospital was the only institution in South Kensington and for quite a large portion of the surrounding area that cared for tuberculosis patients at that time, and the hospital records, complete as far back as 1841, do not include Thompson's name. Many hospitals, on the other hand, could have been found to admit a drug addict.

Thompson's death was more to do with drugs than disease. That Thompson was dying of lung disease and had had this condition for some time is supported, some say, by Thompson's own admission, but if Thompson was dying of tuberculosis, he was dying of every other disease as well. Thompson presents himself, from 1896, the date of the last of the possibly genuine Ripper letters, as a hypochondriac. Either that or he deliberately wanted people to think he was ill or perpetually dying. In August of that year Thompson wrote, in a letter to Everard Meynell, 'I have been unwell this last week, or I would have answered your kind letter before. I have been troubled by a return of the sickness and flooding of blood to the brain.' By September, that flooding brain, as well as rain had him write to Meynell, 'I got drenched through on my way home, and have been unwell with a bad cold.' Thompson again caught a 'cold' in April the following year, 'I was taken very ill last week and was totally unable to get to my work.' Still, in November 1897, he complained, 'Continual occupation intermittent ill-health, which allow me in these days little leisure.' In January 1898 Thompson was in a pedestrian incident when he was struck on the road by a passing horse-drawn taxicab. It was a close shave. To Meynell, he wrote, 'I was not run over, only knocked down; sustaining several scalp wounds and concussion.' In May he explains, again to Meynell, how the woes of his health have continued unabated, 'Thereon forthwith followed the severe and most unhappy cab accident. I have had a year of disaster.' The next year of 1899 Thompson's illness returns, 'found myself taken ill to-day with a violent cold, so that I was unable to write a line ... it was like argue-fits of violent shivering.' By July 1900 he still hasn't gotten any better, 'My work has been too much delayed by ill-health.' When October arrives his sickness has now made him bedridden, 'I have been very unwell all the weekend; and today it came to a climax. I was confined to bed all day.' A month later Thompson writes, not only that he cannot get out of bed, but that he can no longer even eat, 'I was taken so sick I had to go to bed, I had no sleep ... I found myself so ill I could not touch my food for an hour

…The drain on my strength has been going on now for nearly three weeks, with rarely a day but I vomit up at night whenever I may have taken during the day. And gradually my stomach gets so weak that I cannot eat.' In December Thompson draws upon his past to try to affect a cure, 'it has gone on to sickness, and I cannot come in unless it should pass off … my hospital knowledge told me the meaning of my symptom.' A year later, in November 1901, he again got sick, 'I caught fresh cold yesterday and have been laid up to-day in consequence.' The following month, in the December winter of 1901, he tells how his illness was a repeat of the same that occurred the winter last, 'But this winter I have had attacks of rheumatic cold.' By June 1902 Thompson's illness begins to travel, 'I was so unwell yesterday that I could not come – neuralgia in the eye.' These bouts of striking pain in his eye were lasting, 'I have been in very bad health suffering from neuralgia for nearly four weeks without relief.' In January 1905, two years before his death, Thompson continues to be sick, 'I was too exhausted & shaken to see you today, after a dreadful time last night … Am not at all well tonight.' Six months, later, in July, the pain has moved down to his foot, 'I am quite run down tonight, my foot so crippled I can scarcely bear to put it on the ground after a painful walk home.' His housebound existence continued. In August 1905, Thompson wrote, 'I am so very unwell yesterday, I could not get to see you at all.' In February of 1906 he describes how the illness had made him partly paralysed, 'my identification of the disease from which I suffered last spring but one with beriberi (devoutly though I hold it) … The first attack was sudden & comparatively rapid. First, a giving & loss of power at the ankles; then – perhaps in about half an hour – it struck suddenly upward, so that only by powerful effort of will did I keep from falling & to some extent shake it off.' In March Thompson's bouts of various illnesses continued, 'Sorry I can't tell you I am rioting in health ... Not so well last 2 or 3 days. But I think mainly stomach. While cramps still knocks now & again.'

These stomach problems continue, and in May Thompson puts then down to indigestion and blames the landlady's cooking, 'I will not again board with a London landlady. It is semi-starvation, especially for a dyspeptic … I have been too ill and exhausted to get to see you.' In the fall of 1906, his stomach ailment switches to his feet again, with a new condition, 'I am very weak & my foot so swollen & painful in walking that I cannot much more than limp.' A year later, in February 1907, Thompson is battling two diseases, 'Yet I have been so completely upset by aggravated renewal of diarrhoea & dyspepsia.' At the arrival of spring he again has the flue, 'I don't know even now whether it be influenza or not, but anyway in its effects on me it has been worse than my first attack at Crawley was.' Medical problems of this strain span the nine years from 1896 until his compelled drug overdose in 1907. A drug overdose that the Meynells and many of their peers instead liked to say was brought on by tuberculosis, oddly the very condition that Thompson disavowed ever having, called any suggestion that he suffered from the chest, ridiculous nonsense.

All this sickness, as well as having a history of hospitalisation, would make people doubt he could even walk, let alone be strong enough to be the Ripper. Added to this is the mention by Everard Meynell, in his biography of Thompson, that he had only one lung. Biographers write that Everard Meynell could only have known this if Thompson was dissected after his death. Because x-rays were not yet used in hospitals, only a dissection would have revealed if Thompson had only one working lung. No dissection, however, has ever been recorded. When we consider if it is true that Thompson had one lung, we should ask if that would have in any way slowed Thompson down if he was committing 'vengeance' on prostitutes in Spitalfields. Another Francis, who it is certain has only one lung, is Pope Francis. Here is how someone with 'Unus Pulmo', like the 78-year-old pontificator who had his lung removed through surgery as a teenager, was described by Stephen D Cassivi of the Mayo Clinic, Scott Kopec of the University of Massachusetts Medical School, and Jonathan B Orens of the Johns Hopkins School of Medicine,

'One might suspect that losing one of two lungs would cut respiratory capacity in half, but it doesn't, because the human body has significant reserves. The surviving lung soon expands to compensate for its missing mate, and regular exercise speeds the process … that deficit is hardly noticeable during ordinary activities. One-lunged runners have even completed marathons.' {Lung}

Yet, some people dismiss this 'confirmed homeless addict to laudanum' of the crimes, and think him innocent of murders that occurred in a quarter-square-mile of each other, because of presumed weaknesses caused by the laudanum. On 6th October 6 1888 Roderick Macdonald, a coroner's assistant for the Ripper victims, told the press that the Whitechapel victims might have been drugged with a form of laudanum. All autopsies on the victims show there was no struggle. They had been strangled with something like a necktie, rendering them unconscious. Once still and prone on a rigid surface, mutilating the women with a sharp knife would not require great strength. It would be particularly less strenuous if one kept a knife that was razor sharp, like Thompson's dissecting scalpel, the one he only needed to reach into his coat pocket for when he had to 'shave'. Thompson was aged 28 when these women were killed. High physical fitness and strength were major requirements needed for Thompson to enter medical school, and the army, as he did. One biographer has told that when he left his Manchester home in 1885 he walked the 300 kilometres to London. In London his odd jobs had him carrying heavy bundles of newspapers, and racing about town on errands for employers. All biographers tell of him being a keen hiker, walking all over London and the hills of Sussex and Wales. People ask if Thompson could walk the quarter-square-mile to any of the murders and performed what, for a trained student doctor many times over, would be easy.

The second myth surrounding Thompson, that puts him out of the picture for sceptics of the Thompson

Ripper theory, is that his mind was so far gone because of drugs and deprivation that he could not even think straight. People might wonder how Thompson could have even written poetry. It would seem he was too scatter-brained to do much else. The truth is that Thompson was an intellectual powerhouse. While at Ushaw Seminary College, that had 300 student priests, our absent-minded Thompson won 16 of the school's 21 competitive exams in essay writing, giving a success rate, against 300 other writers, of 76%. The master of the school announced that Thompson's essays were 'the best production from a lad his age I have ever seen in this seminary.' This simpleton, before the age of 18, had become fluent in German, French, Italian, Latin and Ancient Greek. This dullard had a reading speed of at least 40 words a second. Apart from his many hundreds of poems, our bimbo Thompson wrote and published 250 reviews and articles in the space of four years, and only 40 of them were with the Meynells help. The total number of essays he wrote and published in his lifetime was near 600. This dopey man's articles were on science, history, biography, politics and sport. When not writing his own essays at a startling speed, he was translating the works of other writers from French, Italian, Greek and even Indian literature. His range of work was admired by the writer Lewis Hind who said, 'He wrote on anything. I discovered his interest in battles and strategy of great commanders was as keen as his concern on cricket. So his satchel was filled with military memoirs, and retired generals ensconced in the armchairs of service clubs wondered. Here was a man who manipulated words as they manipulated men.' Yet the myth has persisted that Thompson, who was 'an argonaut of literature' was not too brainless to pick up one of the hundreds of prostitutes in his own parish who were looking for men, and take her down one of dark alley where she plied her trade.

The Meynells like to say that Thompson required looking after. Thompson called himself a 'versatile genius'. Any problems with taking care of himself financially are imaginary; Everard Meynell's *Life of Francis Thompson* paints a picture of a poor poet who was only prevented from returning to the streets due to his father's charity and almost parental care, but this is not the case. Biographers like Walsh and Boardman, in their books on Thompson, describe how he was earning a steady income in the years before his death. For the 10 years before 1907, Thompson needed £8 per month to pay for expenses, including rent, food and laudanum. This did not add up to £100 per year. Thompson was a prodigious writer and was paid for submitting hundreds of essays and critical reviews on various subjects. Many of these were published, without the Meynells' knowledge, under pseudonyms. In those 10 years Thompson earned:

£750 from periodicals.

£155 from a biography of St. Ignatius.

£100 from miscellaneous sources.

And this is only what was recorded. With well over £1,000 in the bank, Thompson was very much financially independent. Only a comparatively very small amount was spent on his laudanum habit.

Wilfrid Meynell, as well as showing an interest in the Ripper crimes and rescuing Spitalfields resident Francis Thompson a few days after the last murder, has other connections with the Ripper case. The publisher for his 1892 book *The Child Set in the Midst by Modern Poets* was Simpkin & Marshall. They also published the first ever story based on the Ripper murders. This was a short 1888 gothic novel called *The Curse Upon Mitre Square: A.D. 1530 – 1888*, written by John Francis Brewer, the son of a well-known medieval historian. The story used the murder of Catherine Eddowes in Mitre Square as a main plot point. Out of the hundreds of publishing houses in London at that time, Simpkin & Marshall also handled the first ever biography on Francis Thompson, in 1912. Another connection between Meynell and the Ripper happened 15 years later, when the 1913 *The Lodger,* written by Marie Belloc Lowndes, was published. It was the first widely successful novelisation of the Ripper, and it made a fortune. This was released by publishers Methuen; again, one of many hundreds of publishers in London. Founded a year after the Ripper murders, Methuen also released the book *Selected Poems* in 1908, a year after Thompson's death. These works of Thompson began with a biographical note by Wilfrid Meynell. In all the expanse of London, Methuen had their offices at Number 36 Essex Street, London. This was the same street that held Meynell's *Merry England* office, at Number 44. This was the office that Thompson visited to personally deliver his first specimens of poems to his future editor. Meynell was the lifelong friend, neighbour and publisher for Lowndes' brother, the writer Hilaire Belloc. In the same year that *The Lodger* was published, Meynell published the three volumes titled *Works of Francis Thompson*. From 1913 onwards Lowndes, with the help of the exploits of a knife murderer, became an established writer, and Meynell, with the help of Thompson's story of a knife murderer, set himself up for life. The coincidences continue. The guilty man in *The Lodger* was a religious maniac believing he is predestined to kill prostitutes. This is the suggestion of this book, for Thompson the poet. Lowndes' killer signs himself the 'Avenger', just as Thompson's loved writer De Quincey had his murderer do in his story. An inquest is held in Lowndes' novel where an eyewitness gives a description of a suspect that conforms eerily to that of Thompson,

'He was a grim, gaunt man, was this stranger, Mr Coroner, with a very odd-looking face, I should say an educated man in common parlance, a gentleman. What drew my special attention to him was that he was talking aloud to himself – in fact he seemed to be repeating poetry.'

We are met by so very many coincidences. If Thompson is really the gentle poet, that the world has been saying he was, then that is all they are. The coincidences, however continue. Perhaps Thompson's murder story, gives a fitting description of these correlations. In his story, the murderer remarks on a series of omens that portend his doom.

'The chain of coincidence was complete ... Of course it is nothing; a mere coincidence that is all. Yes; a mere coincidence, perhaps if it had been one coincidence. But when it is seven coincidences! It may be a coincidence; but it is a coincidence at my marrow sets.'

If the world were to finally decide on a suspect for Jack the Ripper, let us hope it is not Francis Thompson. Any other suspect, apart perhaps from royalty with Prince Albert Victor, does little to change anything of history. Certainly, a consensus on a suspect would solve the Ripper case, and affect the Ripper industry with its books, tours, museums and films, but the rest of the world would carry on like it did before. Not if we conclude it was Francis Thompson. Because he was influential in his fame, his words have already altered history. Saying he killed at least five women would change history again. This is clear when we understand Thompson's impact, years after his death, in American history. In 1955 the US Supreme Court handed down the Brown v. Board of Education decision. This was a landmark ruling that segregation between blacks and whites in schools was unconstitutional. Most agree it was the most important decision made by the Supreme Court in US history. The ruling turned on a phrase taken from Thompson's poem *The Hound of Heaven*. The judges, instead of giving a specific time-frame for segregation to end, purposely relied on the words 'with all deliberate speed'. This vague description taken from Thompson's poem, by not providing a clear period for the southern states to comply, hindered de-segregation.

Significant reforms were never achieved. It took another decade of protests, KKK lynching, imprisonment and needless suffering before the Supreme Court made a new ruling. Many civil rights historians say that this painful delay reverberates in the psyche of America and its lasting effects can still be felt in social disunity, overt racism, and distrust between African Americans and whites. What will happen to the social fabric of the most powerful nation on earth if they find out that among history's most important decision, made by their courts of law, was inspired by Jack the Ripper?

Thompson's words have indeed influenced our times. His name is associated closely with the histories of great writers. Just some of these literary superstars include DH Lawrence, GK Chesterton, YB Yeats, TS Eliot, Aleister Crowley, Robert Frost, Ezra Pound, Coventry Patmore, and JR Tolkien. A fitting example can be seen with the JR Tolkien, who is known for his *Middle Earth* novels. Tolkien admitted that the 'profound expressions' in Thompson's poems had an important influence on his own writing. Tolkien came to know Thompson's work in 1910, and in 1914 he gave a long talk at Exeter College's Essay Club where he praised Thompson and said that he was 'in perfect harmony with the poet'. Tolkien took inspiration from Thompson. Tolkien's elf-maiden, Lúthien, came from Thompson's coinage of the word Luthany in his poem *The Mistress of Vision*. Tolkien's use of the word 'Southron' for 'southerner people' in his *Lord of the Rings* comes from Thompson's poem *At Lords*. Thompson's friends knew prime ministers, diplomats and billionaires. What happens if their names are forever tainted with the actions of a multiple murderer?

Chapter 21
Murders in the Sanctuary

'On a clear day you can see a long long time ago.'

Francis Thompson.

This book often explores obscure facts that relate to Francis Thompson and the Jack-the-Ripper murders. It interprets these facts largely focusing on historical, religious and occult significance. If Thompson were not so fascinated with the topic, this author might have kept them out of this book. The first and most salient feature of the crimes is that they happened in a district named Whitechapel. It is a fact that, despite great risk to him, the killer stuck to this area. Here, police concentrated their patrols., Individuals and gangs of vigilantes, outraged by the crimes, scoured this area for the killer. Yet, despite these extra threats of his capture, the assassin clung stubbornly to this half-square kilometre. Such a concentrated focus on the murders prompted an inspector for the Whitechapel murders investigation, Henry Moore, to remark upon it. In 1905 Moore was interviewed by reporter Henry Cox from America's

Thompson's Weekly News. Moore told the reporter of the Ripper's obsession with this locality,

'In nearly every case the murders were committed on the actual spot where the bodies were found, or very close to it ... This, as I say, seems to point to the murderer having a system ... The murderer never shifted his ground.'

It is true that the majority of serial killers strike within a small area and usually close to home. This is because they are familiar with the area, and with their refuge so close they believe that they can quickly reach safety after they commit their crime. The most pressing question, if we are to have any chance of closing the case, is what sort of killer of prostitutes would have been drawn to live in Whitechapel? Francis Thompson's West-End prostitute vanished in early June from her Chelsea room, soon after Thompson told her that he had become a published poet. Probably his prostitute came to Whitechapel primarily for the business and because there were many women of her profession to hide amongst.

It explains why Thompson headed east. We know that Thompson had lived in the West End before this. His home was either along the embankments of the Thames, footpaths and doorways, common lodging houses and, for a short time, a lodging room supplied by McMaster. Then, in the middle of 1888, he suddenly shifted his home ground to the other side of the city, to Whitechapel and surrounding districts. His movements are blurry but we know his haunts included Mile End Road, The West Docks district, Limehouse and finally

Spitalfields. Jack the Ripper's kill zone was within a small perimeter of about a half-square kilometre in Spitalfields. Even if we think that Thompson was seeking out his prostitute friend, or someone like her, there must be something more to it. There may have been something special about the place to have strictly limited him to such a small area; knowing what it was may help us determine the identity of the killer.

Assuming Thompson's prostitute was alive and Whitechapel was where she had moved to, it is beneficial to question whether Thompson thought it necessary to kill her here, rather than simply take her somewhere else. Something about Whitechapel and Spitalfields cast some spell on the murderer, preventing him from moving away and killing somewhere else, despite the risk that staying put posed across five successive murders. Every place in London has unique attributes, but the killing field of the Ripper happened to have two very important features that the average person would never have thought twice about; two landmarks that, although unnoticed to almost everyone else, would have made a world of difference to Thompson.

The first is that Spitalfields held London's only homeless refuge that was Catholic-friendly. Providence Row night refuge, although promoted as non-denominational, was essentially Catholic. It was run by the Sisters of Charity, an order of nuns, and back then, as it is today, above the front doors are the statues to the Virgin which is an icon of Catholicism. This refuge would have been very attractive to Thompson, a man brought up as a devoted Catholic and with past aspirations of joining the Catholic clergy. For reasons later explained, Thompson would have no doubt sought this shelter much earlier, if he had met its entry requirements sooner.

The second landmark, which would have drawn a failed medical student and failed priest here, is the very special place that Spitalfields holds in English history. Some research into this parish and the district of Whitechapel in which it lay, shows how someone, and in particular someone of Thompson's background, wanting to bring a religious campaign of violence against prostitutes, could not have chosen a better location.

Many people, including those who played a part in the Jack-the-Ripper murder investigation, thought the killer had medical knowledge. This was echoed in the *Dear Boss* letter supposedly written by the murderer himself who taunted the police with the phrase, 'They say I'm a doctor now Ha Ha'. As it happens, the name of the area that the murders happened in, Spitalfields, means 'Hospital Fields'. This was because it was where England's largest and longest running hospital once existed. It was first known as the New Hospital of St Mary without Bishopsgate, latterly known as St Mary Spital. The Catholic Church ran this hospital. There could be no more suitable parish to house Francis Thompson – a dissecting-scalpel carrying, ex-medical student and practising Catholic – if he were to 'operate' on his victims.

If the reader were to be transported to 1888, set down on a Spitalfields street, and ask a passer-by what they knew of the area's history, the passer-by would tell you only what they knew from the limitation of their short lives. Much of the population was illiterate and unschooled. This meant that knowledge of the past was from what they had seen or been told second-hand by older relatives. They would have told the reader that this place, very long ago in the eighteenth century, had many large weaving houses, and that people came from all over to buy cloth. They would have said that in their lifetime the government had torn down the meanest, dirtiest streets, where criminal gangs once reigned supreme. Some would say that its many old churches and graveyards tell that once the land must have been very important to religious sorts. That many streets still had religious sounding names would be proof of that – names like, Paternoster, Church, Bell, Christabell, and Angel. Hardly anyone alive would have known more. Even the few people who could read would not normally have been able to access histories specific to this parish. The only library that contained a proper history of the areas was the Guildhall Library.

We would be forgiven for thinking that, in a city such as London with its many churches, religious sounding names would abound, but, of the 85 names of districts of London and its surrounds in the 1880s, Whitechapel is the only one whose name means a place of religious worship.

An examination of the old books at the Guildhall Library would have revealed what many would not have known: that the very origin of the name Whitechapel has a history that mirrors the Ripper crimes. The district of Whitechapel was named after Saint Mary's Church. It was built long before the Protestant Reformation, in a time when Roman Catholicism was the religion of the land. Its full name was St Mary Matfelon Spital. The church was later renamed Whitechapel, for its tower painted in whitewash. This building stood in the centre of a religious sanctuary that had operated for six centuries.

The name Matfelon, for this church whose order ran a hospital that primarily treated lepers, means soiled felon. The origins of this church's strange name were discussed by historian John Stowe in his *Survey of Westminster*. This volume tells that in 1428, during the time of Henry VI, a parish widow in Whitechapel was murdered while she slept. The felon fled with her jewels and he was pursued to the Church of St George in Southwark, where he claimed the right of sanctuary. The constables ignored his claim and brought him back to the city of London. As the criminal was being transferred, the women of Whitechapel were so incensed by his murdering ways and disregard for the sanctity of the church land that they flung the filth and dung of the street upon him. Whitechapel's most well-known murder case, the Jack the Ripper murders and also its oldest murder case, a woman killed for her jewels, bear striking coincidences. Both exhibited horrific killings involving that of a woman in her own room and a hunt for the criminal. Both murders had jewellery stolen from their victims, the parish widow in 1428 and Annie Chapman, with her rings, in 1888. Of course, this piece of knowledge of the obscure past, with features that mirror the Ripper crimes, was unknown to most. It would be odd though if Thompson did not know about it. This homeless ex-seminary student had an appreciation of history, both ecclesial and secular.

Records on Spitalfields are held at the Guildhall Library, including the historian Stow's books. This is the same library where Thompson spent much of his spare time when he was homeless. Thompson would have been one of a comparatively low number of people with the ability to understand church lore, an interest in history and access to this historical material. Francis Thompson was a voracious reader, being not only Roman Catholic but also an ex-seminary student who gained prominence in his college for being well versed in religious history. In the *Ushaw Magazine*, published by his seminary college, a fellow student of Thompson wrote, 'Most of his leisure hours were spent in our small reading-room amongst the shades of dead and gone authors.' Francis Thompson had studied ecclesiastical history extensively at his Catholic seminary for several years to become a Catholic priest.

Thompson's school library was not your average. It was annexed to the church treasury that contained England's largest collection of relics in private ownership, including what is believed to be a large part of the True Cross upon which Jesus died and a ring worn by one of England's most venerated saints, Saint Cuthbert. There also existed an extensive library, resplendent with rare manuscripts and considered to be one of the largest religious libraries in Britain. Thompson spent hours at a time, over the course of several years, pouring through dusty documents, parchments and scrolls. No doubt, having been starved of literature as a homeless Londoner, he would have done the same at the Guildhall where he spent great amounts of time. The Guildhall Library had only recently become open to the public and in a short time it became a drawing card for homeless tramps who would seek refuge from the cold winter days by resting in the stalls of the reading room. The Guildhall, where Thompson read the library's material for months, had London's possibly best public map room. Thompson was almost a permanent fixture there where he would pour over its old books and historical documents; until the head librarian grew suspicious of him and had him thrown out onto the streets by the police, whom he said were against him.

That Thompson perhaps saw another special significance in Whitechapel, and outcomes if he were to kill there, can be traced to a chance remark from Thompson to Everard Meynell. He began it by citing the historical significance of murder on church land when he began his letter like so,

'DEAR Ev, I told your father I should come to-morrow, but I send you a line to mak siccar ...'

The words 'mac siccar', Scottish for 'make sure', were derived from the murder of Red Comyn at Greyfriars Church in 1306. The term was made infamous during the time of the Scottish clan wars in 1306. After years of bitter fighting, two main factions remained. One was under Robert the Bruce, the other was led by Red Comyn. Robert wished for Scottish Independence while Red Comyn was ready to accept English rule, under Edward I. Both Bruce and Comyn were Catholics who understood that shedding blood on holy ground was considered sacrilege. This was why both men agreed to meet and settle their differences in the Greyfriars Church in the Scottish border town of Dumfries. When they met an argument broke out with Robert the Bruce becoming incensed by Comyn's refusal to reject Edward I's plans of English domination. In a fit of anger, Robert drew his sword, fatally wounding Comyn before the altar. He left the church and met his men at its entrance. Meanwhile the Franciscan friars rushed into the church and lifted Comyn onto the altar, attempting to staunch the wound. Outside, Bruce told his men about what he had done. 'I doubt I have killed him,' he said, and his friend Kirkpatrick replied, 'I will make it certain.' This was the 'mak siccar' alluded to in Thompson's letter. Kirkpatrick and some other of Bruce's followers then went into the church and restrained the Franciscan monks. Comyn was left, like the Ripper's victims, to bleed to death. In the eyes of the Catholic Church, Bruce's murder of Comyn was not only detestable in itself but also abominable since it had been committed on holy ground. The reigning Pope had no choice but to excommunicate

Bruce for his deed. Still, it seemed that this stabbing in the church by Bruce, instead of bringing the wrath of God, rather sealed the destiny of Bruce's kingship. Thompson's letter to Everard told of his thoughts of the importance of this historical event,

'The critic in question considered that Bruce had left off too soon. But to Bruce's taste (evidently) there was a suggestion in the hinted tragedy of "I doubt I have killed Red Comyn" more truly effective than the obvious ending substituted by his confrere. History, by the way, has curiously failed to grasp the inner significance of this affair.'

The suggestion by Thompson was that while Bruce could be blamed for stabbing Comyn, it was not up to Bruce to stop the bleeding. Preventing the blood loss was not his responsibility and thus he needn't feel remorse. It may well have been that his editor's son, upon reading Thompson's deviation into the history of killing on sacred ground, may have failed to grasp the significance of a retelling of a story. A story related to him by a Thompson who lived in the very streets of Whitechapel. The very area that someone known as Jack the Ripper was stabbing prostituting women to death on what was once sacred and holy ground.

That the land of Whitechapel was once a religious sanctuary is pertinent to Thompson, and perhaps the crimes. When Thompson's faith of Roman Catholicism held power, the entire area was predominately a religious sanctuary.

It was once a universally held law that if a person suspected of a crime reached consecrated ground and claimed sanctuary, then they could avoid arrest. It was reasoned that if a suspect was truly guilty then their fate was under the jurisdiction, not of the sheriff, but of God. The use of sanctuaries in England is first recorded as far back as the fifth century BC. This centuries-old rule insisted that any accused criminal that fled to a place of worship was to be pardoned by the accuser upon departure. The code of sanctuary was dealt a lethal blow in 1538 when Protestant Henry VIII decreed the dissolution of the monasteries.

Thompson not only appreciated the religious power of sanctuaries but also the meaning they had as a refuge for a suspected criminal. He also expressed his distaste that this age-old right of justice was dispensed with the coming of the Reformation. To Thompson the idea that holy laws could be done away with by the stroke of a pen was appalling.

In 1888, Whitechapel, once a place of rolling fields, gardens and monasteries, had become a hotbed of crime and vice where thousands of women sold their bodies for a few coins and drink. One can only imagine how Thompson, a profoundly conservative would-be Catholic priest, must have felt as he roamed homeless and penniless along the East-End streets while all about him, men and women, flaunted every vice imaginable on what he still considered to be church land reserved for God. For Thompson the decay all about him was a direct result of the fall of Catholic dominance over the land.

Thompson's attitude was recorded in his essay on Paganism, which he hand-delivered to his editor. At that time, a year before the murders, he was still homeless. In his essay he told of how he was forced to 'tread as on thorns amidst the sordidness and ugliness, the ugly sordidness and the sordid ugliness, the dull materiality and weariness of this unhonoured old age of the world.'

Thompson's reverence for the importance of sanctuaries was only equal to his dismay that the code of olden days was now refuted. To him it was abhorrent that sanctuaries were now marketplaces that sold human flesh, in the form of these women who gave their bodies for sex for the price of a jug of beer. Before his very eyes was a modern citizenry, polluting places like Whitechapel with every imaginable sin. Thompson recorded this in an unpublished poem of his, *Against Woman Derogating from Herself,* which bore the alternative title of simply *Holy Ground*. It holds these words,

'Yourselves have to the heathen greed betrayed the inaccessible gate; yourselves the laughing dances lead through your shamed cloisters desecrate. When unclean aliens like to these, one word had chidden from your bound, your chaste insulted mysteries, "Avaunt profane! This holy ground!".'

That Spitalfields' unique mixture of history-of-church influence and importance as a hospital is similar to the background of Thompson. His own history was mixture of church and hospital experience. Can this be put down to yet another of the long line of coincidences?

This book relies on a mountain of what may be coincidences or circumstantial evidence. Such evidence has led to many successful prosecutions, including that of American bomber Timothy McVeigh. Speaking on the strength of this sort of evidence, University of Michigan law professor Robert Precht who, was a defence attorney in the World Trade Center bombing, has said, 'Circumstantial evidence can be, and often is much more powerful than direct evidence.' This is because a long sequence of coincidences can reasonably infer a person's guilt. When the chain of circumstances, pointing away from innocence, is long enough the implication towards guilt becomes clear. This book contains a great deal of what might be seen as coincidence, but they all arrive at one inevitable conclusion. Even the 'most bizarre coincidences of Thompson's life', that he was seeking a prostitute and had medical training at the time that the Ripper was killing prostitutes.

To verify if the coincidences, on Thompson being the Ripper, are in fact circumstantial evidence, this writer asked an expert's opinion. In 2002, even before recent research that shows Thompson was living in Providence Row and carried a dissecting scalpel, this author wrote to expert Ken Anderson on probabilities of coincidence. He is the writer of books *Coincidences: accident or design?* (1991) and *Extraordinary Coincidences* (1993). Anderson was given information on Thompson's background, and the crimes, in a slim book that the author had written, simply titled *Jack the Ripper*. The book detailed Thompson and De Quincey and how they shared many life coincidences. It also told how the murders were committed on the grounds of what was once a Catholic hospital and that Thompson, a Catholic, worked in a hospital. Part of Anderson's reply to this author was,

'Dear Richard,

Thank you for sending me a copy of 'Jack the Ripper'. I do not think your connections between Thompson and the Ripper crimes can be dismissed as pure coincidence, as the facts you have gathered are quite substantial and do not appear to rely on chance as their basis ... the facts you have gathered are far more important and it is these I would, had I been the author, stress ...'

This writer also informed Anderson of another incredible coincidence that had to do with the dates of the murders and the types of Catholic saints worshipped on those days. The book this author wrote and gave Anderson suggested that while Thompson was seeking his prostitute friend in the East End, he may have vented his frustrations on similar women of her profession by choosing to kill on this old Catholic Church land. The book also described a pattern of coincidences concerning the choices of each murder location. The first murder happened on Buck's Row. It was not long before named Ducking Pond Lane. where accused woman would be strapped to a wooden chair at the end of a long wooden lever. This chair and woman would be ceremonially dunked into the water in front of a crowd of onlookers. This form of water torture often proved fatal through drowning. By 1888 such ideas about witchcraft were outdated to most people, but not to Thompson, who wrote in another letter, 'I live pretty well as much in the past and future as in the present, which seems a very little patch between the two.' Maps housed in the Guildhall, where Thompson read voraciously, include Richard Horwood's map of 1799-1819. It shows the street with the pond situated where the Ripper's victim would one day be found. To Thompson witches were how he described manifestations of women he disliked, such as his stepmother. The second murder on Hanbury Street was at the rear of a shop whose owner held her weekly Protestant Millennialist Church meeting on the night of the murder. Thompson was a Catholic who professed his hatred of the Protestant revolution that confiscated Catholic Church land, like Spitalfields. The third site on Berner Street was beside the rooms of a meeting hall; the night's topic of the hall, owned by Jews was on the necessity of socialism, an economic theory whose primary tenant was Atheism. This 'ungodly' doctrine, that denied the existence of God, was loathed by a devoutly religious Thompson. The fourth murder occurred in Mitre Square, just a few yards from the Great Jewish Synagogue. Christians, of course, have long blamed the Jews for their role in the execution of Jesus Christ. The fifth murder took place in Miller's Court, less than a hundred metres from Protestant Christ Church, built as a bastion against Catholic dissenters. She died in lodgings under the shadow of its steeple.

Chapter 22
At War with the Saints

'Now I carry the war into the enemy's country'

Francis Thompson.

So far, we have looked at where the murders happened and how they relate to Thompson's strong beliefs. That Jack the Ripper was on some moral crusade, targeting prostitutes, is an idea as old as the crimes themselves and an opinion that was held at the time by the bulk of the population. This reasoning was primarily because the victims were all 'fallen women' and the public readily saw that their killings might have been the work of someone who despised this profession and had taken up a lone mission to cleanse the streets of them. Of the 500 known suspects, that cover almost every walk of life and profession, Thompson, the failed priest with surgical skill, is an easy contender for this sort of killer.

An examination of the dates, and of interest to Ken Anderson, was that, mathematically, speaking there is only a 0.000003 chance that the Whitechapel murderer was not someone who held some kind of religious fanaticism. In Catholicism, occupations are protected by patron saints that are venerated on different days of the year. In 1888, when the murders occurred, before the Catholic calendar was modernised, almost every day was devoted to different saints. It just so happens that the days for the worshiped saints of butchers, soldiers, midwives and doctors fell upon dates of the Ripper murders. Because these occupations used knives and needed anatomical skill to ply their trade, the police suspected, questioned and detained them. It is conceivable that an unhinged person with knowledge of these saints could have chosen to kill on these dates in the belief that they were fulfilling some kind of divine mission. Here are the dates of each murder and their respective saints:

August 31st. – Saint Raymond the patron of midwives.

September 8th. – Saint Adrian the patron saint of Butchers and Soldiers.

September 30th. – (The night of the double murders) Saint Jerome one of the four doctors of the church.

November 9th. – Saint Theodor the patron saint of Butchers and Soldiers.

It can be argued that in Medieval Catholic England, a doctor of the church was a very different thing to what a doctor was in 1888, but to Thompson both would have held the same role of having the authority to intervene in someone's sickness. In a year there were only 15 venerated days in total matching those knife-wielding occupations, that the police considered the Ripper would have held. This means that for any given day, there is a one in 24 chance that any date would fall on these saint days.

Thompson, this book's suspect, was a fanatically religious man. He had skill with knives. He lived in the heart of Whitechapel where the Ripper murders happened. It is clear that the one in 85 probability of Whitechapel having a religious name is significant.

The chances that four dates in a row would fall on saint days, whose occupations, match those the police thought the murderer had, is far more than one in 80. That this could occur purely by random chance is an astronomical one in 344,861.

Further exploration of Thompson as a crazed religionist killer supports the possibility that he justified the murders by killing in certain places, on specific days and in a particularly ways. He may have thought that crime is relative and murder can be forgiven. A bit of doggerel written in his unpublished poem *A Larger Hope* might strongly hint at this,

'Sinned but in proper time and place and kept official hours of grace. Made of his sin no vulgar rumpus. But profligate by chart and compass.'

Ask any self-confessed Ripperologist about any aspect of the crimes and they are bound to tell you that most of what we know is open to conjecture. The histories of the victims, the conclusions of the medical experts, the motivations of the investigators; all are debated and argued. Even the number of victims that died by the killer's hand is a topic of contention. One book will argue that there was in fact no Jack the Ripper, and that all the murders were the work of criminal gangs, or unrelated to each other. Another book will state categorically that there were many murders, before and after the so-called canonical five, and that a single assailant did them all. This book does not claim to have solved the case that Francis Thompson must be the guilty person. This book's aim is to simply show how a supposedly well-known nineteenth-century personality, who is also a comparatively recent suspect, could have been the Ripper. This author is happy to let others try to prove his guilt or innocence. This dissertation does dwell on religion and occult mysticism. To most suspect-driven books launching into a discussion on religious matters would be bizarre and out of place, but this is because other suspects did not deal in religion like Francis Thompson did. He believed in demons as real entities. He was fascinated with the occult and esoteric lore. He saw himself as a prophet, and claimed to have seen ghosts and fairies. Thompson openly studied, shared and practised these beliefs. In a letter to the secretary and his colleague Elizabeth Blackburn in 1892 Thompson wrote, 'I am a Zoroastrian, a Mage, a Pharisee.' To understand why Thompson might be the Ripper, and, even more importantly, to begin to decipher what he sought to achieve through the killings, apart from satiating some unhinged bloodlust, we need to view the bare essentials of the case. This means putting aside speculation, conjecture and opinion. It means looking at the plain facts from the perspective of those who were on the ground; the actual police who investigated case first-hand. Doing anything else risks wishful thinking and misguided judgment to lead us further away from, not closer, to the truth.

Chapter 23
Murder Pattern

'Hate, Terror, Lust and Frenzy Look in on me with faces
... I hear on immanent cities the league-long watches
armed, dead cities lost ere the moon grows a ghost,
phantasmal, viewless, charmed.'

Francis Thompson.

Covered so far in this book has been the district where
the murders happened and their specific locations of
killing as they relate to Francis Thompson. They match
his peculiar attitudes and where he resided. We have
looked at the dates for the murders and they too share an
affinity with Thompson's ideals and staunch religious
upbringing. Ironically, these aspects, where and when
the murders happened is investigation in its most
elementary form. The next aspect, the number of
victims, is child's play compared to a proper
investigation and should not ordinarily lead us to naming
a suspect, if it were not for Francis Thompson. That the
Ripper killed five women was widely accepted by
investigators. This was due to the numerous similarities
of modus operandi, the type of women killed, and

proximity to each other in time and place. Did the number 'five' mean something to Thompson? A year after the Ripper murders Sir Melville Macnaghten became the London Assistant Chief Constable of Scotland Yard. He witnessed, first-hand, the fallout of these crimes. On the Ripper case, Macnaghten wrote in his *Days of My Years* on the canonical five victims,

'Suffice it at present to say that the Whitechapel murderer committed five murders and – to give the devil his due – no more. These being Nichols, Chapman, Stride, Eddowes and Kelly.'

Thompson was a self-confessed admirer of the eighteenth-century poet Samuel Taylor Coleridge. Of the more than a hundred poems that Coleridge wrote, Thompson singled out five pieces that he thought stood out from the rest. Thompson saw an occult significance in these poems and their relationship to the number 'five'. In his essay *Coleridge*, Thompson spoke of the English poet and the power of these five poems,

'He did influence my development more than any other poet ... necromancy is performed, so to speak ... There remain of him his poems ... striving to the last to fish up gigantic projects ... over the wreck of that most piteous and terrible figure of the all five star of his glorious youth; those poor five resplendent poems, for which he paid the devil's price of desolate life and unthinkably blasted powers.'

The answer to where exactly Thompson thought great poems came from was told in the writer JC Reid's book, *Francis Thompson Man and Poet*, published on the centenary of the poet's birth. It quoted Thompson, 'Every great poem is a human sacrifice.' {Reid p99}

As a practising numerologist, Thompson undoubtedly saw great significance in the number 'five'. In one of his notebooks, found in Boston College, he recorded its power,

'Five among the ancients was called the number of Justice as "justly" dividing the digits & for mathematical reasons ... Also that they called it the conjugal number; because resolvable into 2 & 3, parity and imparity the active & passive digits, the material & formal principles "in generative societies" five wise and foolish virgins, Romans allowed but five torches in their nuptial solemnities. The most generative animals created on the fifth day. In kabala, the fifth letter of the Hebrew alphabet is the character of generation.'

The five canonical Ripper murders were said to have struck London's social fabric. These women were crucified onto the infamous pages of history. Being born and bred a Roman Catholic also meant Thompson saw the number as symbolic, reflecting the five wounds that Christ suffered on the cross while dying. That Thompson could well imagine this suffering being transferred onto a female form was expressed clearly in his *The Passion of Mary* poem. This, along with his *Witch Babies* murder poem, was sent in February of 1887 to his future editor, Wilfrid Meynell. In the poem, Thompson described the dying mother of Christ, bleeding in sorrow, as if she herself had suffered Christ's five wounds. The verses tell of the sublime suffering of this woman, who was at one with Christ's dying, while he, the poet, is doomed to walk apart from man, upon lonely, dark streets,

'Thou hung'st in loving agony … The red rose of this passion-tide, Doth take a deeper hue from thee, In the five wounds of Jesus dyed, And in thy bleeding thoughts, Mary … O thou who dwellest in the day! Behold, I pace amidst the gloom, Darkness is ever round my way with little space for sunbeam-room!'

When people look at solving a crime they try to find a pattern of murder. It is an offshoot of the human condition to try to make sense of what seems to be senseless acts of random violence. Whether the Ripper was an opportunistic and disorganised serial killer or worked according to some diabolical master plan has always been an issue of debate. It has been the dream of many Ripper theorists to uncover some recognisable symbolic, overriding pattern to the crimes. A method used over the years has been to examine maps of where the murders occurred with the aim to see this pattern. This leads some people to connect each successive murder location to the next, and by doing so form shapes ranging from pentagons, associated with Satanism, letters of the alphabet, believed to be initials for particular suspects, and crosses, either upright or inverted as if the killer were trying to pervert sacred geometry and holy symbols.

Following the same age-old tradition, here's yet another pattern for the Jack-the-Ripper murders that may well shine a spotlight on Francis Thompson. After the murder of Nichols, the killer turned west with the murder of Chapman. He then went southeast and killed Stride, before again making his way west to slay Eddowes. Finally, the killer returned to the northeast with Kelly's murder. If a line is drawn to follow these directions, given that they are true and equidistant, it forms two triangles that make a crude figure-of-eight pattern. Such a pattern not only relates directly to Thompson, but, if he had a flag, it would have been its sign.

Thompson took time, in his notebooks, to write down the words of the seventeenth-century English author Sir Thomas Brown, on the magical significance of these two meeting triangles,

'If Egyptian philosophy may obtain the scale of influences was thus disposed & the genial spirits of both worlds do trace their way in ascending & descending pyramids, mystically apprehended in the Letter X.'

Thompson certainly saw the 'magical' properties of compass bearings in relation to worship and ritual. Beginning in 1894 Thompson, in lengthy written correspondence, expressed an abiding interest in this subject and the powers claimed by directions of the compass,

'On the matter of the "North" note that verse, "Promotion cometh not from the South, nor the East, nor the West." That is, it cometh from the North. The North seems always to signify the original Godhead, the "Father "– or the "Devil" ... This honouring of the "North" may very likely have been at the bottom of the seeking of the points of the compass from that quarter ... the North represents the simple Divine virility, the South the Divine womanhood, the East their synthesis in the Holy Spirit and the West the pure natural womanhood' full of grace ... I wanted to know if there had been any actual progressive development among the nations with regard to the quarters in which they worshipped-as an historic fact, apart from symbolic meaning.'

This twin-triangle that meets at its apex could be the Vesica Piscis. Also called the Vessel of the Fish, this symbol is a sacred and central symbol to Christian religion. It is believed to be a common practise for those engaged in satanic rituals to somehow pervert a holy symbol or object. These include such acts as holding a black mass where objects such as a crucifix are hung upside down or are otherwise defiled. Thompson knew this and understood its power in the practise of the dark arts. This is why it was a central motif in his only story, his *Final Crowning Work* murder story. In a key scene it was just at the point that his hero Florentine defiles the cross, that the devil appears, and a pact to sacrifice a woman in exchange for poetic immortality is made. As Thompson recorded,

'His face grew hard; with an air of sudden decision he began to act. Taking from its place the crucifix he threw it on the ground ... and, stepping back, he set his foot upon the prostrate cross. A darkness rose like a fountain from the altar, and curled downward through the room as wine through water, until every light was obliterated.'

The Vesica Piscis, being essentially symmetrical, even if flipped vertically or horizontally, retains its shape. Perverting such a shape can only be achieved by tilting it on its side to form the shape found in the murder pattern of the Jack-the-Ripper murders.

Thompson was obsessed with this symbol that predates the cross. The Vesica was printed on the cover of Thompson's 1913 three volume complete works. Engraved upon Francis Thompson's tomb is the same symbol carved as linked crowns, one of laurels, and the other of thorns. A central part of Thompson's longest poem *Sister Songs* depicts dryads, which are mythical, winged spirits. As the narrator in the poem shares the poem's central message, these spirits trace two circles in a linked figure-of-eight pattern in the air,

'Sister Songs' records:

Gyre in gyre their treading was, ...

Wheeling with an adverse flight,

In twi-circle o'er the grass,

All the band linked by each other's hand;'

Thompson perceived the tilted Vesica Piscis to hold potent powers. Here is given just a small section of his studies on the topic, which is contained in his notebooks, stored in the Burns Library at Boston College. It is given here, as he wrote it to highlight the depth of observations,

'Antipodal Triangle 1= first progeny of any given triangle in its evolution towards perfection. (i.e. towards equilateral triangle). Tendency of successive progenies to oscillate twist plus and minus; difference of half each time, as measured by angle of equilateral Δ = 60 degrees. Thus one progeny will equal (say) +70 degrees, the next =5.5 degrees; next +62 ½, next -58 ¾ (plus +minus). Thus progress in a regular 2 ratio till an equilateral Δ is evolved. Reversing the process you pass through the "Δ of reference" (or starting-point Δ), & reach ultimately a point = degenerated triangle. But, in certain cases the triangles tend to degenerate into an oscillating straight line, the basic ends closing up simultaneously with the apex (apex point>) & thus coalescing in the point = the degenerated triangle. (Hegelian law) ...the straight line only manifests the oscillation.'

Thompson had little qualms in professing his own dark fascination of the shape and its control over his life. It can be seen in this snippet of verse written by him,

'Oh, I believe astrology,

Tis destiny prevails,

And my evil stars are the fishes, with

The Virgin and the Scales!'

Thompson's fixation on this symbol was lifelong. The idea that he may have sought to superimpose it on a large scale by a series of murders over a landscape seems incredible. However, the more we study Thompson the more likely it seems to be that he may have acted on such extremes. It appears he attempted to engineer some sort of new order upon the face of society. On the face of it, Thompson's possible motive was simply to avenge a prostitute who abandoned him. More likely, however, whatever brought him take on the persona of the Ripper and kill again and again were multiple motives converging into a vast diabolical plan. A plan requiring a spoilt genius who had much knowledge of history, the right set of skills and nothing to lose. As has been explained Thompson was essentially a hermit and knew but very few people. During the 1890s he kept largely to himself and rarely strayed from his lodgings; still he did not fail to make an impression on the handful of people who knew him. One such person was an Indian named Sarath Kumar Ghosh. Thompson and Ghosh shared the same lodging house for a time. Thompson so fascinated this foreigner that he became part of a novel that Ghosh wrote and published in 1909, two years after Thompson's death. In his story *The Prince of Destiny: The New Krishna*, Ghosh borrowed events and meetings from real life in his portrait of Thompson. Ghosh devoted much of this in sharing with his readers Thompson's fascination with the same image shown by the geometry of the twin triangle evident in the placing of the Ripper murders. Ghosh's book detailed many meetings between Barath, his book's protagonist, and the novelised Thompson.

In the story Barath approaches Thompson one night to enquire as to his thoughts on how human civilisation might best move forward. Thompson answers it through the meeting of opposing forces, best illustrated mathematically by the meeting of triangles. A graphic example can be found in the Jack-the-Ripper murders and the police's attempt to capture him. Many now say that the inadvertent result of these high-profile murders was the instigation of much social change that led to the improvement of living conditions in the East End, with the clearance of the slums, as well as evolved policing methods and better social welfare including improvement in education and health. Ghosh, in his novel, has Thompson, in laborious detail, explain the function of the triangle in spurring human evolution. Thompson's description of his doctrine in Ghosh's story runs into many pages. Here are parts of it, severely shortened. Even so, we can see how Thompson would have been almost alone in seeing why the Ripper may have wished to make use of this shape throughout the murders. In the story, Thompson answered with deep emotion:

'To him the Infinite Equilateral Triangle was the end of all things … Instead of abstract functions we shall take a graphic example in illustration, for instance the triangle. Now taking any triangle at random, we can evolve from a second triangle, from that third, and so on. But of all triangles the equilateral the perfect type and the astonishing thing that, begin with what poor specimen of the species we will, the series of triangles evolved must end in this particular process in an infinite equilateral triangle. Wondrous, yet inevitable … as a sort of mathematical illustration of the theory of evolution, by showing that any given species must ultimately end in the perfect type ... let this be the line-of-perfection to be ultimately reached ... Exactly what should happen in progressive civilisation, [the] great doctrine of human progress ... In its evolution the point broke itself up into two parts, which, however, remained in contact; these two parts began to oscillate about the point of cleavage, while each elongated at its free end, the length of the oscillation forming the base of the triangle. The true interpretation of these motions as applied to the evolution of species in the physical world.'

If the Ripper did place importance in the doctrines as espoused by Thompson, once again some the case's mysteries, even the most minuscule, are suddenly resolved. For example, why, as the papers said, the killer might have paused after the murder of Annie Chapman in Hanbury Street, to place two coins side-by-side next to her body to form an infinity symbol. Answered, too, is why, when the body of Catherine Eddowes was found in Mitre square, investigators were perplexed as to why the killer, who was working under such strict time constraints, took the chance to cut two matching V-shapes beneath her eyelids.

On the morning of the double murder in Mitre Square, Eddowes' killer brought the tip of his knife against her neck, and laying her down he cut her throat open. He then pulled open her black jacket and nicked at other parts of her body including her face where he left matching V-shaped marks below her eyelids. Finally, he tore off a piece of her apron and walking away, wiping his knife clean. Some see the Vs as some sort of symbolic gesture by the killer; this sort of thinking springs from the spiritualists and occultists in 1888 who said that the Ripper murders were some sort of dark ritual. A few people still believe the killer might have made the double Vs by cutting through the nose on purpose, to simultaneously make a sign like, for example, the two parts of a symmetrically balanced infinity symbol ><. Others explain that the two cuts were made circumstantially as the killer sliced down into the nose; the blade would then just happen to cut both cheeks simultaneously. If Thompson were the murderer, then as trained surgeon three times over, performing such cuts would have been easy to do, and especially with his working knowledge in the emergency surgery of a large hospital.

Thompson's vast interest in more than just the standard religious texts, and his fascination in the occult, were better understood after his death. When his executors went into his lodgings to go through his meagre possessions, Thompson's landlady pointed out the hole that Francis Thompson had worn in the carpet over which he would pace until the early morning, muttering chants to himself. Thompson's notebooks, found in his room, contained 30 pages of notes and symbols. Within were details on the planets and the Jewish Kabbalah. Thompson had also collected pieces on the Anima Mundi, which is the ancient idea that the world and all it contains is in essence a single soul. He had also collected bird and animal imagery related to Hindu, Assyrian and Egyptian gods and the symbolic meaning of gases, precious stones, jewellery and the Tao Cross. This cross, shaped like the letter T, is thought by many to hold mystic significance and is thought by some to be the shape of the cross on which Jesus may have been crucified. Even the swastika, a symbol adopted by the Nazis, can be found in his notebooks, of which Thompson noted, 'It is in a height & breath, & inscribed in a perfect square in a magic quaternary. Four points = birth, life, death, immortality.'

Included in his collected writings was the subject of the transmigration of the soul, more commonly known as reincarnation. Also in his gathered notes from obscure occult journals were articles upon Paracelsus, an alchemist. Paracelsus believed that human essences could be used to create a tiny human-like life form. In his 1572 book *De Natura Rerum,* the alchemist advised feeding the creature known as a homunculus with human blood. Thompson also collected treatises on gnostic religion, pagan rites and the symbols of worship among the Knights Templars. Finally, Thompson's notes contained numerous references to the Faust legend in which a man sells his soul to Satan. Mrs Blackburn, who helped him gather his notes, wrote a comment upon it, 'such an awful revelation of wickedness.'

Perhaps Thompson was the Ripper, with clear aims. In a thesis Thompson wrote about his ideal form of world government, he wished for one in which the old ways of pagan human sacrifice and modern Christianity would join together,

'When the federation of the world comes as come I believe it will ... I see only two religions constant enough to effect this ... Paganism and Christianism ... We offer sacrifice to the Queen of Heaven.'

If Thompson was a criminal mastermind then he might have been more than a murderer, also a terrorist. Perhaps it were better for us all if this highly educated and trained, renowned religious poet is not the Ripper, and we can all sleep safe. If the killer was a simple man who had just gone mad then we could view the crimes as momentary aberration, limited to the autumn of 1888. If the killer was some uneducated tradesman, a street-gang member or drunken sailor without any pretentions beyond the killings themselves, we could ignore these murders as a mere mysterious anomaly of the industrial age. If Thompson is reckoned as the killer, though, then we are forced to contend with a murderer with pretensions of greatness; a killer who did indeed consort with the highest in the land and left his mark on so many truly great figures of the Victorian and modern age. In his own time, the ways of Thompson were mostly indecipherable. His works were taken as odd contraptions, his poems as strange pieces that often obscured gibberish. The newspaper *Pall Mall* dismissed the works in Thompson's book *New Poems*, published in 1897, as nonsense. This typifies common reaction. His *New Poems* were mainly on mysticism, myths and magic. The *Pall Mall* called one of the poems within *The Anthem of Earth* a 'terrible poem ... without form and void, rhymeless'. The *Anthem* related Thompson's distaste of the world's adoration of science and its forsaking of the mystical arts. To the paper's critic, the poem was just an outburst from a poet who had never dealt in anything of any significance, but if the poet was also the same man who, in 1888, had terrified an entire city, the mere metaphors might have held a darker sentiment than the paper's critic may have dared believed. Part of Thompson's *An Anthem of Earth* equates science to a decrepit pig with a surgeon's knife cutting away flesh in vain. Going on to describe the interior of his mind, Thompson tells of how he sees himself as a stranger lost in a vast maze of dark burial chambers. In verses typical of Thompson, he asks a hungry world to be patient, for soon it will feed on the flesh of the slaughtered until it vomits. He wonders if the reader can hear the rattle of knives crying to be set free. In 1897 the idea that the world would become caught up in some universal conflict was far-fetched. In 1914, within a year of Thompson's death, his seemingly absurd prophecy took shape as World War One. Thompson's poem did not end there. In words echoing the Ripper murders and accompanying threatening letters, on a grand scale, Thompson assured that all humankind held no importance and he promised that all mankind will perish in blood. Here is *An Anthem of Earth* by Francis Thompson,

'Science, old noser in its prideful straw,

That with anatomizing scalpel tents

Its three-inch of thy skin and brags 'All's bare'...

All which I am; that am a foreigner

In mine own region? Who the chart shall draw

Of strange courts and vaulty labyrinths

The spacious tenements and wide pleasances,

Innumerable corridors far-withdrawn,

Wherein I wander darkling, of myself?

Darkling I wander, nor dare explore

The long arcane of those dim catacombs,

Where the rat memory does its burrows make...

Tarry awhile lean Earth, for thou shalt drink,

Even till thy dull throat sicken,

The draught thou grow'st most fat on; hear'st thou not

The World's knives bickering in their sheaths? O patience!

Much offal of a foul world comes thy way

And man's superfluous cloud shall soon be laid

In a little blood ...'

Astrology holds that the position of the constellations influence earthly affairs. Thompson, our Spitalfields ex-student doctor with the knife, wrote in small notebooks during the crimes. Many of them show how he proscribed in astrology in his autobiographical poems, such as this one,

'The shadows plot against me,

and lie in ambush for me;

The stars conspire

and a net of fire …

and the maws of mists

are opened to undo me.'

If the Ripper of 1888, like my suspect, believed that any of the 88 spinning constellations foreshadowed events, it might not be a coincidence which constellation was directly above all throughout the four-month murder period. In the sky's zenith, when five women were killed through fatal injuries to the throat and then sexually mutilated, was the Perseus constellation. The constellation is said to depict the mythical hero of Ancient Greece, resting his foot on Algol. A star system has held a long fascination. Its unusual, varying brightness held an interest to ancient peoples who called it the 'Blinking Demon'. To astronomers it is Beta Persei who explain this phenomenon to be caused by the orbits of a binary, possibly triple, star. In 1888 it had the nickname of 'Demon Star'. Astrologers around the world believe that its powers are of primitive female sexuality, and that its energies become manifested in strangulation, beheading, and danger to the throat and to the neck. It is very commonly referred to as the 'Evil One'. The Arabs called it the 'Monster's Head'. The

Ancient Greeks also named it after a monster. To them it represented the severed head of the Gorgon Medusa, who Perseus killed with a blade. Many cultures connect this star, whose highest accession was reached during the Ripper murders, with evil. The Hebrew astrologers call it 'Rōsh ha Sāṭān', which translates as 'Satan's Head'. The Romans knew it as 'Caput Larvae', meaning 'Spectre's Head'. Eastern astrologers dubbed it the 'Piled-up Corpses'. While the Chinese knew these stars, that shone down onto five fresh graves, as 'Tseih She', or the fifth star of the mausoleum.

Conclusion

'Yet there is more, whereat non guesseth love! Upon the
ending of my deadly night.'

Francis Thompson.

If Francis Thompson was Jack the Ripper, then one of
the greatest crime mysteries has been laid to rest. On the
surface, the connection with Thompson to the crimes
should have been made long ago. The Ripper and
Thompson shared 1888 as the pivotal year in which both
came to prominence, and they happened to have done
this in the comparatively tiny area of Spitalfields. Both
their names share the characteristic of being unknown.
The Ripper's anonymity became the eternal mystery and
Thompson's reclusive existence allowed others to
rewrite his life story as they saw fit. Typical of the praise
awarded to Francis Thompson, within months after his
death in 1907, is this from *The Stylus*, printed on the 1st
March 1908,

'there died quietly in a London hospital a man of the
rarest genius ... The poet relates how the anatomy
classes so sickened him that he never attended them after
the first day. Instead of studying medicine, he spent his

whole day in the public libraries ... To have felt and loved Francis Thompson's poetry is one of those spiritual gains in our life which, come what may, can never be lost entirely. He was rather a soul, a breath, than a man. It is the mind of a woman in the character of a child, so that we feel for him less admiration than tenderness and gratitude. Francis Thompson has done the world an inestimable good, if the world will but recognize it, for he has succeeded in cloaking all things with the divine presence, and so vividly that we can almost see God in our midst. Truly a miracle was performed by this poet inspired of the Holy Ghost, "And the Word was made flesh, and dwelt among us.'"

On the face of such star-struck renditions on Thompson's life, is it any wonder that no one thought Thompson was Jack the Ripper, and if they did, that they would think twice before telling someone? When Mary Kelly was murdered, Thompson's home was less than 100 yards away. His only reason for roaming those streets at night was that he was looking for a prostitute. In one of the pockets of his coat were notes for his poem on hunting and disembowelling them, so he could find and kill their foetuses. In the other pocket was his razor-sharp dissecting blade, that he had been trained for years with, to make the exact same wounds that were made on the victims. That he was probably Jack the Ripper is a conclusion that comes from looking at the most likely explanation for what he wrote and how he lived before, during and after the murders.

If any book is guilty of painting Thompson at his very worst, it is this one. The comparing of this work by a 'suspectologist' to any other will show this one speculates with a very long bow and makes leaps of logic with the best of them. How it differs to the mountain of books, poems, articles, plays, songs and symphonies devoted to Thompson's genius and goodness is that it does the exact opposite. In keeping with this principle, this writer will strive to conclude with a summary of why he might have killed all these women and why he might have gone about doing it the way he did.

Maybe Thompson killed these five women because he believed God had chosen him to do so; he thought that he was the voice of God. Perhaps, for Thompson, by killing these five women he would be inflicting five wounds, like those upon Christ at his crucifixion. These wounds would strike at what he perceived as to be a crumbling society, an ineffectual church and a corrupt government, thus smiting the English people and their worship of science. For, by 1888, society had beaten him into the gutter. It had forced him to the streets, it had ignored him, it had made him a beggar, and it had spurned him. Francis was a mystic whose life was full of impossible loves. Thompson believed in magic and God, pain and sacrifice, and heaven and hell. In his wake he believed he had made those prostitutes, once thought of as criminals, into innocent victims; his poetry turned pain into beauty and filled night with fear.

When Francis Thompson arrived, at the age of 25, to make his fortune in the London of 1885, he saw it as more than a mass of people and street signs. London was the city that promised both his fortune and the deity for whom he nightly prayed. Like his kindred spirit De Quincey, a century earlier, Thompson was convinced that it would be here that the muse of literature would inspire him with a kiss. For Francis Thompson, the three years leading to 1888 were years of darkness. Thompson, as a mystic, was a man of extremes in both thought and deed. He was in love with riddles and secrets and he saw in London a vessel that held all his answers. For Thompson, his paradox was that God is real but he lets him set a church on fire, forsake the priesthood, lie, run away from home, take drugs, be with a prostitute and steal. Yet, he does not smite him but he hides from me, in her, the prostitute who hides from him.

Maybe Thompson felt his father and the Holy Father, his mother and the Holy Mother, and love, had forsaken him. Only his dream remained; that he could find an everlasting and pure love in capturing his fled prostitute. It is possible that Thompson, in a drug-affected state and after three years of destitution, may have come to see himself as a 'messiah'-type figure acting out a crucifixion on a large scale; by killing five 'sinners', he was projecting the wounds of Christ's crucifixion as a stigmata upon society. Perhaps it was felt, by Thompson, that by killing within a religious site, upon the feast days of selected martyred saints who were eastern crusaders and patron saints of butchers, soldiers, doctors and scholars, he would be cleansed of guilt. Thus, as the crusading knight like 'Francis Tancred', he could elect himself a key player in his perceived apocalypse and be forgiven for his sins. Thompson saw that in crucifying womankind he could bring forth a new entity encased within his poetry and within the enigma of Jack the Ripper; an entity to one day preside over a new 'heaven and a new earth'. It was what Thompson sought in madness, in drugs, in destitution, and in pain and death.

Prepared to open the brazen gates of hell he may have snatched his poetry through the sacrifice of five women to hold his own dark Mass. Even the inconceivable is possible, for when the Ripper murdered Mary Kelly she may have already submitted to his desire to kill her. By 9th November, many Londoners, and prostitutes in particular, were in dire dread and fear of the Ripper, with all wondering, would it ever end. The girls of Spitalfields asked if they were to be his next. Some of the more wretched even begged for the Ripper to come and snatch them away from their terrible lives of poverty. This is leads to a horrible, contemplation. If Thompson spoke kindly to Kelly before her fireplace, maybe with her sordid life flashing before her flaming eyes, she allowed herself to be persuaded by an account of her redemption. Words fashioned possibly like these ones, this writer imagines,

'Look what at what your life has become my poor Mary. Look in the squalor you live. How many more years can you be pretty? You have sinned and are all undone and fallen. Will you not seek forgiveness and by hand sinister become as a one of innocence? Be another martyr to be elected to sit amongst the saints? Stay your cries, rest your weary limbs, and let me carry you away. I will make you my last and greatest offering. Trust in me and consent to be seduced by the ritual of pain and of ecstasy. As Veronica did for sweet Jesus with her pitying veil, my instrument will cover your face with the balm of oblivion. I shall keep the secret to my grave Mary. I'll make you famous.'

Thompson may have ripped, and torn, and written a rough draft that was burned to ash until only the final proofs remained. When Thompson published what he penned, he may have combined twin truths. These were the genius of him, as a poet and the monstrous Ripper, but also separate lies, one of his innocence and the other in the myth of the superman murderer. Thompson, fleeing the loss of his soul, may have tried to turn his own horror into fiction by feeding on the fear of others. Thompson played make-believe in his love of death, yet he contradicted himself with every breath, He lived a lie in life and rhyme; the rest he left to us as meagre evidence.

One can speculate that, in June of 1888, when Thompson lost his prostitute, he decided to bring her back, but he was anxious about what she would do. What would prevent her from leaving him again? Maybe, to his warped reasoning, there was only one way that she could not. He would bring her back in such a way that her spirit would encompass the earth. He would kill in the heart of an empire – London. A city that was then the cultural and political centre of the earth.

Thompson would do so by following ancient occult rites, so that when his lost love – his prostitute came back – her spirit would spread outwards. She would live again on the waves of energies until she would be like a spirit existing everywhere. It could have been his plan from the start, that by killing these five women on special days, in particular places and in a certain way he would engineer a sort of resurrection. It would take yet another volume, by this author, to adequately explain the conclusion from two decades of study of Thompson. Incredible as it sounds to ordinary ears, it seems that he may have believed that after the last murder was committed, his longed for vanished prostitute would rise up in an ideal form. His possible wish was that when he would step in a puddle the sound of the water splashing would be her laughter, when he felt a table he would feel her skin, when he sipped a cup of tea he would taste sweet kisses. Oh, and the wind would echo his name whispered by her. But to Thompson's dismay, what was finally revealed was far from what he had hoped. As with any being, there was in Francis Thompson things to admire, and may he be seen as the singular individual that he was. Thompson's life was incredible and his poems reflect profundity. However, what may be more extraordinary, than this poet and his poetry, are we for letting history fall victim to his crimes.

Here is Francis Thompson's, 1895 *Sister Songs,*

'O Princess of the Blood of Song!

In her pulse mine shall thrill;

And the quick heart shall quicken from the heart that's still.

Ah! help, my Daemon that hast served me well! ...

A passionless statue stands.

Oh, pardon, innocent one!

Pardon at thine unconscious hands!

"Murmurous with music not their own," I say?

When the embrace has failed, the rapture fled,

Not he, not he, the wild sweet witch is dead!

So between thy father's knees

I saw THEE stand.

And now? -

The hours I tread ooze memories of thee, Sweet!

Beneath my casual feet.

With rainfall as the lea,

The day is drenched with thee;

In little exquisite surprises

Bubbling deliciousness of thee arises

From sudden places, ...

And, though he cherisheth

The babe most strangely born from out her death,

Some tender trick of her it hath, maybe, -

It is not she!

Even so

Its lovely gleamings

Seemings show

Of things not seemings; …

My living heart is laid to throb and burn,

Till end be ended, and till ceasing cease.

I have you through the days!

You are mine through the times!

I have caught you fast for ever in a tangle of sweet
rhymes.

You may scorn,

But you must be

Bound and sociate to me;

With this thread from out the tomb my dead hand
shall tether thee!

For we do know

The hidden player by his harmonies,

And by my thoughts I know what still hands thrill
the keys.'

Francis Thompson's *Finis Coronat Opus*: The Final Crowning Work

[Because Thompson's 1889 murder story may be the closest thing we have to a confession by Jack the Ripper and may serve readers interest, it has been included in this book.]

In a city of the future, among a people bearing a name I know not, lived Florentian the poet, whose place was high in the retinue of Fortune. Young, noble, popular, influential, he had succeeded to a rich inheritance, and possessed the natural gifts which gain the love of women. But the seductions which Florentian followed were darker and more baleful than the seductions of women; for they were the seductions of knowledge and intellectual pride. In very early years he had passed from the pursuit of natural to the pursuit of unlawful science; he had conquered power where conquest is disaster, and power servitude.

But the ambition thus gratified had elsewhere suffered check. It was the custom of this people that among their poets he, who by universal acclaim outsoared all competitors, should be crowned with laurel in public ceremony. Now, between Florentian and this distinction there stood a rival. Seraphin was a spirit of higher reach than Florentian, and the time was nearing fast when even the slow eyes of the people must be opened to a supremacy which Florentian himself acknowledged in his own heart. Hence arose in his lawless soul an insane passion; so that all which he had seemed to him as nothing beside that which he had not, and the compassing of this barred achievement became to him the one worthy object of existence. Repeated essay only proved to him the inadequacy of his native genius, and he turned for aid to the power which he served. Nor was the power of evil slow to respond. It promised him assistance that should procure him his heart's desire, but demanded in return a crime before which even the unscrupulous selfishness of Florentian paled. For he had sought and won the hand of Aster, daughter to the Lady Urania, and the sacrifice demanded from him was no other than the sacrifice of his betrothed, the playmate of his childhood. The horror of such a suggestion prevailed for a time over his unslacked ambition. But he, who believed himself a strong worker of ill, was in reality a weak follower of it; he believed himself a Vathek, he was but a Faust: continuous pressure and gradual familiarisation could warp him to any sin. Moreover his love for Aster had been gradually and unconsciously sapped by the habitual practise of evil. So God smote Florentian, that his antidote became to him his poison, and love the regenerator love the destroyer. A strong man, he might have been saved by love: a weak man, he was damned by it.

The palace of Florentian was isolated in the environs of the city; and on the night before his marriage he stood in the room known to his domestics as the Chamber of Statues. Both its appearance, and the sounds which (his servants averred) sometimes issued from it, contributed to secure for him the seclusion that he desired whenever he sought this room. It was a chamber in many ways strongly characteristic of its owner, a chamber 'like his desires lift upwards and exalt,' but neither wide nor far-penetrating; while its furnishing revealed his fantastic and somewhat childish fancy. At the extremity which faced the door there stood, beneath a crucifix, a small marble altar, on which burned a fire of that strange greenish tinge communicated by certain salts. Except at this extremity, the wails were draped with deep violet curtains bordered by tawny gold, only half displayed by the partial illumination of the place. The light was furnished from lamps of coloured glass, sparsely hung along the length of the room, but numerously clustered about the altar: lamps of diverse tints, amber, peacock-blue, and changefully mingled harmonies of green like the scales on a beetle's back. Above them were coiled thinnest serpentinings of suspended crystal, hued like the tongues in a wintry hearth, flame-colour, violet, and green; so that, as in the heated current from the lamps the snakes twirled and flickered, and their bright shadows twirled upon the wall, they seemed at length to undulate their twines, and the whole altar became surrounded with a fiery fantasy of sinuous stains.

On the right-hand side of the chamber there rose – appearing almost animated in the half lustre – three statues of colossal height, painted to resemble life; for in this matter Florentian followed the taste of the ancient Greeks. They were statues of three poets, and, not insignificantly, of three pagan poets. The first two, Homer and Aeschylus, presented no singularity beyond their Titanic proportions; but it was altogether otherwise with the third statue, which was unusual in conception. It was the figure of Virgil; not the Virgil whom we know, but the Virgil of medieval legend, Virgil, magician and poet. It bent forwards and downwards towards the spectator; its head was un-circled by any laurel, but on the flowing locks was an impression as of where the wreath had rested; its lowered left hand proffered the magician's rod, its outstretched right poised between light finger-tips the wreath of gilded metal whose impress seemed to linger on its hair: the action was as though it were about to place the laurel on the head of someone beneath. This was the carved embodiment of Florentian's fanatical ambition, a perpetual memento of the double end at which his life was aimed. On the necromancer's rod be could lay his hand, but the laurel of poetic supremacy hung yet beyond his reach. The opposite side of the chamber had but one object to arrest attention: a curious head upon a pedestal, a head of copper with a silver beard, the features not unlike those of a Pan, and the tongue protruded as in derision. This, with a large antique dock, completed the noticeable garniture of the room. Up and down this apartment Florentian paced for long, his countenance expressive of inward struggle, till his gaze fell upon the Figure of Virgil. His face grew hard; with an air of sudden decision he began to act. Taking from its place the crucifix he threw it on the ground; taking from its pedestal the head he set it on the altar; and it seemed to Florentian as if he reared therewith a demon on the altar of his heart, round which also coiled burning serpents. He sprinkled, in the flame which burned before the head, some drops from a vial; he wounded his arm, and moistened from the wound the idol's tongue, and, stepping back, he set his foot upon the prostrate cross.

A darkness rose like a fountain from the altar, and curled downward through the room as wine through water, until every light was obliterated. Then from out the darkness grew gradually the visage of the idol, soaked with fire; its face was as the planet Mars, its beard as white-hot wire that seethed and crept with heat; and there issued from the lips a voice that threw Florentian on the ground: 'Whom seekest thou?' Twice was the question repeated; and then, as if the display of power were sufficient, the gloom gathered up its edges like a mantle and swept inwards towards the altar; where it settled in a cloud so dense as to eclipse even the visage of fire. A voice came forth again; but a voice that sounded not the same; a voice that seemed to have withered in crossing the confines of existence, and to traverse illimitable remotenesses beyond the imagining of man; a voice melancholy with a boundless calm, the calm not of a crystalline peace but of a marmoreal despair, 'Knowest thou me; what I am?'

Vanity of man! He who had fallen prostrate before this power now rose to his feet with the haughty answer, 'My deity and my slave!'

The unmoved voice held on its way:

'Scarce high enough for thy deity, too high for thy slave, I am pain exceeding great; and the desolation that is at the heart of things, in the barren heath and the barren soul. I am terror without beauty, and force without strength, and sin without delight. I beat my wings against the cope of Eternity, as thou thine against the window of Time. Thou knowest me not, but I know thee, Florentian, what thou art and what thou wouldst. Thou wouldst have and wouldst not give, thou wouldst not render, yet wouldst receive. This cannot be with me. Thou art but half baptised with my baptism, yet wouldst have thy supreme desire. In thine own blood thou wast baptised, and I gave my power to serve thee; thou wouldst have my spirit to inspire thee — thou must be baptised in blood not thine own!'

'Any way but one way!' said Florentian, shuddering.

'One way: no other way. Knowest thou not that in wedding thee to her thou givest me a rival? Thinkest thou my spirit can dwell beside her spirit? Thou must renounce her or, me: aye, thou wilt lose not only all thou dreadest to sin for, but all thou hast already sinned for. Render me her body for my temple, ~ and I render thee my spirit to inhabit it. This supreme price thou must pay for thy supreme wish. I ask not her soul. Give that to the God Whom she serves, give her body to me whom thou servest. Why hesitate? It is too late to hesitate, for the time is at hand to act. Choose, before this cloud dissolve which is now dissolving. But remember: thine ambition thou mightest have had; love thou art too deep damned to have.'

The cloud turned from black to grey. 'I consent!' cried Florentian, impetuously.

*****

Three years—what years since I planted in the grave the laurel which will soon now reach its height; and the fatal memory is heavy upon me, the shadow of my laurel is as the shadow of funeral yew. If confession indeed give ease, I, who am deprived of all other confession, may yet find some appeasement in confessing to this paper. I am not penitent; yet I will do fiercest penance. With the scourge of inexorable recollection I will tear open my scars. With the cuts of a pitiless analysis I make the post-mortem examine of my crime.

Even now can I feel the passions of moment when (since the forefated hour was not till midnight), leaving her under the influence of the merciful potion which should save her from the agony of knowledge and me from the agony of knowing that she knew, I sought, in the air of night and in hurrying swiftness, the resolution of which she had deprived me. The glow-worm lamps went out as I sped by, the stars in rainy pools leaped up and went out, too, as if both worm and star were quenched by the shadow of my passing, until I stopped exhausted on the bridge, and looked down into the river. How dark it ran, bow deep, how pauseless; how unruffled by a memory of its ancestral hills! Wisely unruffled, perchance. When it first danced down from its native source, did it, not predestine all the issues of its current, every darkness through which it should flow, every bough which it should break, every leaf which it should whirl down - in its way? Could it, if it would, revoke its waters, and run upward to the holy hills? No; the first step includes all sequent steps; when I did my first evil, I did also this evil; years ago had this shaft been launched, though it was but now curving to its mark; years ago had I smitten her, though she was but now staggering to her fall. Yet I hesitated to act who had already acted, I ruffled my current which I could not draw in. When at length, after long wandering, I retraced my steps, I bad not resolved, I. had recognized that I could resolve no longer.

She only cried three times. Three times, O my God I—no, not my God. It was close on midnight, and I felt her only, (she was not visible,) as she lay at the feet of Virgil magician and poet. The lamp had fallen from my band, and I dared not relume it. I even placed myself between her and the light of the altar though the salt-green fire was but the spectre of a flame. I reared my arm; I shook; I faltered. At that moment, with a deadly voice, the accomplice-hour gave forth its sinister command. I swear I struck not the first blow. Some violence seized my hand, and drove the poniard down. Whereat she cried; and I, frenzied, dreading detection, dreading, above all, her wakening, — I struck again, and again she cried; and yet again, and yet again she cried. Then—her eyes opened. I saw them open, through the gloom I saw them; through the gloom they were revealed to me, that I might see them to my hour of death. An awful recognition, an unspeakable consciousness grew slowly into them. Motionless with horror they were fixed on mine, motionless with horror mine were fixed on them, as she wakened into death.

How long had I seen them? I saw them still. There was a buzzing in my brain as if a bell had ceased to toll. How long had it ceased to toll? I know not. Has any bell been tolling? I know not. All my senses are resolved into one sense, and that is frozen to those eyes. Silence now, at least; abysmal silence; except the sound (or is the sound in me?), the sound of dripping blood; except that the flame upon the altar sputters, and hisses, and bickers, as if it licked its jaws. Yes, there is another sound— hush, hark!—It is the throbbing of my heart. Not—no, nevermore the throbbing of her heart! The loud pulse dies slowly away, as I hope my life is dying; and again I hear the licking of the flame.

A mirror hung opposite to me, and for a second, in some mysterious manner, without ever ceasing to behold the eyes, I beheld also the mirrored flame. The hideous, green, writhing tongue was streaked and flaked with red! I swooned, if swoon it can be called; swooned to the mirror, swooned to all about me, swooned to myself, but swooned not to those eyes.

Strange, that no one has taken me, me for such long hours shackled in a gaze! It is night again, is it not? Nay, I remember, I have swooned; what now stirs me from my stupor? Light; the guilty gloom is shuddering at the first sick rays of day. Light? Not that, not that; anything but that. Ah! The horrible traitorous light, that will denounce me to myself, that will unshroud to me my dead, that will show me all the monstrous fact. I swooned indeed.

When I recovered consciousness, it was risen from the ground, and kissed me with the kisses of Its mouth. They told me during the day that the great bell of the cathedral, though no man rang it, had sounded thrice at midnight. It was not a fancy, therefore, that I heard a bell toll there, where—when she cried three times. And they asked me jestingly if marriage was ageing me already. I took a mirror to find what they meant. On my forehead were graven three deep wrinkles; and in the locks which fell over my right shoulder I beheld, long and prominent, three white hairs. I carry those marks to this hour. They and a dark stain on the floor at the feet of Virgil are the sole witnesses to that night.

It is three years, I have said, since then; and how have I prospered? Has Tartarus fulfilled its terms of contract, as I faithfully and frightfully fulfilled mine? Yes. In the course which I have driven through every obstacle and every scruple, I have followed at least no phantom-lure. I have risen to the heights of my aspiration. I have overtopped my sole rival. True, it is a tinsel renown; true, Seraphin is still the light-bearer, I but a dragon vomiting infernal fire and smoke which sets the crowd a-gaping. But it is your nature to gape, my good friend of the crowd, and I would have you gape at me. If you prefer to Jove. Jove's imitator, what use to be Jove? 'Gods,' you cry; 'what a clatter of swift-footed steeds, and clangour of rapid rolling brazen wheels, and vibrating glare of lamps! Surely, the thunder-maned horses of heaven, the chariot of Olympus; and you must be the mighty Thunderer himself, with the flashing of his awful bolts! 'Not so, my short-sighted friend: very laughably otherwise. It is but vain old Salmoneus, gone mad in Elis. I know you, and I know myself. I have what I would have. I work for the present: let Seraphin have the moonshine future, if he lust after it. Present renown means present power; it suffices me that I am supreme in the eyes of my fellow-men. A year since was the laurel decreed to me, and a day ordained for the ceremony: it was only postponed to the present year because of what they thought my calamity. They accounted it calamity, and knew not that it was deliverance. For, my ambition achieved, the compact by which I had achieved it ended, and the demon who had inspired forsook me. Discovery was impossible. A death sudden but natural: how could men know that it was death of the Two-years-dead? I drew breath at length in freedom. For two years It had spoken to me with her lips, used her gestures, smiled her smile:—ingenuity of hell!—for two years the breathing Murder wrought before me, and tortured me in a hundred ways with the living desecration of her form.

Now, relief unspeakable! That vindictive sleuth-hound of my sin has at last lagged from the trail; I have had a year of respite, of release from all torments but those native to my breast; in four days I shall receive the solemn gift of what I already virtually hold; and now, surely, I exult in fruition. If the approach of possession brought not also the approach of recollection, if— Rest, O rest, sad ghost! Is thy grave not deep enough, or the world wide enough, that thou must needs walk the haunted precincts of my heart? Are not spectres there too many, without thee?

Later in the same day. A strange thing has happened to me—if I ought not rather to write a strange nothing. After laying down my pen, I rose and went to the window. I felt the need of some distraction, of escaping from myself. The day, a day in the late autumn, a day of keen winds but bright sunshine, tempted me out so, putting on cap and mantle, I sallied into the country, where winter pitched his tent on fields yet reddened with the rout of summer. I chose a sheltered lane, whose hedge-rows, little visited by the gust, still retained much verdure; and I walked along, gazing with a sense of physical refreshment at the now rare green. As my eyes so wandered, while the mind for a time let slip its care, they were casually caught by the somewhat peculiar trace which a leaf-eating caterpillar had left on one of the leaves. I carelessly outstretched my hand, plucked from the hedge the leaf, and examined it as I strolled. The marking—a large marking which traversed the greater part of the surface—took the shape of a rude but distinct figure, the figure 3. Such a circumstance, thought I, might by a superstitious man be given a personal application; and I fell idly to speculating how it might be applied to myself.

Curious! I stirred uneasily; I felt my cheek pale, and a chill which was not from the weather creep through me. Three years since that; three strokes—three cries—three tolls of the bell—three lines on my brow—three white hairs in my bead! I laughed: but the laugh rang false. Then I said, 'Childishness,' threw the leaf away, walked on, hesitated, walked back, picked it up, walked ox ~ again, looked at it again. Then, finding I could not laugh myself out of the fancy, I began to reason myself out of it. Even were a supernatural warning probable, a warning refers not to the past but to the future. This referred only to the past, it told me only what I knew already. Could it refer to the future? To the bestowal of the laurel? No; that was four days hence, and on the same day was the anniversary of what I feared to name, even in thought. Suddenly I stood still, stabbed to the heart by an idea. I was wrong. The enlaurelling had been postponed to a year from the day on which my supposed affliction was discovered. Now this, although it took place on the day of terrible anniversary, was not known till the day ensuing ~ Consequently, though it wanted four days to the bestowal of the laurel, it lacked but three days to the date of my crime. The chain of coincidence was complete. I dropped the leaf as if it had death in it, and strove to evade, by rapid motion and thinking of other things, the idea which appalled me. But, as a man walking in a mist circles continually to the point from which he started, so, in whatever direction I turned the footsteps of my mind, they wandered back to that unabandonable thought. I returned trembling to the house.

Of course it is nothing; a mere coincidence, that is all. Yes; a mere coincidence, perhaps, if it had been one coincidence. But when it is seven coincidences! Three stabs, three cries, three tolls, three lines, three hairs, three, years, three days; and on the very date when these coincidences meet, the key to them is put into my bands by the casual work of an insect on a casual leaf, casually plucked This day alone of all days in my life the scattered rays con-verge; they are instantly focused and flashed on my mind by a leaf! It may be a coincidence, only a coincidence; but it is a coincidence at which my marrow sets. I will write no further till the day comes. If by that time anything has happened to confirm my dread, I will record what has chanced. One thing broods over me with the oppression of certainty. If this incident be indeed a warning that but three days stand as barriers between me and nearing justice, then doom will come upon me at the unforgettable minute when it came on her.

The third day—It is an hour before midnight, and I sit in my- room of statues. I dare -not sleep if I could sleep; and I write, because the rushing thoughts move slower through the turnstile of expression. I have chosen this place to make what may be my last vigil and last notes, partly from obedience to an inexplicable yet comprehensible fascination, partly from a deliberate resolve. I would face the lightning of vengeance on the very spot where I most tempt its stroke, that if it strike not I may cease to fear its striking. Here then I sit to tease with final questioning the Sibyl of my destiny. With final questioning; for never since the first shock have I ceased to question her, nor she to return my riddling answers. She unrolls her volume till my sight and heart ache at it-together. I have been struck by innumerable deaths; I have perished under a fresh doom every, day, every hour—in these last hours, every minute. I write in black thought; and tear, as soon as written, guess after guess at fate till the floor of my brain is littered with them.

That the deed has been discovered—that seems to me to probable, that is the con-jecture, which oftenest recurs. Appallingly probable! Yet how improbable, could I only reason it. Aye, but I cannot reason it. What reason will be left me, if I survive this hour? What, indeed, have I to do with reason, or has reason to do with this, where all is beyond reason, where the very foundation of my dread is unassailable simply because it is unreasonable? What crime can be interred so cunningly, but it will toss in its grave, and tumble the sleeked earth above it? Or some hidden witness may have beheld me, or the prudently-kept imprudence of this writing may have encountered some unsuspected eyes. In any case the issue is the same; the hour which struck down her will also strike down me: I shall perish on the scaffold or at the stake, unaided by my occult powers; for I serve a master who is the prince of cowards, and can fight only from ambush. Be it by these ways, or by any of the countless intricacies that my restless mind has unravelled, the vengeance will come:

its occasion may be an accident of the instant, a wandering mote of chance; but the vengeance is pre-ordained and inevitable. When the Alpine avalanche is poised for descent, the most trivial cause—a casual shout—will suffice to start the loosened ruin on its way; and so the mere echoes of the clock that beats out midnight will disintegrate upon me the precipitant wrath.

Repent? Nay, nay, it could not have been otherwise than it was; the defile was dose behind me, I could but go forward, forward. If I was merciless to her, was I not more merciless to myself; could I hesitate to sacrifice her life, who did not hesitate to sacrifice my soul? I do not repent, I cannot repent; it is a thing for inconsequent weaklings. To repent your purposes is comprehensible, to repent your deeds most futile. To shake the tree, and then not gather the fruit—a fool's act! Aye, but if the fruit be not worth the gathering? If this fame was not worth the sinning for—this fame, with the multitude's clapping hands half-drowned by the growl of winds that comes in gusts through the unbarred gate of hell? If I am miserable with it, and might have been happy without it? With her, without ambition—yes, it might have been. Wife and child! I have more in my heart than I have hitherto written. I have an intermittent pang of loss. Yes, I, murderer, worse than murderer, have still passions. that are not deadly, but tender.

I met a child to-day; a child with great candour of eyes. They who talk of children's instincts are at fault: she knew not that hell was in my soul, she knew only that softness was in my gaze. She had been gathering wild flowers, and offered them to me. To me, to me! I was inexpressibly touched and pleased, curiously touched and pleased. I spoke to her gently, and with open confidence she began to talk. Heaven knows it was little enough she talked of! Commonest common things, pettiest childish things, fondest foolish things. Of her school, her toys, the strawberries in her garden, her little brothers and sisters—nothing, surely, to 'interest any man.' Yet I listened enchanted. How simple it all was; how strange, how wonderful, how sweet! And she knew not that my eyes were anhungered of her, she knew not that my ears were gluttonous of her speech, she could not have understood it had I told her; none could, none. For all this exquisiteness is among the commonplaces of life to other men, like the raiment they imbue at rising, like the bread they weary of eating, like the daisies they trample under blind feet; knowing not what raiment is to him who has felt the ravening wind, knowing not what bread is to him who has lacked all bread, knowing not what daisies are to him whose feet have wandered in grime. How can these elves be to such men what they are to me, who am damned to the eternal loss of them? Why was I never told that the laurel could soothe no hunger, that the laurel could staunch no pang, that the laurel could return no kiss? But needed I to be told it, did I not know it? Yes, my brain knew it, my heart knew it not. And now—

At half-past eleven.

O lente, lente currite, noctis equi!

Just! they are the words of that other trafficker in his own soul. Me, like him, the time tracks swiftly down; I can fly no farther, I fall exhausted, the fanged hour fastens on my throat: they will break into the room, my guilt will burst its grave and point at me; I shall be seized, I shall be condemned, I shall be executed; I shall be no longer I, but a nameless lump on which they pasture worms. Or perhaps the hour will herald some yet worser thing, some sudden death, some undreamable, ghastly surprise—ah! what is that at the door there, that, that with her eyes? Nothing: the door is shut. Surely, surely, I am not to die now? Destiny steals upon a man asleep or off his guard, not when he is awake, as I am awake, at witch, as I am at watch, wide-eyed, vigilant, alert. Oh, miserable hope! Watch the eaves of your house, to bar the melting of the snow; or guard the gateways of the clouds, to bar the forthgoing of the lightning; or guard the four quarters of the heavens, to bar the way of the winds: but what prescient hand can close the Hecatompyloi of fate, what might arrest the hurrying retributions whose multitudinous tramplings converge upon me in a hundred presages, in a hundred shrivelling menaces, down all the echoing avenues of doom? It is but a question of which shall arrive the fleetest and the first. I cease to think. I am all a waiting and a fear. Twelve!

At half-past two. Midnight is stricken, and I am unstricken. Guilt, indeed, makes babies of the wisest. Nothing happened; absolutely nothing. For two hours I watched with lessening expectance: still nothing. I laughed aloud between sudden light-heartedness and scorn. Ineffable fool that I was, I had conjured up death, judgement, doom—heaven knows what, all because a caterpillar had crawled along a leaf! And then, as I might have done before had not terror vitiated my reason, I made essay whether I still retained my power. I retain it. Let me set down for my own enhardiment what the oracle replied to my questioning.

'Have I not promised and kept my promise, shall I not promise and keep? You would be crowned and you shall be crowned. Does your way to achievement lie through misery?—is not that the way to all worth the achieving? Are not half the mill-wheels of the world turned by waters of pain? Mountain summit that would rise into the clouds, can you not suffer the eternal snows? If your heart fail you, turn; I chain you not. I will restore you your oath. I will cancel your bond. Go to the God Who has tenderness for such weaklings: my service requires the strong.'

What a slave of my fancy was I! Excellent fool. What! Pay the forfeit of my sin and forgo the recompense, recoil from the very gates of conquest? I fear no longer: the crisis is past, the day of promise has begun, I go forward to my destiny; I triumph.

• • • • •

Florentian laid down his pen, and passed into dreams. He saw the crowd, the throne, 'the waiting laurel, the sunshine, the flashing of rich robes; he heard the universal shout of acclaim, he felt the flush of intoxicating pride. He rose, his form dilating with exultation, and passed, lamp in hand, to the foot of the third statue. The colossal figure leaned above him with its outstretched laurel, its proffered wand, its melancholy face and flowing hair; so lifelike was it that in the wavering flame of the lamp the laurel seemed to move. 'At length, Virgil,' said Florentian, 'at length I am equal with you; Virgil, magician and poet, your crown shall descend on me!'

One... Two... Three! The strokes of the great clock shook the chamber, shook the statues; and after the strokes had ceased, the echoes were still prolonged. Was it only an echo?

Boom!

Or—was it the cathedral bell?

Boom!

It was the cathedral bell. Yet a third time, sombre, surly, ominous as the bay of a nearing bloodhound, the sound came down the wind.

Boom!

Horror clutched his heart. He looked up at the statue. He turned to fly. But a few hairs, tangled round the lowered wand, for a single instant held him like a cord. He knew, without seeing, that they were the three white hairs. When, later in the day, a deputation of officials came to escort Florentian to the place fixed for his coronation, they were informed that he had been all night in his Chamber of Statues, nor had he yet made his appearance. They waited while. the servant left to fetch him. The man was away some time, and they talked gaily as they waited: a bird beat its wings at the window; through the open door came in a stream of sunlight, and the fragmentary song of a young girl passing:

'Oh, syne she tripped, and sync she ran

(The water-lily's a lightsome flower),

All for joy and sunshine weather

The lily and Marjorie danced together,

As he came down from Langley Tower.

There's a blackbird sits on Langley Tower,

And a throstle on Glenlindy's tree;

The throstle sings' Robin, my heart's love!'

And the blackbird,' Bonnie, sweet Marjorie!'

The man came running back at last, with a blanched face and a hushed voice. 'Come,' he said, 'and see!' They went and saw. At the feet of Virgil's statue Florentian lay dead. A dark pool almost hid that dark stain on the ground, the three lines on his forehead were etched in blood, and across the shattered brow lay a ponderous gilded wreath; while over the extinguished altar-fire the idol seemed to quiver its derisive tongue. 'He is already laurelled,' said one, breaking at length the silence; 'we come too late.' Too late. The crown of Virgil, magician and poet, had descended on him.

Notes

(1) = O lente, lente currite, noctis equi: (Oh, slowly, slowly, run, horses of the night.) From the last scene of Marlowe's play *Faustus*. A tale about Faustus who trades his soul to the devil in return for everlasting youth.

Hecatompyloi: Better known as Hecatompylos. Ancient Patina city in western Khurasan and capital of the Iranian. Arsacid dynasty. Name means 'City of 100 gates' in Greek. Once lost to history before being 'rediscovered' by modern archaeologists. Mentioned in Thompson's poem *An Anthem of Earth*,

'Rabble of Pharaohs and Arsacidae

Keep their cold house within thee; thou hast sucked down

How many Ninevehs and Hecatompyloi,

And perished cities whose great phantasmata

O'erbrow the silent citizens of Dis:'

Vathek: A character in a novel *Vathek: An Arabian Tale from an Unpublished Manuscript, with Notes Critical and Explanatory*, written by William Beckford and published in 1786. Vathek is a supposed descended of Caliph Haroun al Raschid (763-809, Caliph of Baghdad). Vathek's two great passions are arcane knowledge and a decadent lifestyle. A magician who offers him great powers if he sacrifices 50 children visits him. It is later revealed that this is a test by Mohammad of his Islamic faith.

Homer, Aeschylus & Virgil: Greek poets and playwrights.

Pan: Pagan nature god.

Necromancer: A magician whose magic deals with the dead.

Langley Tower A medieval fortress built in AD 1350 near Hexham. Has four towers and seven-foot-thick walls.

Olympus: Home to the Greek gods.

Salmoneus: Of Greek mythology. King of the land of Elis. Pretended to be the god Zeus and demanded sacrifices to himself. He and his kingdom of Elis were destroyed by Zeus with a thunderbolt.

Notes: Richard. A. Patterson. Saturday, 01 January 2005.

Was Francis Thompson Jack the Ripper?

BY Joseph C Rupp, MD PhD NUECES COUNTY MEDICAL EXAMINER

[Dr Joseph Rupp, the first person to publicly ask if Francis Thompson was Jack the Ripper, wrote the following article in the *Criminologist* journal, in 1988. Dr Rupp has graciously given this author permission to reprint it here.]

November 1988 marked the hundredth anniversary of the most celebrated series of murders committed in the 20th century. Within a three-month period between August 31 and November 9 1888, Jack the Ripper killed and mutilated five women in the East End of London. A series of crimes so bizarre and so brutal, committed by a killer so nebulous and elusive, that these murders have fascinated amateur and professional sleuths for a hundred years. The murderer was never apprehended and the case never solved, and yet there is enough information available to provide us with grist for endless speculation as to the identity and motive of the killer. Herein lies much of the fascination of this series of crimes.

In 1910 Dr Thomas Stowell caused a sensation when he published, in 'The Criminologist', his solution to the Ripper mystery. He proposed that Prince Albert Victor, Duke of Clarence, the eldest son of the future King Edward VII, was in fact Jack the Ripper. While an interesting theory, it did not really stand up too well under close scrutiny. But it was all great fun and provided many Ripper aficionados with entertaining bedtime reading. As the centennial approaches perhaps now is the time to take another look at the Ripper ease in the hope that renewed interest will be generated in solving this series of murders.

In 1968 John Walsh authored a biography of the poet Francis Thompson titled 'Strange Harp, Strange Symphony'. Francis Thompson is best known for his celebrated poem 'The Hound of Heaven', which is required reading in every survey of English literature course. In 1968, I knew very little about Thompson except that he was an opium addict and was rescued from the streets of London by a literary benefactor. Early in Walsh's book in discussing Francis Thompson's rescue from the streets of London the author states, 'It was Everard Meynell who first glimpsed the connection between 'The Hound of Heaven' and Thompson's search for his friend (a prostitute) during August-September 1888 ...' This was followed by a footnote,

'At this time (August-September, 1888) occurred the most bizarre coincidence in Thompson's life. During the very weeks he was searching for his prostitute friend, London was in an uproar over the ghastly deaths of five such women at the hands of Jack the Ripper. In these circumstances, his concern for his prostitute friend's welfare would naturally have been heightened. The police threw a wide net over the city, investigating thousands of drifters, and known consorts with the city's lower elements, and it is not beyond possibility that Thompson himself may have been questioned. He was, after all, a drug addict, acquainted with prostitutes and, most alarming, a former medical student! A young man with a similar background and living only a block away from McMaster's shop was one who early came under suspicion, see Cullen, T., "When London Walked in Terror".'

Needless to say this footnote made a great impression upon me and as I read the biography I could not help but read it in light of the possibility that Thompson himself might have been the Ripper. Upon finishing the biography, it was clear that Francis Thompson was at least as good and perhaps a far better candidate for the role of Jack the Ripper than was the Duke of Clarence or any number of other suspects that have been put forward over the past one hundred years. With these thoughts in mind, let us review the life of Francis Thompson, taking particular cognizance of those facts and incidents in his life which fit him for the role of the Ripper.

Francis Thompson was born on December 18, 1859, in the town of Preston in Lancashire. He was born into a devout Catholic family and his father Charles Thompson was a practising doctor of homeopathy. Francis was a frail and delicate child and until he was nearly 11 years old, was educated at home with his two sisters. A precocious child, by the age of seven or eight he was already reading Scott Macaulay, Shakespeare and the Bible. He was allowed to read anything that interested him and at a young age was particularly taken by Coleridge's poems, 'The Rhyme of the Ancient Mariner' and 'Christabel'.

When Francis was nearly 11 years old, he was sent away to school at Upshaw College near Durham to begin the fall term in September of 1870. At Upshaw he was one of three hundred boys. Later in his life, Thompson said of his first association with his schoolmates,

'Fresh from my tender home and my circle of just-judging friends, these malignant schoolmates, who danced round me with mocking, evil distortion of laughter … were to me devilish apparitions of a hate now first known; hate for hate's sake, cruelty for cruelty's sake. And as such they live in my memory, testimonies to the murky aboriginal demon in man.' {LIFE p18)

Thompson made a satisfactory adjustment to his school life for he was to remain at Upshaw for seven years. His school record was good, especially in Latin, Greek, and English. His teachers spoke of him as a 'good, quiet shy lad'. Thompson pursued a four-year course in Christian humanism that led to a three-year college programme in preparation for entry into the priesthood. After seven years in school at Upshaw, his teachers decided that he was unsuited for the priesthood.

The reasons given to his parents were 'his strong nervous timidity' and a 'natural indolence, which has always been an obstacle with him'. The officials at the school concluded that it was 'not the holy will of God' that he should be a priest.

In July 1877, a failure in his own eyes and disappointment to his parents, he returned home. It was now decided that Francis should follow in his father's footsteps and become a doctor. The boy acquiesced in his parent's wishes and after passing the entrance examinations for medical school was accepted as a student of Owens College in Manchester. On September 27, 1877, two months short of his 18th birthday he signed the Owens College Register and was admitted to the Medical Department for both summer and winter sessions.

Francis now began to live a double life, which was to last for six years. As a medical student, he communed each day from his home in Ashton-under-Lyne to Manchester. He pretended to study but attended only as many lectures as allowed him to convince his family that he was an earnest student. During the hours when he should have been attending lectures he was walking the streets of Manchester, dozing in the sun, reading books and poetry, visiting the library and spending long afternoons watching the cricket matches. In June, 1879, after two years in medical school, he went to London to sit for his examinations and failed.

His health now began to break under the pressures of his pretence, and in 1879 he suffered his first long illness from tuberculosis. He lay in bed for days and it was probably during this period than he first began to take laudanum [a mixture of 90% alcohol and 10% opium). It was at this time also that his mother, for no known reason, gave her son a copy of De Quincey's 'Confessions of an English Opium Eater'. It was her last gift to her son before she died on December 19, 1879, as the result of some sort of liver ailment from which she had been suffering for about six months. The indications are that Francis began using laudanum because of his illness and continued to use laudanum because of his reading of De Quincey.

In any event, by the end of 1880 Francis had acquired the laudanum habit. Upon his recovery from his illness, he returned to medical school, renewing his life of deception with the new added burden of his drug addiction. In 1881, he went lo London and again failed his medical examinations. His tolerant father sent him back to medical school for yet another two years, and in 1884, he went to sit for his examinations in Glasgow, rather than London, in the hope that the examinations in Scotland would be easier. Thompson's father finally determined, after the third failure and at the age of 25, that his son should leave school and go to work.

Francis's first job was with surgical instrument makers in Manchester. This job lasted only a couple of weeks and was followed by a job as an encyclopaedia salesman, which lasted only a couple of months. During this time, he read the entire encyclopaedia, but sold not a single volume. After these failures, Francis enlisted as a soldier. He was examined and put through a course of basic training and then rejected as physically unfit for military service, presumably because of his drug addiction. It finally dawned on the tolerant Dr Thompson that something was the matter with his son and he suspected alcoholism as the problem. One Sunday in November 1885, he confronted Francis with his suspicions and was met with denials but no explanations. Of course, Francis's denials were truthful concerning alcohol since his real problem was his addiction to laudanum. On the following day, November 8, 1885, Francis left home and went to Manchester where he spent about a week in his old haunts disposing of some of his books in order to sustain his laudanum habit. Several days later, he wrote home for his fare to London and arrived in London about November 15, 1885.

He arrived in London with no plans. 'I made the journey to the Capital,' he wrote, 'without hope and with the gloomiest foreboding in the desperate spirit of an enfant perdu.' His arrival in London was the beginning of three years of penury and suffering from which experience forms the basis for much of his wonderful poetry.

He made no attempt to contact relatives in London who might have helped him. His love of books drew him to a job as a 'collector' for a bookseller. He picked up books from the wholesale book dealers that had been ordered by his employer and delivered the books back to the bookstore or directly to the customers. He soon lost this job, partly through indolence and partly because he read more books than he delivered. By July, 1886. Francis was living on the streets with enough money only for food and drugs.

The streets of London did not provide many opportunities to find the eleven pence a day, which he needed to exist. He was reduced to near beggary. He was a bootblack, a newspaper and match seller, he ran after cabs in hope of a tip for loading and unloading baggage or holding the horses while passengers alighted. Many nights he had no money for a bed, even in the poorest lodging house. Sometimes he spent the night in a shelter provided on the Embankment for the homeless, sleeping on a mattress in a boxlike, lidless coffin covered with a leather blanket. His love of books continued and an observer at the Guildhall Library recalled, 'He was so poorly clad that it fell on my lot to have to perform the painful duly of asking him to forego his visit.' He lived in the gutter, sheltering from the elements in doorways and porches and wandering the streets by day and by night.

In August of 1866, after nine months on the streets of London, Thompson met John McMaster, owner of a boot shop at 14 Panton Street just off Leicester Square. McMaster took him in his shop and gave him employment. He received his food and five shillings a week for his services as messenger, odd job Boy, and for opening and closing the shop. Mr. McMaster did all he could to rehabilitate Thompson. He gave him a boy's work to do and Thompson was more a guest than an employee. In the bookmaker's shop and within the circle of the McMaster family Thompson began to write and talk as he had not done for a long time.

In December 1888, it was arranged that Francis should return home to his family for the Christmas holidays. Francis spent two weeks with the family, however his family was changing. His sister Mary planned to enter a convent and his father announced his intention to take a second wife.

When Thompson returned in McMaster's shop in January, he had increased his use of laudanum, although his benefactor, like his father, mistook the symptoms for those of alcoholism. Upon his return, Francis was even less of a satisfactory employee than before. Disappointed with what he considered as 'his only failure', McMaster decided that he could no Longer keep Thompson in his home. By the middle of January 1887, clothed in a brown overcoat, which he was to wear for several years, the poet left the bookshop to return to his vagrant life. On the streets of London during the bitter winter of 1886, he reached the nadir of his life. Starving and near death, charity came to him from an unexpected source. A young prostitute took him home to share her food and lodging. With her Thompson found companionship and warmth, which filled the gap left by the death of his mother.

In February of 1887, Francis had some kind of unexplained good fortune. 'With a few shillings to give me breathing space', he began to pull together the manuscript of his essay entitled 'Paganism' and some poems. 'Next day I spent my half penny on two boxes of

389

matches (to sell) and began the struggle for life.' At the end of February 1887, he sent the manuscript and the poems to a small Catholic magazine called 'Merry England'.

The editor of the magazine Wilfrid Meynell was too busy to read unsolicited manuscripts and so for six months the package remained unopened. When it was finally examined, Meynell was struck by the quality of the essay, although the poetry did not impress him. He wrote at once to Thompson's return address, the post office at Charing Cross. This letter was unclaimed, and after more delay and finally without the author's permission one of Thompson's poems, 'The Passion of Mary', was published in 'Merry England', in April 1888, fourteen months after its submission.

In the meantime, Thompson's circumstances had become truly desperate. With hope virtually gone, decimated by cold and hunger and with the drug tearing at him, he decided upon suicide. Thompson's account of his suicide attempt is not without interest. He went to a dump behind Covent Garden when he planned to take one large dose of laudanum. After swallowing half of the laudanum, he felt a hand laid on his wrist and, looking up half conscious, saw the figure of the dead poet Thomas Chatterton (1752-1770) – the marvellous boy who had committed suicide by taking arsenic before his 18th birthday and who has become the romantic symbol of suffering genius. Restrained by the figure from drinking the other half of the laudanum, Thompson recalled the legend that money had arrived for Chatterton the day after his suicide and so Thompson resolved not to take his own life. The very next day he learned that his poem, 'The Passion of Mary', had appeared in 'Merry England' in the April issue, which had reached its subscribers in the third week in March.

On April 14, 1888, Thompson wrote a letter to Wilfrid Meynell. Meynell immediately responded to Thompson's letter, however, it was many days before Thompson appeared in Meynells office. At this encounter Meynell described Thompson as 'a waif of a man more ragged and unkempt than the average beggar, with no shirt underneath his coat and bare feet in broken shoes'. During June and July of 1888, Thompson continued to visit Meynell at the 'Merry England' office. He refused either to accept the offer of a regular sum of money or to leave his life in the streets.

Apparently the rescue of Thompson by Meynell had precipitated a crisis in the life of the poet, for he was faced with breaking off his relationship with the prostitute who had for so long sustained him. However, it was the girl herself who finally resoled the problem, for she disappeared without a word and without a trace. According to his biographers, Thompson was desolate.

During August and September of 1888, he searched for her day and night through the streets of London. There is evidence that during this period of searching in the closing months of 1888, that concept of *pursuit by* and *flight from* a loving and forgiving God began to crystallise his ideas for his finest poem, 'The Hound of Heaven'. By mid-October, 1888, Thompson had tentatively accepted the fact that the girl had vanished for good. The girl was never found nor was her name ever discovered.

Thompson now became more amenable to Meynell's offers of help. He allowed himself to be examined by a doctor and late in 1888 entered a private hospital. We know that Thompson underwent the pangs of withdrawal in the hospital and was there for several weeks. He was discharged as cured some time in December of 1888. After his release from the hospital, Thompson was so weak and depressed that Meynell, after taking him under his roof for a while, arranged for him to convalesce in the free Premonstratensian Monastery at Stonington in Sussex. It was there that Thompson went early in 1889 and remained until February of 1890. This period of time, free of drugs and recuperating, was one of the most productive and creative of his life.

Thompson, who had begun taking laudanum, about 1880, underwent withdrawal in 1888, which affected a temporary cure. He reverted to the drug habit after several years, underwent another cure and was drug free for about four years. Then, in 1896, he began using the drug again and continued until his death, in 1907, as a result of tuberculosis and addiction.

The first of the Ripper murders occurred on August 31, 1888. By this time Francis Thompson had been living on the streets of London for about three years. The second Ripper murder occurred September 3. The third and fourth murders occurred on September 30. It was during August and September of 1888 that Thompson was conducting his desperate search by day and night through the streets of London for his prostitute girlfriend. The last of the Ripper murders occurred in November, after which no more was heard from Jack the Ripper. Francis Thompson left home on November 9, 1885, after a bitter argument with his father. He entered hospital sometime around the middle of November, 1883, for treatment of his drug addiction, which accounts for his sudden departure from the London scene.

All of the authorities on the Ripper agree that the murderer quite likely had some sort of medical training. Francis Thompson spent six years in medical school: in effect, he went through medical school three times. It is unlikely, no matter how disinterested he was or how few lectures he attended, that he did not absorb a significant amount of medical knowledge. Indeed, we know that he learned enough medicine to deceive his father, a practising physician, for a matter of six years.

By 1888 Thompson had been a drug addict for eight or nine years. There is no need to reiterate what drug addiction does to the personality and patterns of behaviour, nor what the drug addict is capable of doing in order to supply his drug habit. One of the most interesting facts pointing to Thompson as a suspect is his poetry itself. One cannot read his poems without seeing the underlying rage and hostility of this otherwise devoted, obedient son and pious Catholic. Francis Thompson certainly possessed a chaotic sexuality. He grew up and was educated with his sisters. He was devoted to his mother. His relationship with women later in life including his prostitute benefactrix was always strange and unusual. In none of the biographic material is there evidence that he ever had a sexual encounter with a woman. These facts also make Francis Thompson a prime suspect in this series of sex murders, particularly if we couple this with his drug addiction.

Another curious coincidence is the fact that the Ripper was able to elude the police so many times in spite of the complete mobilisation of many volunteer groups and law enforcement agencies in London. If we look at Thompson's background, having lived in the streets for three years prior to this series of crimes, there is no doubt that he knew the backstreets of London intimately, and that his attire and condition as a derelict and drug addict would not arouse suspicion as he moved by day and night through the East End of London.

It is of importance to look at the origins of his most famous poem, 'The Hound of Heaven'. There has been a great deal written concerning where the idea originated of comparing God and his pursuing love to a hound of heaven. Meynell felt that the idea began to crystallize during August and September of 1888 when he was searching for his prostitute girlfriend through the streets of London. If this is true, it is possible that all the talk of press of using bloodhounds in the East End of London to track the Ripper was in fact part of the material that provided the fleeing Thompson with the idea for his most celebrated poem. Finally, in regard to the matter of the sudden and complete disappearance of Thompson's prostitute girlfriend, his biographers would have us believe that this woman, upon realizing that Thompson's rehabilitation was being delayed by his attachment to her, suddenly and with altruistic intent, disappeared out of Thompson's life. In fact, the hooker with the 'hooker with the heart of gold' is a fiction almost as universally accepted as the ineffectuality of capital punishment. It is just as likely to suppose that Thompson, in the grips of an avaricious streetwalker, decided that she should disappear.

Was Francis Thompson Jack the Ripper? Perhaps the matter can be settled since handwritten notes from the Ripper and handwritten manuscripts by Francis Thompson are easily accessible.

Everard Meynell, 'The Life of Francis Thompson'. St. Clair Shores, Michigan: Scholarly Press Inc. 1971.

Meynell, Viola. 'Francis Thompson and Wilfrid Meynell', New York E. P. Dulton & Co, Inc. 1953.

Reid. J. C. 'Francis Thompson, Man and Poet.' London England: Routledge & Kegan Paul Ltd. 1959.

Rumbelow, Donald. 'The Complete Jack the Ripper', Boston, Massachusetts: New York Graphic Society, 1975.

Thomson, Paul Van Kuykendall, 'Francis Thompson, A Critical Biography,' New York: Thomas Nelson & Sons, 1961.

Walsh, John. 'Strange Harp Strange Symphony,' London, England: W.H. Allen & Co., 1968

Bibliography

James Chen, Poetic Justice, 29 Cardozo Law Review (2007). Paper on Supreme Court. Brown vs Brown.

'The Poems of Francis Thompson'. London University Press. 1960. Reprint of 1913 edition.

Beverly Taylor 'Francis Thompson'. 1987. G.K. Hall & Company.

Blunt. Wilfrid Scawen 'My Diaries. Being a Personal Narrative of Events 1888-1914'. Part Two 1900-1914. New Knopf. York. Alfred A. 1822. Uncut edition.

Boardman. Brigid M. 'Between Heaven and Charing Cross'. The Life of Francis Thompson.' 1988. {Charing}

Boardman. Brigid M. 'Poems of Francis Thompson'. Bloomsbury Academic; 1 edition. 2002. {Boardman}

Connolly. Rev. Terence L.S.J., Ph.D. 'Poems of Francis Thompson.' 1941 Appleton Century-Crofts, Inc. New York. {Poems}

'Francis Thompson, In His Paths.' The Bruce Publishing Company Milwaukee.

397

Darrell. Figgis. (1882-1925) 'Bye-Ways of Study.' 1918. Talbot Press.

Megroz. R.L 'Francis Thompson the Poet of Earth in Heaven, A Study in Poetic Mysticism and the Evolution of Love-Poetry.' 1927. Faber & Gwyer.

Meynell Everard. 'The Life of Francis Thompson' 1913. 1st edition. {LIFE}

& 1926 5th revised. Burns Oats & Washbourne. Ltd.

Meynell. Viola. 'Francis Thompson and Wilfrid Meynell'. 1952. London. Holis & Carter.

'Francis Thompson and Wilfrid Meynell' A memoir by Viola Meynell. London Hollis & Carter, 1952.

The 'Works of Francis Thompson'. Vols. I, II, III. London. First Impression, May 1913.

Thompson. Francis 'Selected Poems'. London. Burns and Oats. Ltd.

Thomson, Paul Van Kuykendall, 'Francis Thompson, A Critical Biography,' New York: Thomas Nelson & Sons, 1961. {Paul Van K}

Walsh. John Evangelist 'Strange Harp, Strange Symphony'. The Life of Francis Thompson. 1967. {Walsh}. Also 'The Letters of Francis Thompson'. 1969. Hawthorn Books, Inc. {Letters}

Jackson. Holbrook. 'The Eighteen Nineties A Review of Art and Ideas at The Close of the Nineteenth Century.' 1913.

'Merry England'. Edited by Wilfrid Meynell. Nov, 1888 edition. London.

Lowndes Marie Belloc. 'The Lodger'. 1913. Methuen & Co. Ltd. First Four Square Edition reprints. December 1966.

'Later Leaves being the further reminiscences of Montagu Williams, Q.C 1891. {Leaves} Quote from University of Nottingham Website. Manuscripts and Special Collections. Transcript of item from: By Sword and Gun.

'John C. Reid, Francis Thompson: Man and Poet (London: Routledge and Kegan Paul, 1959), {Reid}